The Book of John

Richmond Shee

Copyright © 2014 by Richmond Shee

All rights reserved. No part of this publication may be reproduced, stored in a retrieval system, or transmitted in any form or by any means, electronic, mechanical, photocopying, recording, scanning, or otherwise, except as permitted under Section 107 or 108 of the 1976 United States Copyright Act, without the prior written permission of the Publisher. Requests to the Publisher for permission should be addressed to TheBookofJohn777@yahoo.com.

Scripture quotations are from the King James Authorized Version.

ISBN-13: 978-069228977-8

Purple
dreamer
Publishers

With gratitude to the Lord Jesus Christ for the gifts of eternal life and wisdom, and to my beloved wife, Jody.

Contents

Foreword 5

Introduction 7

Chapter 1 – Emmanuel 9

Chapter 2 – True Joy 30

Chapter 3 – Love 42

Chapter 4 – Living Water 67

Chapter 5 – Healer 87

Chapter 6 – Bread of Life 103

Chapter 7 – Teacher 122

Chapter 8 – Forgiver 139

Chapter 9 – Sent One 162

Chapter 10 – Good Shepherd 177

Chapter 11 – Resurrection and Life 196

Chapter 12 – King of Israel 214

Chapter 13 – Servant 234

Chapter 14 – Way, Truth, Life 253

Chapter 15 – True Vine 269

Chapter 16 – Advisor 285

Chapter 17 – Advocate 299

Chapter 18 – Truth 315

Chapter 19 – Lamb of God 332

Chapter 20 – The Christ 345

Chapter 21 – Master Fisherman 357

Works Cited 370

About the Author 371

Foreword

I had been praying for and witnessing to my coworker and dear friend for a number of years. He was not interested in the salvation of Jesus Christ and would often brush me off by telling me that he would look into it at age 50. But God was faithful and continued to draw him to Christ. Through the course of events, one day he was ready, and I had the privilege of leading him to the Lord.

As many Bible believers do, I recommended that he read the Gospel of John. When I followed up a couple of weeks later, he happily reported that he had read the book. When I asked him what he got out of it, he said, "A bunch of history."

It dawned on me that I needed to help young believers in Christ to get more out of the Bible and to learn how to apply God's truth to their lives.

Every passage in the Bible has three applications: historical (past), inspirational (present), and doctrinal or prophetic (future). The Bible is indeed an accurate history book. It is also a book of prophecy by which we may know the future and chart the course of our lives appropriately. More importantly, the Bible is an inspirational book, where we can imagine ourselves in the story and profit through personal application of its truth.

In this book I set out to explain the Gospel of John at the young-believer level in the blended format of a Bible study and commentary. There are 21 chapters, corresponding to each chapter in the gospel. The title of each chapter reflects who Jesus Christ is in that chapter. Each contains four sections: Historical Synopsis, Key Spiritual Lessons, Prophecies (if applicable), and Summary. The

Historical Synopsis briefly describes the history covered in the chapter. The Key Spiritual Lessons is the meat of the chapter. The Prophecies section exposes the future events that are encoded in the chapter.

This book is recommended as a reference commentary for the Gospel of John and as an example of how to outline and study the Bible. It is my sincere hope that new believers in Christ may be able to study and understand the Bible and feed themselves with the truth of God.

Introduction

The Apostle John was one of the original 12 disciples of Jesus Christ. Jesus called John and his brother James while they were mending fishing nets on a ship with their father Zebedee, according to *Mark 1:19-20*. Immediately, the brothers left the ship to follow Jesus.

The Apostle John was also the beloved disciple of Jesus Christ, according to *John 13:23, John 19:26,* and *John 21:7, 20*. Today he is also known as the Apostle of Love by his extensive writings on love in the book of *1John*.

John was the only original disciple who was spared from martyrdom. He spent the latter years of his life in exile in Patmos, a small Greek island in the Aegean Sea. There he penned the book of Revelation. John was uniquely used by God to document His outreach and plan of salvation for mankind, His love, and His wrath.

The Gospel of John is the fourth gospel in the New Testament, following the gospels of Matthew, Mark, and Luke. Each disciple presents Jesus in a different light. Matthew presents Jesus as the King of the Jews. Mark presents Jesus as a servant. Luke presents Jesus as the Son of man. John presents Jesus as the Son of God from heaven.

The gospels of Matthew, Mark, and Luke are collectively known as the synoptic gospels because they include and describe events from a similar point of view, as contrasted with that of John. John omits many of the accounts in the synoptic gospels and includes a considerable amount of material not found in them. John's purpose for the readers is noted in *John 20:30, "And many other signs truly did Jesus in the presence of his disciples, which are not written in this book: (31) But these are written, that ye might believe that Jesus is the Christ, the Son of God; and that believing ye might have life through his name."*

The Gospel of John can be outlined as such:

I. Christ's outreach to the lost world – chapters 1–12
II. Christ's ministry to His own – chapters 13–17
III. Christ's sufferings and glory – chapters 18–21

1 – Emmanuel

Historical Synopsis

The Apostle John exposes Jesus Christ as the divine Word from heaven, who was God Himself. He describes the creativity of the Word as the one who crafted and owns the entire creation. He then reveals the outreach of the Word with His quickening virtue, having life as the light of men. Following, he talks about the humanity of the Word as the Savior of the world.

The Apostle John then describes John the Baptist, who was the forerunner of Jesus Christ and was sent by God to the Jews to bear witness of Jesus as the true Light.

Included in this chapter is the record of Christ's manifestation to the nation of Israel through baptism. John the Baptist was privileged to baptize Jesus and witness the Spirit of God descend from heaven and abide upon Jesus when He came up out of the water.

This chapter concludes with the calling of the first disciples—Andrew, Philip, Nathanael, and an unnamed man, who is believed to be the penman of this gospel.

This chapter can be outlined as such:

    I.   Christ's identity – *John 1:1-18*
   II. Christ's forerunner – *John 1:6-8, 19-28*
  III. Christ's manifestation – *John 1:29-34*

The Book of John

IV.   Christ's followers – *John 1:35-51*

Chapter 1 – Emmanuel

Key Spiritual Lessons

The opening scene of the Gospel of John is as dramatic as the first two verses of the book of Genesis. In the first five verses, the Apostle John takes us from the most awesome God to the most awful darkness and from a lively creation to a deadly destruction. The rest of the verses deal with God's outreach to the fallen human race.

This chapter provides crucial foundational biblical concepts for young believers. Following are the key spiritual lessons:

    I.   The ruin of mankind – *John 1:1-5*
    II.   The rescue of mankind – *John 1:5-51*

The Ruin of Mankind

[Verse 1] When the curtain lifts, the spotlight is on the Word. The identity of the Word is immediately established—*"the Word was God."* Yet the middle of the verse suggests that God and the Word are two separate entities—*"the Word was with God."* Furthermore, the Word is personified with the "him" pronoun in verse 3 and was made flesh (took on human form), according to verse 14. Who is this Word-God?

John the Baptist identified Him as Jesus Christ in verses 15-18. Jesus was the Word (100% God) who came into the world in human form. The Godhead is a Trinity that consists of God the Father, God the Son, and God the Holy Spirit. They are not three separate Gods; they are the same God. Jesus Christ is the second person of the Trinity.

It is important to emphasize that *"the Word was God."* We can only know God and how to interact with and live for Him through His Word. Strictly speaking, we have the incarnate Word (Jesus Christ) and the written word. The Bible is the inspired word of God. (Inspiration is the mechanism that God used to communicate His mind to man.) *2Timothy 3:16 All scripture is given by inspiration of God, and is profitable for doctrine, for reproof, for correction, for instruction in righteousness.* We should not pretend to know God if we do not know what the Bible says. Our relationship with God is as good as our obedience to His word. Sadly, nowadays the Bible is not relevant to many Christians. Pause and meditate on *Hosea 4:6, "My people are destroyed for lack of knowledge: because thou hast rejected knowledge, I will also reject thee, that thou shalt be no priest to me: seeing thou hast forgotten the law of thy God, I will also forget thy children."*

[Verses 2-3] Having revealed the identity of the Word, the Apostle John takes us to the beginning of creation to set straight the record on the origin of the universe and its rightful creator and owner. He also highlights the significance and centrality of the Word in creation.

The Word was in the beginning with God. The phrase *"in the beginning"* refers to the beginning of creation and not the beginning of the Word, for God does not have a beginning. To better understand this, consider "in the beginning" and "from the beginning." *Genesis 1:1* says, *"In the beginning God created the heaven and the earth,"* meaning God and the Word existed in eternity before the beginning of creation. The universe we now have exists from (or since) the beginning.

Verse 3 says, *"All things were made by him; and without him was not any thing made that was made."* As God spoke, the Word brought things into existence. Of God and by the Word, all things came into existence. Creation was not a random act, but according to wisdom and purpose. *Proverbs 8:22-31* and *Ephesians 3:9* are good cross references.

Chapter 1 – Emmanuel

Nothing was ever created or made without the Word, from the highest angel to the finest dust. *Psalms 33:6 By the word of the LORD were the heavens made; and all the host of them by the breath of his mouth. Colossians 1:16 For by him were all things created, that are in heaven, and that are in earth, visible and invisible, whether they be thrones, or dominions, or principalities, or powers: all things were created by him, and for him: (17) And he is before all things, and by him all things consist.*

Everything owes its existence to the Word. This truth destroys the Big Bang theory and the theory of evolution.

[Verse 4] The spotlight shifts to the life in the Word—*"In him was life; and the life was the light of men."* King David knew all along that the fountain of life was with God, and he wrote in *Psalms 36:9, "For with thee is the fountain of life: in thy light shall we see light."* As the fountain of life, the Word is the source of natural and spiritual life of all living creatures. Every living thing borrows life from the Word. Read *John 14:6, John 11:25*. Life is given, and as such we do not own it. We are stewards of it, and we must account for it in the end.

Consider Adam's building blocks. *Genesis 2:7 And the LORD God formed man of the dust of the ground, and breathed into his nostrils the breath of life; and man became a living soul.* Adam's body was made of lifeless, inert material. It became a living being when God injected life into his body. Through the life that was in the Word, Adam was able to live, function, and fellowship with God. *Acts 17:28a* says, *"For in him we live, and move, and have our being."*

According to the latter part of verse 4, *"The life was the light of men."* The life in the Word with respect to mankind is a spiritual light that illuminates mankind to the knowledge of God. King David wrote in *Psalms 43:3, "O send out thy light and thy truth: let them lead me; let them bring me unto thy holy hill, and to thy tabernacles.*

(4) Then will I go unto the altar of God, unto God my exceeding joy: yea, upon the harp will I praise thee, O God my God." Read *2Corinthians 4:6, Psalms 119:105*. Without the spiritual light of life from the Word of life, mankind has no access to God and no hope of eternal life. Jesus says in *John 8:12, "I am the light of the world: he that followeth me shall not walk in darkness, but shall have the light of life."* Adam and Eve lost the light of life when they sinned.

Do you have the light of life from the Word of life? Unlike natural sunlight that falls on everyone, spiritual light is personal and must be obtained individually. *1John 1:1 That which was from the beginning, which we have heard, which we have seen with our eyes, which we have looked upon, and our hands have handled, of the Word of life; (2) (For the life was manifested, and we have seen it, and bear witness, and shew unto you that eternal life, which was with the Father, and was manifested unto us;)"* Read *John 3:36, John 5:24, John 6:47, John 14:6*.

In the first four verses we learn Jesus is the Word, God, the Creator, and the Life. There is no God besides the Lord Jesus Christ. *Isaiah 45:5a I am the LORD, and there is none else, there is no God beside me.* We must not serve any other gods. The Bible says, "No man can serve two masters." When I was a Taoist I wore a bronze pendant that bore the image of a monk for protection and blessing. After receiving Jesus Christ as my Lord and Savior, I threw the pendant into a sewer drain.

[Verse 5] All was well in the preceding verses, but then darkness appeared—*"And the light shineth in darkness; and the darkness comprehended it not."* What darkness is this that prevents people from comprehending the light of God? Those affected by the darkness do not know the truth and their loving Creator, who wants to restore them and give them eternal life. God is not willing that any should perish, but that all should come to the knowledge of truth and repent. But how can people know God if they cannot comprehend the divine light because of the darkness?

Chapter 1 – Emmanuel

This darkness is evil and is associated with spiritual wickedness in high places and the power of Satan, according to *Ephesians 6:12* and *Acts 26:18*. Darkness shrouds the minds of sinners who are not regenerated and illuminated by the Spirit of God. Like a blind person who is unable to perceive physical light, these sons of Adam are spiritually blind and are incapable of comprehending the rays of divine light, no matter how smart they may be. The truths of God are foolishness to such minds. Consequently they establish their own system of righteousness and reject the true Messiah (Anointed or Savior), as is evident in verses 10 and 11—*"He was in the world, and the world was made by him, and the world knew him not. He came unto his own, and his own received him not."*

What happened that plunged mankind into darkness, alienating individuals from the light and life of God? Where does this evil come from?

Sometime in eternity past, darkness broke out in heaven. There was an anointed cherub that covered the throne of God whose name was Lucifer. Lucifer is a good name. It means "light-bearer." He was the epitome of God's creative design. God commended Lucifer as follows:

- *"Thou sealest up the sum, full of wisdom, and perfect in beauty"* – Ezekiel 28:12b.
- *"Thou wast perfect in thy ways from the day that thou wast created"* – Ezekiel 28:15a.

Lucifer's body was magnificently adorned with precious stones of sardius, topaz, diamond, beryl, onyx, jasper, sapphire, emerald, carbuncle, and gold, for glory and beauty. Imagine the reflection of God's light on him. Lucifer was also equipped with musical instruments. He far exceeded the other angelic beings in all aspects and was the showcase of God's workmanship. He was No. 2

in heaven and enjoyed freedom and access to God's throne, holy mountain, and garden.

Tragically Lucifer was corrupt. *Ezekiel 28:17a Thine heart was lifted up because of thy beauty, thou hast corrupted thy wisdom by reason of thy brightness.* Instead of honoring and glorifying God with his beauty and wisdom, Lucifer was vain, prideful, and consumed with self. Despite all the blessings, he wasn't satisfied being No. 2. He wanted to take God's place. According to *Isaiah 14:12-14*, Lucifer said in his heart, *"I will ascend into heaven, I will exalt my throne above the stars of God: I will sit also upon the mount of the congregation, in the sides of the north: I will ascend above the heights of the clouds; I will be like the most High."*

Not surprisingly, God disagreed and said, *"I will destroy thee, O covering cherub, from the midst of the stones of fire"* in *Ezekiel 28:16b*. God also said, *"Yet thou shalt be brought down to hell, to the sides of the pit"* in *Isaiah 14:15*.

Lucifer rebelled against God and drew one-third of the angels with him. A galactic war erupted in heaven where life and light battled death and darkness, which continues even to this day. Lucifer, who became Satan and darkness, took the earth. When God looked on the earth that once was His footstool, He said, *"I beheld the earth, and, lo, it was without form, and void; and the heavens, and they had no light"* in *Jeremiah 4:23*. Darkness overtook creation. Read *Ezekiel 28:13-19, Isaiah 14:12-15, Revelation 12:3-4, Jeremiah 4:19-26, Genesis 1:2, Isaiah 45:18*.

God began the restoration by plunging the earth into water for cleansing. And *"the Spirit of God moved upon the face of the waters."* God then shined His spiritual light in darkness. He said in *Genesis 1:3-4, "Let there be light: and there was light. And God saw the light, that it was good: and God divided the light from the darkness."*

Chapter 1 – Emmanuel

Fast forward a few days, God created Adam and Eve and gave them a mission—*"Be fruitful, and multiply, and replenish the earth."* Wait a minute, what was there to replenish if it was a perfect world? Something had to be missing. The truth is, Adam did not get a perfect world. Evil was in his garden. Adam and Eve were tasked to replenish that which was lost to Satan, but Satan was determined to destroy God's seed. He appeared to Eve in the form of a serpent and beguiled her. She ate the forbidden fruit and shared it with Adam, who was not deceived, but willfully sinned against God by knowingly eating the forbidden fruit. The light of God departed from Adam and Eve, and they went dark. Without the light covering, they were cut off from the life of God, and they discovered their nakedness. They both died spiritually that day, even though Adam lived to be 930 years old before he physically died. In his lifetime, Adam produced sons and daughters after his own likeness and image, which was sinful in nature. Read *Genesis 3:1-19, Genesis 5:1-5, Romans 5:12, 1Timothy 2:14.*

Sinful Adam set off a new human kind that is contrary to God's original design. His descendants are born with his sin nature in the realm of spiritual darkness alienated from the light and life of God. Below are some of their traits:

1. None by default have access to God. Fellowship with God is destroyed because *"what communion hath light with darkness?"*

2. None by default can comprehend the light (or truth) of God because everyone is born with hereditary spiritual blindness.

3. Everyone is a spiritual child of the devil and is inclined to fulfill his will. Read *John 8:44, 2Timothy 2:25-26.* The saying, "We are all God's children" is a lie, because all are born in the realm of spiritual darkness and resemble

their spiritual father the devil. The proof is right at home. Parents need not teach children to be bad. Children are born fully equipped to sin—lie, disobey, steal, hate, kill, etc., because of the sin nature they inherit from Adam. Left unchecked, they will turn into monsters, to the dismay of their loving parents. Adoption by Jesus Christ is the only way out of the devil's family. (Learn more about God's family and the devil's family in Chapter 8.)

Thank God, He did not give up on sinners. He wanted them to know Him and have fellowship with Him. He employed human witnesses to proclaim the Light. He manifested Himself to mankind in human form and established a rescue team that consisted of John the Baptist, Jesus Christ, and the disciples. They were to give to sinners the knowledge of salvation that they might be reconciled to God. Fast forward about 4,000 years from *Genesis 1:2*, John the Baptist appeared as prophesied. Read *John 3:16-17, Isaiah 40:3*.

Following are the members of God's rescue team.

1. John the Baptist—herald of the Light
2. Jesus Christ—the Light
3. Jesus' disciples—proclaimers of the Light

The Rescue of Mankind

John the Baptist—herald of the Light

[Verse 6] The son of Zacharias and Elisabeth, John the Baptist, is described as righteous and blameless before God. John's conception was the fulfillment of prophecy as well as a miracle, because his parents were well past their child-bearing years. The angel Gabriel appeared to Zacharias while he was performing his priestly duty of burning incense in the temple of God. Gabriel told

Chapter 1 – Emmanuel

Zacharias that his wife Elisabeth would bear a child and he should name him John, which means "Jehovah is a gracious giver."

Elisabeth was a cousin to Mary, the mother of Jesus. That made John the Baptist a second cousin to Jesus. John was six months older than Jesus. Read *Luke 1:5-80*.

John the Baptist was a unique individual:

- He was the fulfillment of prophecies in *Isaiah 40:3* and *Malachi 3:1*.
- He was filled with the Holy Ghost while he was in the womb – *Luke 1:15*.
- He was endowed with the spirit and power of Elijah – *Luke 1:17*.
- He was called the prophet of the Highest. Jesus credited John as such: *"Among those that are born of women there is not a greater prophet."* Read *Luke 1:76, Luke 7:28*.
- He had the ability to see the Spirit of God descending upon Jesus – verse 32.
- He stood for righteousness, even when it cost him his life. He reproved king Herod Antipas to his face for wanting to marry Herodias, the wife of his brother Philip, and for all the evils he had done. John was put in prison and later beheaded. Read *Matthew 14:1-12*.

[Verses 7-8] John the Baptist had a specific ministry to the Jews and lived a purposeful life. In his ministry he turned many Jews back to God through his preaching and baptism. Read *Matthew 3:1-12*. Jesus was the Word and John was the voice. Following is a brief summary of John's purpose and ministry.

- To be a forerunner of Jesus Christ – verses 19-28
- To bear witness of the true Light – verses 7-8, 15-18, 29-36

19

- To administer the baptism of repentance – verse 31
- To give the knowledge of salvation to the Jews – *Luke 1:77*
- To give light to them that sat in darkness – *Luke 1:79*
- To guide the Jews in the way of peace – *Luke 1:79*

John's prospect in the work of ministry was to be fruitful—*"that all men through him might believe."* His goal was that the Jews to whom he preached might believe that Jesus was the Light and Messiah. Twice the Pharisees asked John *"Who art thou?"* and he told them he was *"the voice of one crying in the wilderness,"* quoting *Isaiah 40:3*.

Can God count on you to be the voice in a dark and dying world? As special as John was, he was a man. God employs common people to be His witnesses in this dark world. You are fearfully and wonderfully made; you have the Holy Spirit of God in you; you are a son of God. God can use you as He used John.

Do you know that you can live a purposeful life as John the Baptist? What is your purpose and prospect in life? Do you know that God saved you on purpose and for a great purpose? Just as He put Adam and Eve in the garden to dress it, He has a purpose for you. Read *2Corinthians 5:18-20, John 15:16*. You are made to matter for God. You are a steward of His truth and He has called and sent you as His witness for the following reasons:

- Because darkness does not comprehend light – verse 5
- Because the world is sinful – verse 29, *John 3:19*
- Because no one has seen God – verse 18
- Because the world does not know God – verses 10, 26
- Because God can be known – verse 12, *Romans 1:19-20*
- Because God should be made manifest to sinners – verse 31

Chapter 1 – Emmanuel

Jesus Christ—the Light

Jesus Christ was born of a virgin, according to the prophecy in *Isaiah 7:14*, which was written about 680 years prior to the nativity. God chose Mary, who at the time was espoused to Joseph from the lineage of David. The angel Gabriel appeared and broke the news to Mary that she would conceive a son and should name him Jesus, which means "Jehovah is salvation." Mary's premarital pregnancy did not bode well with Joseph, who being a just man, thought of putting her away privately. But the angel of the Lord appeared to Joseph in a dream and confirmed that the child in Mary was of the Holy Ghost. So Joseph took Mary as his wife, but did not have an intimate relationship with her until after Jesus was born. Read verses 1, 14, *Matthew 1:18-25*.

[Verses 9-13] Jesus Christ is the true Light that shines on everyone who comes into this world, in order that sinners may know the truth and be reconciled to God. Unfortunately mankind in its sinful corruption is incapable of comprehending the Light and chooses darkness. They try to establish their own righteousness through religion. But we who receive Jesus Christ by faith are given the power (right or privilege) to become the sons of God and are ensured eternal life. We are born again by the Spirit of God—a spiritual operation that results in a second birth. See Chapter 3 for what it means to be born again by the Spirit. Read *John 8:12, John 12:46, John 3:19-21*.

Following are the salient points:

1. Jesus Christ is the true Light. This reveals that there is false light, such as false Christs, bibles, teachers, prophets, and disciples. Beware that you are not deceived by genuine-looking counterfeits. *Matthew 24:24 For there shall arise false Christs, and false prophets, and shall shew great signs and wonders; insomuch that, if it were possible, they shall deceive the*

The Book of John

very elect. Read *Matthew 7:15-20*. You need to know the truth, which reveals falsehood. This means you need to have a working knowledge of the Bible.

2. Jesus Christ *"was in the world,"* but He was not of the world like us. Jesus Christ was of the Father. He was God the Son. The Jews struggled with Jesus' origin in chapters 7 and 8. They mistook Him as an ordinary man, the son of Joseph, and did not own Him as the Messiah. John the Baptist, whom the religious rulers of the Jews held in high regard, positively testified of Jesus' superiority three times in this chapter (verses 15, 27, 30). John also said that Jesus was before him, even though Jesus, as a man, was six months younger than John. This was because Jesus was an eternal being from everlasting. Jesus was before Abraham and Adam. Read *Proverbs 8:22-31. Psalms 90:1-2, John 8:58*.

3. Jesus Christ debunks the following false teachings with the phrase *"as many as received him"* in verse 12.
    a. God has a certain quota for the number of souls in heaven.
    b. God only saves those of a certain race or skin color.
    c. God predestinated certain persons to be saved.

4. Jesus Christ is the only way of salvation and eternal life.

[Verse 14] We learn so many things about Jesus from this verse alone—*"And the Word was made flesh, and dwelt among us, (and we beheld his glory, the glory as of the only begotten of the Father,) full of grace and truth."*

Jesus was the embodiment of the Word, who was the Almighty God. *Isaiah 9:6 For unto us a child is born, unto us a son is* *given: and the government shall be upon his shoulder: and his name shall be called Wonderful, Counsellor, <u>The mighty God</u>, The everlasting Father, The Prince of Peace.*

Jesus was Emmanuel, meaning "God with us." *Matthew 1:23 Behold, a virgin shall be with child, and shall bring forth a son, and they shall call his name Emmanuel, which being interpreted is, God with us.* God was ready to dwell with man. In the Old Testament, God dwelled with man in the tabernacle as described in *Exodus 25* and *26*. In the New Testament, God dwells with man through Jesus Christ. Thus no one can claim to have God in their lives without Jesus Christ.

Jesus also was the glory of the Father and the express image of His person, according to *Hebrews 1:1-3*. No one has ever seen the Father, but what can be known of Him has been declared by Jesus in the pages of the Bible. Verse 18 says, *"No man hath seen God at any time; the only begotten Son, which is in the bosom of the Father, he hath declared him."* This means to know God is to know His Word.

Christians should have a working knowledge of the word of God, otherwise, we will default to trusting in feelings and practicing things that are unbiblical. The Bible gives specific instructions and counsel for us to live by. We are not to live by feelings. We may know the God we serve and His dealings with mankind by His words and testimonies. The Bible says, *"Ye shall know that I am the LORD."* We may know the truth that delivers us from falsehoods, for the word of God is truth, according to *John 17:17*. We may know the reason for our existence, the plan for our life, and find true happiness and contentment in this utterly vain world by navigating our lives according to the precepts of the word. *Psalms 119:105* says, *"Thy word is a lamp unto my feet, and a light unto my path."* We may know Old Testament Bible stories that serve as examples for our admonition, according to *Romans 15:4* and *1Corinthians 10:11-12*. We may know the future by the prophecies in the Bible. A biblical view of end times helps us set proper affections and

The Book of John

priorities in life. Perhaps above all, we may make known to our children the praises of the Lord, His strength, and His wonderful works that they may set their hope in God – *Psalms 78:1-8*.

Jesus was the only begotten of the Father. The Father had no other Savior besides Jesus, the Lamb of God who takes away the sins of the world. Read verses 29, 36, *John 3:16, 1John 4:9*. All other so-called saviors are antichrists. Your future is in jeopardy if your salvation is based on anything or anyone besides Jesus alone.

Jesus was full of grace and truth. Verse 16 says, *"And of his fulness have all we received, and grace for grace."* The grace (favor with God) and truth that we get from Jesus is of His fullness. How full? According to *Colossians 1:19, "For it pleased the Father that in him should all fulness dwell."* This means Jesus is more than sufficient. We absolutely need not (and should not) go to another source to obtain grace and truth, because Jesus is the personification of grace and truth. If we want favor with God, the answer is Jesus—period. If we want truth, the answer is also Jesus—period.

Jesus offers *"grace for grace"* (or grace upon grace). Verse 17 says, *"For the law was given by Moses, but grace and truth came by Jesus Christ."* Thank God we are not under the law, but under grace. No one can fulfill the law. Just think of the times you have broken the Ten Commandments. *Romans 3:20 Therefore by the deeds of the law there shall no flesh be justified in his sight: for by the law is the knowledge of sin.*

In verses 32-34, John confirmed that Jesus was the Son of God. God Himself validated this with His Spirit descending and remaining on Jesus. So if Jesus was the Son of God and the Word was God the Father, and now they are joined by the Spirit of God, what do we have here? *Colossians 2:9* gives the answer, *"For in him dwelleth all the fulness of the Godhead bodily."* Jesus Christ was 100% God in the flesh.

Chapter 1 – Emmanuel

Other titles of Jesus in this chapter include the Messiah, the King of Israel, and the Son of man. Read verses 41, 49, and 51. A prophecy is revealed by building up the titles of Jesus as follows.

Verse 1	Word = God The Word was God.
Verses 14, 17	Word = God = Jesus Christ Jesus was God in human form.
Verses 29, 36	Word = God = Jesus Christ = Lamb of God Jesus, as the innocent Lamb of God was sacrificed for the sins of the world.
Verse 34	Word = God = Jesus Christ = Lamb of God = Son of God Jesus will return as the Son of God to establish His kingdom on earth.
Verse 41	Word = God = Jesus Christ = Lamb of God = Son of God = Messiah The Jews will acknowledge that Jesus is the Messiah.
Verse 49	Word = God = Jesus Christ = Lamb of God = Son of God = Messiah = King of Israel Jesus will be hailed as the King of Israel.
Verse 51	Word = God = Jesus Christ = Lamb of God = Son of God = Messiah = King of Israel = Son of man Jesus is the Son of man prophesied in *Daniel 7:13*. As the Son of man, Jesus will be the King of Kings and Lord of Lords, according to *Daniel 7:14*.

What is the word of God to you? You would do well to resolve this early in your Christian life. One of the things that separates Christianity from other religions is its claim to an absolute written authority from God. The Bible is the word of God; it is the word of truth.

The word of God is essential to your growth in the grace and knowledge of Jesus Christ. There is so much treasure in the Bible that can only be seen and understood by those whose spiritual eyes are enlightened by the light of the gospel of Christ. The treasures are yours to mine. Read the Bible daily and ask the Holy Spirit of God to teach you how to apply the principles to your life. The Bible is not just a collection of stories, it is God's words to live by and should be your final authority. Remember that no one can violate the word of God and not fall.

Finally, are you able to explain the gospel to others? You must be able to explain how you received Jesus Christ for the pardoning of your sins and show others the salvation verses in the Bible.

The disciples—proclaimers of the Light

[Verses 35-51] Andrew, Peter, Philip, Nathanael, and an unnamed person (who could be the Apostle John, the penman of this gospel) were the early disciples of Jesus Christ. A disciple is a learner. If you are to know and grow in the knowledge of the truth and be fruitful, then you need to be a disciple.

A disciple learns from a master. What better master can one have than the Lord Jesus Christ? Andrew, Nathanael, and the unnamed disciple called Jesus Rabbi, a title used by the Jews to address their teachers. They came to Jesus to be His students. You too can learn at the feet of Jesus. Pick up your Bible and read it daily. You can learn from another person, but eventually you must learn from Jesus. Read *Proverbs 2* about receiving wisdom and understanding. Notice the transfer of mastership from John the Baptist to Jesus in verses 35-37. (See the definition of discipleship in Chapter 21.)

A disciple confirms Jesus' identity by the word of God. According to verse 37, Andrew and his pal first heard John the Baptist speak concerning Jesus, for John had testified, *"This was he," "This is he," "This is the Son of God,"* and *"Behold the Lamb of God,"* in verses 15, 30, 34, and 36 respectively. Thereafter they

Chapter 1 – Emmanuel

followed Jesus and examined Him by spending time with Him, and confirmed that they had found the Messiah. Philip also was able to authenticate that Jesus was the Messiah by searching the scriptures—*"We have found him, of whom Moses in the law, and the prophets, did write, Jesus of Nazareth, the son of Joseph."* In *John 5:39*, Jesus advised the Jews who had trouble believing in Him: *"Search the scriptures; for in them ye think ye have eternal life: and they are they which testify of me."* You should do likewise. Search the scriptures and confirm for yourself that Jesus is precisely who the Bible says He is. Don't simply believe what others say. Remember the Bible is our final authority.

A disciple follows Jesus. Consider the principle in *John 10:27*, *"My sheep hear my voice, and I know them, and they follow me."* Jesus said to Philip, *"Follow me,"* and He would say the same to you. The first disciples couldn't have imagined how their lives would change once they decided to follow Jesus. Their faith and obedience transformed the world.

Below is what it means to follow Jesus based on *Luke 9:57-62*. See additional notes in Chapter 21.

- *Luke 9:57 And it came to pass, that, as they went in the way, a certain man said unto him, Lord, I will follow thee whithersoever thou goest. (58) And Jesus said unto him, Foxes have holes, and birds of the air have nests; but the Son of man hath not where to lay his head.*
  Following Jesus is not about getting more of the world and its comforts. It is about gaining or winning Christ. After all, nothing in this world is worth anything compared to knowing and following the Lord Jesus Christ. The Apostle Paul wrote, *"Yea doubtless, and I count all things but loss for the excellency of the knowledge of Christ Jesus my Lord: for whom I have*

suffered the loss of all things, and do count them but dung, that I may win Christ."

- *Luke 9:59 And he said unto another, Follow me. But he said, Lord, suffer me first to go and bury my father. (60) Jesus said unto him, Let the dead bury their dead: but go thou and preach the kingdom of God.*
  Following Jesus is to be about the Father's business and to let nothing distract us from it.

- *Luke 9:61 And another also said, Lord, I will follow thee; but let me first go bid them farewell, which are at home at my house. (62) And Jesus said unto him, No man, having put his hand to the plough, and looking back, is fit for the kingdom of God.*
  Following Jesus means no turning back. We cannot serve two masters. Read *Matthew 6:24*. We must burn the bridges to the past.

A disciple also evangelizes the lost. As a result of spending time with Jesus, Andrew told his brother Simon Peter, that he had found the Messiah and brought him to Jesus. In like manner, Philip brought Nathanael to Jesus. What about you? Remember that you are a member of God's rescue team. Share your faith in Christ with your family. Show them the pathway to salvation and how they can obtain forgiveness of sins. Your testimony is extremely important. Be careful to maintain a pure and blameless life so that people see Jesus through you. The light of God is in you. You, the earthen vessel that encapsulates the light of the glorious gospel of Christ, must be broken for the light to shine through. Read *2Corinthians 4:6-7*. The most effective evangelism is accomplished through the demonstration of your life (your priorities, decisions, and choices) and communicated in love, humility, and brokenness of spirit.

Summary

The Word is God, the Creator of the universe, and the source of life. The Word is the light of life that illuminates mankind to the knowledge of God. Unfortunately the minds of sinners are shrouded by darkness disallowing them to comprehend the divine light of God. In His great mercy, the Word reached out to mankind in human form in the person of Jesus Christ.

God is not willing that any sinner should perish, but that all should come to repentance. God uses human witnesses to bear witness of the true Light, beginning with the prophets in the Old Testament, to John the Baptist, to Jesus Christ, to the early disciples and apostles, and to you and me. We are a member of God's rescue team and we have a responsibility to testify the Word (Jesus Christ) to unbelievers that they might be reconciled to God. *Romans 10:14 How then shall they call on him in whom they have not believed? and how shall they believe in him of whom they have not heard? and how shall they hear without a preacher? (15) And how shall they preach, except they be sent? as it is written, How beautiful are the feet of them that preach the gospel of peace, and bring glad tidings of good things! (16) But they have not all obeyed the gospel. For Esaias saith, Lord, who hath believed our report? (17) So then faith cometh by hearing, and hearing by the word of God.*

2 – True Joy

Historical Synopsis

There was a marriage in Cana of Galilee where the bride or the groom might have been related to Jesus because Mary seemed to be a principal person at the wedding. Since Joseph is not mentioned, he is thought to have died by this time. It was at this marriage that Jesus performed His first miracle of turning water into wine.

Following a brief stop at Capernaum, Jesus went up to Jerusalem to keep the Passover. There He discovered the Jews had turned the temple into a merchandise mart. He was enraged because the temple was meant to be *"my Father's house,"* a house of prayer. He drove the buyers and sellers out of the temple and overthrew the tables of the moneychangers and the seats of them that sold doves. He also gave a sign to the Jews who quarreled with Him.

This chapter can be outlined as such:

I. Jesus turns water into wine at a wedding in Cana – *John 2:1-11*
II. Jesus purges the temple in Jerusalem – *John 2:12-17*
III. Jesus foretells His death and resurrection – *John 2:18-22*
IV. Jesus is accepted by many Jews when they see the miracles – *John 2:23-25*

Chapter 2 – True Joy

Key Spiritual Lessons

Packaged in this chapter is the secret to true joy. While the world uses the word "joy" and "happiness" interchangeably, "joy" is a fruit of the Spirit, according to *Galatians 5:22*. Believers can be joyful regardless of their circumstances. Unbelievers seek joy in worldly things like parties, food, alcohol, drugs, sports, wealth, power, ownership, relationships, and so forth. Unfortunately the joy they seek is still as far away as ever.

The secret to true joy is as follows:

I. Be a believer of Jesus Christ – *John 2:1-4*
II. Be a vessel for the water-wine – *John 2:5-11*
III. Be careful not to defile the temple of God – *John 2:12-16*
IV. Believe in the living Christ and His words – *John 2:17-25*

Be a Believer of Jesus Christ

[Verses 1-2] There was a marriage in Cana of Galilee on the third day, which is generally thought to be the same day that Jesus found Philip and Nathanael in *John 1:43-51*. The bride or groom might have been related to Mary, the mother of Jesus, as she seemed to be somewhat in charge, and she didn't need a wedding invitation as did Jesus and His disciples.

[Verse 3] The joyous wedding ran into its first setback when Jesus arrived. Mary said to Jesus, *"They have no wine."* (They ran out of wine.)

Wine is a type of joy. Read *Psalms 104:15, Proverbs 3:9-10, Judges 9:13*. (A type is a symbol that may represent a person, thing,

Chapter 2 – True Joy

or event. The Bible is full of types, which makes it very interesting and lively.) The two types of wine presented in this chapter are the traditional wine from grapes and Jesus' water-wine. Respectively, they represent worldly joy and true joy.

Compare the wine from the blood of the grapes (*Genesis 49:11, Deuteronomy 32:14*) with the wine from the blood of Christ. Read *John 6:53-56*. Consider *John 6:54, "Whoso eateth my flesh, and drinketh my blood, hath eternal life."* The saying is symbolic. It is not meant to be physical, but spiritual by faith. The Jews didn't understand and they struggled with it. Today biblical churches serve wafers and grape juice during communion to symbolize the body and blood of Christ. (They don't become the body and blood of Christ after a priest does some hocus pocus.)

Below are the lessons:

- Worldly joy is grossly inadequate to truly make anyone happy because it deteriorates over time. Observe in verse 10 that good wine is traditionally brought out at the beginning of a feast when the guests' heads are clear and their appetites fresh. Lower quality wine is served when the guests are well drunk and their heads are confused. This depicts the degradation of worldly joy.

- Worldly joy will eventually run out regardless of how much you have. Do not focus on getting more from the world in order to be happy. Instead get true joy from Jesus Christ by inviting Him into your life and letting His words abide in you.

- Worldly joy should be replaced by true joy if Jesus is your Lord. Notice that the traditional wine ran out when Jesus arrived at the wedding.

[Verse 4] Jesus responded to Mary's suggestion by saying, *"Woman, what have I to do with thee? mine hour is not yet come."*

This strange response comes across as disrespectful to Mary for some readers. This is not so because Jesus used the occasion to teach the people that true joy could only be obtained through a blood relationship with the risen Christ. During the wedding it wasn't time for Jesus to suffer, bleed, and die for the sins of the world, therefore He said to Mary, *"Mine hour is not yet come."* In lieu of His blood, Jesus turned water into wine, symbolizing His blood. (Note the parallel between Moses' miracle and Jesus' miracle. Moses turned water into blood [*Exodus 7:19-21*], Jesus turned water into wine [blood].)

Jesus also said, *"Woman, what have I to do with thee?,"* because the timing of the offering of His blood on the cross was according to God's determination and no one, not even Mary, could influence it.

To experience true joy, you must first invite Jesus Christ into your life. You will not find true joy outside of Jesus Christ, certainly not in anything the world has to offer, including religion. Sadly many who claim to be Christians simply live a Christian lifestyle and have no personal relationship with the Christ of Christianity. Some have a zeal for God, but not everyone has a relationship with God.

Be a Vessel for the Water-Wine

[Verses 5-11] Mary took the rebuke, knowing that Jesus would still help her friends (or relatives) in this strait. She told the servants to observe His orders. Jesus instructed them to fill the six stone water pots with water to the brim and then to draw some out and serve the governor of the feast. The governor, who wasn't aware of the miracle, tasted the water-wine and was surprised that

Chapter 2 – True Joy

the bridegroom had kept the good wine until last rather than serve it at the beginning of the feast, as was customary.

Notice in verse 9 that the servants who filled the pots with water witnessed the miracle. Imagine their joy. You too can experience true joy as follows:

1. Obey the word of God. Mary said to the servants, *"Whatsoever he saith unto you, do it."* The servants filled and drew from the water pots according to Jesus' instructions. Learning the Bible is easy, but obeying it is tough, because the flesh is a self-serving me-monster. Read *Romans 7:14-25*. It is not how much you know about the Bible that matters, but how much you practice what it says. You will blow it from time to time. You will feel bad and may want to do something good for God to get back in His good grace. But the best thing you can do is ask God for forgiveness and repent, because the Bible says in *1Samuel 15:22b*, *"Behold, to obey is better than sacrifice, and to hearken than the fat of rams."* (Repent simply means changing course 180 degrees, turning from the course of sin to God.)

2. Fill the water pots with water. Water is a type of the word of God. Read *Ephesians 5:25-26*. You are the water pot. (There are six water pots. In Christian numerology, six is the number of man.) You don't want to be an empty water pot. The Bible says in *Proverbs 19:2a*, *"The soul be without knowledge, it is not good."* You want to be filled with the word of God to the brim. This takes time. It is precept upon precept, line upon line, here a little, and there a little, like children when they are first instructed in the rudiments of a language. Read *Proverbs 24:3-4, Isaiah 28:9-10*. Have daily fellowship with God.

Remember RPM – Read, Pray, and Meditate on the word of God.

3. Draw out what God has taught you and serve. Look for an opportunity to serve in the local church. You will experience the joy of ministering the word of God and seeing lives supernaturally transformed and enriched like a fine aged wine.

Be Careful Not To Defile the Temple of God

[Verses 12-16] After the wedding, Jesus, along with His mother, kinsmen, and disciples, spent a short time in Capernaum. The name Capernaum means "Village of comfort." Thereafter Jesus went up to Jerusalem to keep the Passover. This was the first Passover after Jesus' baptism.

At Jerusalem, He discovered the Jews had turned the temple of God into a house of merchandise. Instead of maintaining the tranquil house of prayer where people come to worship and meet with God, the Jews profaned the temple and used it as a merchandise mart. They sold oxen, sheep, and doves, and transacted foreign currency exchanges. Imagine the smell. The religious rulers allowed it, possibly because they had a share of the profits.

Jesus made a scourge of small cords and drove the merchants and the animals out of the temple and overthrew the money changers' tables. He said to the merchants who sold doves, *"Take these things hence; make not my Father's house an house of merchandise."*

The main lesson here is that a clean vessel is necessary in order to experience true joy. Your body is the temple of the Holy

Ghost. Read *1Corinthians 3:16-17, 1Corinthians 6:12-20*. Keep it sacred and holy, otherwise you can expect discipline from God.

The most miserable people in the world are Christians who are out of fellowship with God. He will show you the things that must be corrected when you read, pray, and meditate (RPM) on His word. You should respond in obedience, even though it may not be easy because of the daily battle with your flesh. You may pray *Psalms 139:23-24 Search me, O God, and know my heart: try me, and know my thoughts. And see if there be any wicked way in me, and lead me in the way everlasting.*

Believe in the Living Christ and His Words

[Verses 17-22] When the disciples heard Jesus reference the temple as *"my Father's house,"* they were reminded of the verse, *"The zeal of thine house hath eaten me up"* in *Psalms 69*, which belonged to the Messiah. Jesus essentially presented Himself as the Messiah to the Jews. (The verses in *Psalms 69* are referenced in the New Testament in *John 15:25, John 19:28,* and *Romans 15:3*, to show that Jesus is the Messiah.)

Jesus' action to purge the temple was gutsy, to say the least. He was alone, unassisted, and armed with only a scourge of small cords. Surprisingly, the religious rulers did not send their officers to arrest Jesus. They supposed He acted by a divine authority and demanded a sign (or miracle) to prove that His actions were authorized and commissioned by God.

Jesus gave them a sign related to His death and resurrection. He said, *"Destroy this temple, and in three days I will raise it up."* The religious rulers scoffed at the answer. It took 46 years to build the temple. It was ludicrous for a man to think that he could raise it up in three days. They did not understand that Jesus was referring to the temple of His body.

For a sign, Jesus could have healed someone or opened the eyes of a blind person as He did to the man at the Pool of Siloam in chapter 9. But He knew that those were the men who would crucify Him, so He gave them a direct prophecy of their future action as well as their demise, because He would rise from the dead.

After Jesus rose from the dead (about three years after this prophecy), the disciples recalled His words and believed the scripture. *Psalms 16:10 For thou wilt not leave my soul in hell; neither wilt thou suffer thine Holy One to see corruption.* Jesus' words agreed with scriptures because He was the Word.

To experience true joy, you must believe in the living Christ and His words. Jesus Christ is alive! He is the only living God. All other so-called gods are dead. You can count on the word of God because it is truth. Read *John 17:17*. The Bible must be your final authority rather than a religion or a religious leader. It is the word to live by, and your view of what's right and wrong must be based on it.

[Verses 23-25] On the feast day in Jerusalem, Jesus performed miracles, and many believed in His name. However Jesus did not commit Himself to all of them because He was omniscient and knew what was in their hearts.

You may say you believe in Jesus. The question is, does Jesus believe in you? God knows your heart. You can fool many people, but you cannot fool God because He reads your heart. The Bible says in *1Samuel 16:7b*, "*For the LORD seeth not as man seeth; for man looketh on the outward appearance, but the LORD looketh on the heart.*"

Chapter 2 – True Joy

Prophecies

The end-time prophecies in this chapter reveal that God is not done with the Jews. The Apostle Paul supported this view in his epistle to the church at Rome in Romans chapters 9-11. Some bad teachings proclaim that God has given up on the Jews. This simply is not true.

The phrase "third day" in verse 1 is the key that unlocks the prophecy in this chapter. Consider *Hosea 6:1, "Come, and let us return unto the LORD: for he hath torn, and he will heal us; he hath smitten, and he will bind us up. (2) After two days will he revive us: in the third day he will raise us up, and we shall live in his sight."*

The phrase "two days" refers to the 2,000-year period after the Jews rejected Jesus Christ as their Messiah. (You should know that one day is as a thousand years. Read *2Peter 3:8.*) Jesus Christ was crucified about 2,000 years ago. After that, the gospel went to the Gentiles. Therefore the 2,000-year period is also known as "The times of the Gentiles." This is the time we live in. We are fast approaching the close of the "two days" period. The "third day" can come at any moment when the Lord Jesus will return to deal with the Jews once again.

The future of the Jews is encoded in the following verses:

- *John 2:2 And both Jesus was called, and his disciples, to the marriage.*
  Jesus Christ will come again to the Jews when they, as a nation, acknowledge their offence and call on Him, just as when they called Him to the wedding in Cana. Jesus Christ will be accompanied by the armies of heaven – *Revelation 19:14.*

- *John 2:3 And when <u>they wanted wine</u>, the mother of Jesus saith unto him, They have no wine.*
  At His second coming, the Lord Jesus will find the Jews in a sorry state. The Jews will be without joy, just as the wine ran out at the wedding. The antichrist is the reason for their sorrow. They will be betrayed and severely persecuted and afflicted by the antichrist. *Hosea 5:15 I will go and return to my place, till they acknowledge their offence, and seek my face: in their affliction they will seek me early.*

- *John 2:6 And there were set there six waterpots of stone, after the manner of the purifying of the Jews, containing two or three firkins apiece. (7) Jesus saith unto them, Fill the waterpots with water. And they filled them up to the brim.*
  The Jews will be without the knowledge of God as represented by the empty water pots at the wedding. However God will miraculously fill them with His truth. *Jeremiah 31:33 But this shall be the covenant that I will make with the house of Israel; After those days, saith the LORD, I will put my law in their inward parts, and write it in their hearts; and will be their God, and they shall be my people. (34) And they shall teach no more every man his neighbour, and every man his brother, saying, Know the LORD: for they shall all know me, from the least of them unto the greatest of them, saith the LORD: for I will forgive their iniquity, and I will remember their sin no more.* Also read *Hebrews 8:10-12, Hebrews 10:16-17.*

- *John 2:14 And found in the temple those that sold oxen and sheep and doves, and the changers of money sitting: (15) And when he had made a scourge of small cords, he drove them all out of the temple, and the sheep, and the*

> *oxen; and poured out the changers' money, and overthrew the tables; (16) And said unto them that sold doves, Take these things hence; make not my Father's house an house of merchandise.*

The temple of God in Jerusalem will be desecrated. The antichrist will use it as a platform to declare himself as God. Read *2Thessalonians 2:3-4, Matthew 24:15, Daniel 9:26-27*. But rest assured, all will be cleaned up when the Lord Jesus Christ returns.

- *John 2:23 Now when he was in Jerusalem at the passover, in the feast day, many believed in his name, when they saw the miracles which he did.*

    Jesus Christ will reappear in Jerusalem. He will deliver the Jews from the antichrist and turn their mourning into joy. Read *Jeremiah 31:10-13, Psalms 30*. They will see the miracle and get to taste the water-wine, the new joy from Jesus Christ. And many will believe Jesus that day, not by faith, but by sight.

Jesus also prophesied of His own death and resurrection in verses 18-22. This prophecy is indeed fulfilled. Praise God that Jesus Christ rose again. Death and hell had no power over Him. Read *1Corinthians 15:12-22*.

Summary

Your selection of wine matters, because the two types of wine represent worldly joy and true joy. Jesus Christ is the only source of true joy. May you find true joy. May the word of God enrich your life like a fine aged wine.

3 – Love

Historical Synopsis

This chapter begins with the famous story of Nicodemus, who visited Jesus by night to learn more of His doctrine. Nicodemus was no ordinary man. He was a man of eminence and authority in Jerusalem, a ruler of the Jews, and a member of the Sanhedrim of the sect of the Pharisees. Among the Jews, the Pharisees were the strictest sect for religion and holiness that focused on external purity and performance. Although corrupt, they highly regarded the Messiah and all the writings of the Old Testament. They believed in doctrines of angels and spirits and the resurrection of the dead, which the Sadducees denied. Yet the Pharisees were irreconcilable enemies of Christ, making it interesting that such a one should come to Jesus and desire a conversation with Him.

This chapter concludes with John the Baptist's discourse with his disciples concerning baptism. Since Jesus' disciples also baptized people, John's disciples weren't sure whom they should follow. This prompted John to clarify his standing with Christ.

This chapter can be outlined as such:

I. Jesus' discourse with Nicodemus concerning spiritual regeneration – *John 3:1-21*
II. John the Baptist's discourse with his disciples concerning baptism and his standing with Christ – *John 3:22-36*

Chapter 3 – Love

GOD

Eternal Life

SIN Death

… The Book of John

Key Spiritual Lessons

This is the most-referenced chapter in the Gospel of John because it contains the most famous, quoted, and displayed verse in the Bible—*John 3:16,* which talks about God's great love and sacrifice for mankind. This chapter is packed with doctrine. The amount of truth challenges the best preacher, writer, and commentator. We could camp here a long time. The chapter explains life's greatest necessity, which is eternal life. After all, what is life without eternal life?

Following are the key spiritual lessons:

I. The necessity of spiritual regeneration – *John 3:1-13*
II. The necessity of Christ's suffering and death – *John 3:14-21*
III. The necessity of making Christ preeminent in your life – *John 3:22-36*

The Necessity of Spiritual Regeneration

[Verse 1] Nicodemus, whose name means "Conqueror," was an ecclesiastical ruler of the Jews and a member of the Sanhedrim, which was an assembly of 20 to 23 men, consisting of wise men, priests, Levites, and elders of the people. Jesus referred to Nicodemus as "a master of Israel" in verse 10.

[Verse 2] Fearing the reproach of his peers, Nicodemus went to see Jesus at night under the cover of darkness. He was attracted to Jesus by the miracles He performed. The Sanhedrim was convinced that Jesus was a teacher who came from God because the miracles were real and no man could perform them except God was with Him. Nicodemus called Jesus Rabbi, a title used by the Jews to address their teachers whom they believed possessed great

Chapter 3 – Love

treasures of wisdom and knowledge. Nicodemus couldn't figure out if Jesus was the Messiah, which could have been the reason for the visit. (The Jews were expecting a political savior who would appear in external pomp and power. Jesus did not fit that image in His first appearance to Israel. He was a meek and lowly person.) Since Nicodemus mentioned God in the conversation, Jesus took the opportunity to present the Kingdom of God and switched the conversation from miracles to the mystery of regeneration or second birth.

Note:

Unlike Gentiles, Jews couldn't deal with faith. They required signs. Therefore the miracles were Jesus' credentials. They were proofs to the Jews that God the Father and Jesus were one. Read *1Corinthians 1:22, John 5:36, John 10:24-25, 37-38, John 14:10-11*.

[Verses 3-5] Jesus positively and vehemently asserted to Nicodemus that *"Except a man be born again, he cannot see the kingdom of God."* Jesus began the speech with "Verily, verily," which means amen, surely, truly, and of a truth. Double that since He said it twice. The matter was non-negotiable and irreversible. This doctrine caught Nicodemus off guard because the Jews rested in the Law of Moses. Read *Romans 2:17-29*. Imagine a master of Israel who knew the Old Testament inside-out being told he would miss the Kingdom of God.

Nicodemus didn't comprehend the idea of a natural and spiritual body and that the new birth was to be a spiritual operation. It was obvious from his statement, *"How can a man be born when he is old? can he enter the second time into his mother's womb, and be born?"* To him, this was absurd, to say nothing of impossible, as any natural person would think. So Jesus expounded the mystery: *"Verily, verily, except a man be born of water* (first birth, physical) *and of the Spirit* (second birth, spiritual), *he cannot enter into the kingdom of God."* Read *1Corinthians 15:39-50*. One cannot be physically born into a relationship with God.

The doctrine of spiritual regeneration is simple:

- Problem of mankind
  The entire human race must be spiritually regenerated because of sin. The first birth (of flesh) is defective. *Romans 3:23 For all have sinned, and come short of the glory of God.* Read *Romans 5:12, Psalms 51:5*. The natural man is not patchable or repairable by worldly or physical means. No amount of education, religion, morality, or good works can erase sin and secure a right relationship with God. Read *Ephesians 2:8-9, Romans 11:6, Hebrews 11:6.*

- Penalty of sin
  The Bible says, *"The wages of sin is death."* Sinners who die in their sins are eternally separated from God. Their unrighteous souls will stand in judgment according to their works instead of according to their faith in Jesus Christ. In this case, they will be found guilty 100% of the time, and they will burn in the lake of fire for eternity. *Ezekiel 18:4 Behold, all souls are mine; as the soul of the father, so also the soul of the son is mine: <u>the soul that sinneth, it shall die</u>.* Any questions? All unregenerated sinners will die a second death. As the faithful saying goes, "If you are born once, you will die twice; if you are born twice, you will die once." Read *Hebrews 9:27, Isaiah 64:6, John 8:23-24, Revelation 20:11-15.*

- Provision of God
  Verse 16 says, *"For God so loved the world, that he gave his only begotten Son, that whosoever believeth in him should not perish, but have everlasting life."* Salvation is

Chapter 3 – Love

God's free gift made available through Jesus Christ only. *Romans 6:23 For the wages of sin is death; but the gift of God is eternal life through Jesus Christ our Lord.*

[Verses 6-8] The natural man's greatest necessity is to be born again by the Holy Spirit of God, which is a spiritual operation through faith in Jesus Christ. The spiritual birth is distinctly different than the first birth by flesh—*"That which is born of the flesh is flesh; and that which is born of the Spirit is spirit."* Unlike physical birth, spiritual birth is invisible. However, the evidence should be very clear.

Seeing that Nicodemus was astonished at the doctrine of the new birth, Jesus used the wind as an illustration. (The wind is a type of the Holy Spirit of God.)

- *"The wind bloweth where it listeth"*—The Holy Spirit of God is a free agent in regeneration. He works how, where, and when He pleases.

- *"Thou hearest the sound thereof, but canst not tell whence it cometh, and whither it goeth"*—No one can tell when the Holy Spirit of God begins and ends the operation, but one should be able to notice a clear change in the person whom the Holy Spirit has regenerated.

Being saved or born again is based on knowledge of the word of God combined with faith and not feelings, good works, visions, experiences, or membership in a certain religion or denomination. Sadly, many overturn Bible truth with their feelings and experiences.

You need to know that you are a sinner bound for hell and that God loves you, sent His Son to die for your sins, and salvation is a free gift available only in Jesus Christ. Salvation is a transaction—a conscious decision to exchange sin and death for forgiveness and eternal life. Be extremely careful, because Christendom has many professing Christians who are not Christians. Their salvation testimonies are uncertain and incorrect. Examples include surviving a terrible accident or near-death experience, speaking in tongues, water baptism, good works, church membership, familiarity with Jesus' stories, someone praying for them, and so on. I once asked a man if he knew the Lord. He replied, "Oh, I was baptized when I was 12." He was basing his salvation on his baptism and was living with a false hope. Just when I thought I'd heard it all, a young lady claimed to be a Christian because she prayed and God healed her sick dog.

Here is a test: If God were to ask you why He should let you into heaven, what would you say?

What is required to be born again? Accepting Jesus Christ as Lord and Savior by faith through a simple prayer with the following understanding:

- Admission of sin before Jesus Christ. Jesus is of no use to the self-righteous, just as doctors are of no use to sick people who refuse to admit they are sick. Read *Mark 2:17*. You must see yourself as lost before you can be saved.

- Understanding the penalty of sin is death.

- Realizing that only Jesus Christ can forgive sins. Read *1Timothy 2:5, John 14:6, 1John 2:23, 1John 5:11-13, Acts 4:10-12, Matthew 7:13-14.*

- Agreeing that God's salvation is a free gift and not a loan or debt that should be repaid through good works. All that is necessary is to simply receive the gift with a sincere prayer and a believing heart. A gift is free to the

- Accepting Jesus Christ as Lord and Savior by faith through a simple prayer. *Romans 10:9 That if thou shalt confess with thy mouth the Lord Jesus, and shalt believe in thine heart that God hath raised him from the dead, thou shalt be saved. (10) For with the heart man believeth unto righteousness; and with the mouth confession is made unto salvation.*

[Verse 9] Unfortunately Nicodemus still couldn't understand the doctrine of regeneration. He said, *"How can these things be?"* The concept of being born again by the Holy Spirit of God in order to enter into the Kingdom of God was too strange and foreign to him. It wasn't because he was a dumb person. Nicodemus was highly educated. His problem, like all unsaved people, was that *"the god of this world hath blinded the minds of them which believe not, lest the light of the glorious gospel of Christ, who is the image of God, should shine unto them."*

[Verse 10] Jesus reproved Nicodemus. It was unacceptable for him as a master of Israel who taught others to not grasp the doctrine. Jesus said, *"Art thou a master of Israel, and knowest not these things?"*

[Verse 11] Yet Jesus continued to assert the certainty of the doctrine to Nicodemus by beginning His speech with "Verily, verily" for the third time. He said, *"We speak that we do know, and testify that we have seen; and ye receive not our witness."* Jesus' words were faithful and true based on the knowledge and testimony of the Godhead (Father, Son, and Holy Ghost), but the Jews did not receive their witness. Verse 32 says, *"And what he hath seen and heard, that he testifieth; and no man receiveth his testimony."* Read *Proverbs 8:5-9, Proverbs 22:17-21.*

[Verses 12-13] Jesus sometimes used similitudes taken from nature, such as human birth, water, and wind in this case, to help people understand spiritual truth. This is because spiritual truth can be known and visualized by familiar earthly elements.

No man had ever gone up to heaven to bring back the knowledge of divine and heavenly things, but the Son of man, who came down from heaven. He presented the spiritual doctrines in a way that people could relate to and understand. Therefore when the Jews would not believe, it no longer was a case of lack of understanding, but a case of willful rejection. It was also silly not to believe, because none had been to heaven to be able to prove what Jesus said was wrong.

God never wanted people to blindly believe His doctrines. The Bible is full of similitudes to help people understand and believe His truth. Each time you come across such words as "like" and "as," God is teaching His truth using a familiar similitude that you can easily comprehend.

Note:

Embedded in verse 13 is the doctrine of God's omnipresence. We are bound by time and space, but not Jesus. Consider verse 13, *"And no man hath ascended up to heaven, but he that came down from heaven, even the Son of man which **is** in heaven."* This is because Jesus and the Father are one, and they are omnipresent.

Nicodemus' response to spiritual birth serves as a window into the minds of unsaved (or lost) people. He represents people (including religious elites) who have no personal relationship with the Lord Jesus Christ. This understanding helps us to be better witnesses. The following can be gleaned from the first 21 verses.

Chapter 3 – Love

- [Verse 2] Lost people are intrigued by the supernatural miracles of Jesus by which they conclude He came from God. They are interested in learning more about the person of Jesus, whom they mislabel, but will not openly inquire.

- [Verses 3-10] Lost people are physically minded and have difficulty grasping the concept of spiritual birth. Once I had a discussion with a lost person about the poor people in India, explaining that their foremost need is to be born again through a relationship with the Lord Jesus Christ. He couldn't understand that and suggested that they needed education the most.

- [Verses 11-18] Lost people are ignorant of heavenly things because they do not receive the witness or testimony of the Son of man who came down from heaven. Yet there is no one else who has been or can go up to heaven to bring back the knowledge of divine and heavenly things. They also do not believe *"in the name of the only begotten Son of God."* As a result, they miss the great love of God and eternal life, and they remain in condemnation. Read verses 31-36.

- [Verses 19-20] Lost people reject God's Light and love darkness because their deeds are evil.

The Necessity of Christ's Suffering and Death

Adam's failure left mankind hopelessly lost in sin and eternally separated from God. In Adam, all die because there is no solution for sin, for it is impossible to produce a sinless person from a sinner. *Job 14:4 Who can bring a clean thing out of an unclean? not one.*

Adam's failure also put God in a seeming tough spot. On one hand, He had to judge sin, which meant the entire human race would be wiped out. On the other hand, He so loved the world. In His infinite wisdom, God found a solution that satisfied both interests. He sacrificed His only perfect, innocent, obedient, and righteous Son Jesus Christ, and made Him to be sin for mankind so that we might obtain God's righteousness in Him. Therefore in Christ, all can be made alive. Read *2Corinthians 5:21, 1Corinthians 15:22*.

God charged our sins to Jesus' account. Sin is painful, ugly, costly, and deadly. Jesus drank the full cup of God's wrath. He was tortured and beaten beyond recognition, humiliated, and cruelly crucified. He suffered, bled, and died to fully pay for our sins.

[Verse 14] The suffering and death of Christ was prophesied and played out in Moses' days. While Israel was wandering in the wilderness, they were bitten by fiery serpents because of their complaining sin, and many died. When the people realized and confessed their sins, they entreated Moses to ask God to remove the serpents. God did not remove the serpents. Instead He instructed Moses to make a serpent of brass and set it on a pole so that when those who were bitten looked upon it, they lived. Read *Numbers 21:4-9*. (Incidentally, the serpent on a pole is the logo of the World Health Organization.) Since the time of Adam and Eve, the serpent is a cursed animal. Christ was made a curse for mankind. Read *Galatians 3:13*. Brass represents God's judgment. The serpent of brass was put on the pole. Christ was judged and put on the cross.

Why did God put Jesus on the cross? Verse 15 gives the answer, *"That whosoever believeth in him should not perish, but have eternal life."*

Chapter 3 – Love

Why did God want sinners to have eternal life? Verse 16 gives the answer, *"For God so loved the world, that he gave his only begotten Son, that whosoever believeth in him should not perish, but have everlasting life."* Let's break this verse down.

- *"For God"*—It was God's own initiative according to His mercy and compassion.

- *"so loved"*—The Greek language has several words for love: "phileo" (φιλία), "eros" (ἔρως), "storge" (στοργή), and "agape" (ἀγάπη). "Phileo" is brotherly or friendship love. The city of Philadelphia is known as the city of brotherly love. "Eros" is where we get the word "erotic," which refers to love of sexual nature. "Storge" is the love that parents have for their children. "Agape" is the highest form of love. It is selfless, sacrificial, and charitable. It is a sacrificial love regardless of the response (acceptance or rejection) from the recipient. God's love is agape love. (The Greek word for love in this verse is "agapao" (ἀγαπάω), which is the verb form of the noun "agape".)

- *"the world"*—God so loved the world of fallen and wicked men. He loves every person from every nation and ethnicity.

- *"that he gave his only begotten Son"*—God's love was fulfilled when He sacrificially gave His only begotten Son to suffer and die for His enemies. It is inconceivable that this sinful world is worth the death of His Son. Read *Romans 5:6-10*. God did not have another Savior besides Jesus Christ. He was and is a gift to sinners.

- *"that whosoever believeth in him should not perish, but have everlasting life"*

- The gift of eternal life is for whosoever will believe in Jesus Christ by faith. This belief is not an intellectual faith as one believes in Abraham Lincoln or George Washington. (No one believes in Jesus Christ more than the devil himself. Read *James 2:19*.) It is also not a temporal faith where one prays and trusts God for safety or blessing. Your belief needs to be a saving faith. This means trusting or casting your faith on Jesus Christ, according to verses 16-17, and accepting Him as Lord.
- There is no limit to the number of people who can come to Christ to obtain forgiveness of sins and eternal life.

This gospel is good news for sinners. It is so wonderful that the prophets of old inquired and diligently searched the scriptures for the exact time when Christ should come to work out the salvation of His people. Even the angels desired to look into this wonderful gospel. Read *1Peter 1:10-12*. Do not miss this great salvation. *Hebrews 2:1 Therefore we ought to give the more earnest heed to the things which we have heard, lest at any time we should let them slip. (2) For if the word spoken by angels was stedfast, and every transgression and disobedience received a just recompence of reward; (3) How shall we escape, if we neglect so great salvation; which at the first began to be spoken by the Lord, and was confirmed unto us by them that heard him.*

> And can it be that I should gain
> An interest in the Savior's blood?
> Died He for me, who caused His pain?
> For me, who Him to death pursued?
> Amazing love! how can it be
> That Thou, my God, should die for me?
>
> Refrain:

Chapter 3 – Love

Amazing love! how can it be
That Thou, my God, should die for me!

He left His Father's throne above,
So free, so infinite His grace!
Emptied Himself of all but love,
And bled for Adam's helpless race!
'Tis mercy all, immense and free,
For, O my God, it found out me. [Refrain]

Long my imprisoned spirit lay
Fast bound in sin and nature's night.
Thine eye diffused a quickening ray;
I woke, the dungeon flamed with light!
My chains fell off, my heart was free,
I rose, went forth and followed Thee. [Refrain]

No condemnation now I dread:
Jesus, and all in Him, is mine!
Alive in Him, my living Head,
And clothed in righteousness divine,
Bold I approach the eternal throne,
And claim the crown, through Christ my own.
[Refrain]

("And can it be that I should gain?"
hymn by Charles Wesley)

If Christ paid the penalty for your sins, this means He not only is your Savior, but your Master. He bought you with a price. He owns you, and you are no longer your own. You are to serve Him the rest of your life. His agenda and priority trump yours. His will, wishes, and wants also trump yours. He must be preeminent in your life. Keep your body and actions holy and right. Employ a steward mindset and invest in things that advance the gospel of Christ and glorify God. He expects you to be fruitful. You don't want God to have buyer's remorse after paying such a high price for you. Demonstrate with your life that you are worth the price rather than

55

a worthless asset. Read *1Corinthians 6:9-20, John 4:34, John 6:38, Luke 12:42-48, Luke 16:1-13.*

[Verse 17] It is important to note that God did not send Jesus Christ into the world to condemn sinners, but that they may be saved through Him. It was a rescue mission. This is because sinners are condemned already. There was no need to further condemn them, but to save them.

[Verse 18] While verses 14-17 give the doctrine of love, verses 18-21 give the doctrine of condemnation. The flip side of love is wrath—*"he that believeth not the Son shall not see life; but the wrath of God abideth on him."* Yes, there is wrath. God is not only about love as some bad preachers like to portray in order to profit from people. Those who reject Jesus Christ reject God's love and remain in condemnation with no hope of eternal life, because there is no other Savior besides the only begotten Son of God.

Those who believe in Jesus Christ escape condemnation. *Romans 8:1 There is therefore now no condemnation to them which are in Christ Jesus, who walk not after the flesh, but after the Spirit. (2) For the law of the Spirit of life in Christ Jesus hath made me free from the law of sin and death.* Read *John 5:24.* All it takes is for one to fully believe in Jesus Christ.

Verses 19-20 explain why sinners remain in condemnation— *"And this is the condemnation, that light is come into the world, and men loved darkness rather than light, because their deeds were evil. For every one that doeth evil hateth the light, neither cometh to the light, lest his deeds should be reproved."*

- The light of the gospel reaches everyone who comes into this world, according to *John 1:9.* No one can accuse God for not revealing Himself and His salvation. *Romans 1:19 Because that which may be known of God is manifest in them; for God hath shewed it unto them.*

Chapter 3 – Love

(20) For the invisible things of him from the creation of the world are clearly seen, being understood by the things that are made, even his eternal power and Godhead; so that they are without excuse."

- Sinners love darkness rather than light because their deeds are evil. They love to sin and persist in it.

- Sinners hate the light of the gospel of Jesus Christ, neither will they come to the light because it reveals their transgressions and convicts and condemns them. It is natural for them to shun the light. They can't stand to be told their faults.

[Verse 21] But some sinners respond to God's call for repentance. They come out of darkness and welcome the light of the gospel. They trade in their evil deeds for works of truth and righteousness. Their deeds are no longer the hidden things of dishonesty.

Christians are to love sinners. We should love all homosexuals, adulterers, drunkards, idolaters, murderers, and such like, but hate their sin. Understand that we too were once lost and were servants of sin. Read *Romans 6:17-18, 1Corinthians 6:9-11*. We need to view sinners, some of whom may be our own relatives, through the gospel lens. The Son of God bled and died for them.

The Necessity of Making Christ Preeminent in Your Life

[Verses 22-26] Having celebrated the Passover in Jerusalem, driven out the buyers and sellers from the temple, done the miracles that caused many to believe on Him, and completed the discourse with Nicodemus concerning regeneration, Jesus and His disciples went into the country, in the land of Judea in southern

The Book of John

Israel. He tarried there with His disciples, and people came to Him and were baptized.

At the same time, John the Baptist also was baptizing in Aenon near Salim. There arose a dispute between John's disciples and the Jews, who had not submitted to John's baptism of repentance. Purification (religious washings) was the core issue. The Jews practiced various washings and purifications; some were instituted by the Law of Moses, while others were imposed by the tradition of the elders. Read *Mark 7:3-4*. It could be that John's disciples, being immature in the faith, touted their baptisms as superior to and superseding all the purifications of the Jews. It was likely that the Jews in this dispute raised a doubt about John's baptism because there was another baptism in Jesus' camp, and people were going to Him. Whose baptism was right and safer to follow, and why were more people going to Jesus? John's disciples were ruffled by the objection and went to him for clarification.

John's disciples might have expected him to debate the Jews, but instead they received a lesson on ministry and preeminence. John explained his place and purpose in ministry, why Jesus was superior, and that the disciples should cheer the increase in Jesus' camp. Responding to the disciples' concern of *"all men come to him"* in verse 26, John gave the following advice:

- Don't worry about what others have.
  [Verse 27]
  Why? Because *"A man can receive nothing, except it be given him from heaven."* God decides who gets what and how much according to His sovereign will. Every person comes into this world naked and everything that the person has, including breath, is a gift from heaven.

  Every minister also receives gifts according to the sovereign will of God. There are diversities of gifts,

Chapter 3 – Love

differences of administrations, and diversities of operations. These are not designed for personal benefit, but for the common good of the body of Christ. Read *1Corinthians 12, 13, 14*.

- Do worry about fulfilling your calling in ministry.
  [Verses 28-29]
  John was very clear on his calling in ministry—*"I am not the Christ, but that I am sent before him."* And John fulfilled his calling—*"He that hath the bride is the bridegroom: but the friend of the bridegroom, which standeth and heareth him, rejoiceth greatly because of the bridegroom's voice: this my joy therefore is fulfilled."* John was the friend of the Bridegroom (Jesus Christ) as one sent by Him to negotiate the match. He was privileged to bring together the Savior and those He came to save. John rejoiced greatly to stand with the Bridegroom, to hear His voice, and to witness the blessed espousals. In other words, John was just happy to see people get saved. He was an evangelist indeed.

  Ministers should be like John, aspiring to be the friend of the Bridegroom, introducing the bride (saved sinners or the church) to Him. Joy in ministry is not based on the number of followers, or the size of the congregation.

- Do remember that Jesus Christ must increase and ministers must decrease.
  [Verse 30]
  The end goal of ministry is that Jesus Christ must increase and ministers must decrease. Jesus Christ alone is exalted. In John's mind, it was a good thing that he was losing people to Jesus, because Jesus came from heaven and was above all.

Always remember *"He must increase, but I must decrease."* The more Christ increases in your life, the better off you are. The more He is in charge of your life, the happier you are. The Bible says, *"Trust in the LORD with all thine heart; and lean not unto thine own understanding. In all thy ways acknowledge him, and he shall direct thy paths."* Many people have trouble trusting the Lord and turning control of their lives over to Him. They want Jesus to take care of them in the afterlife, but won't let Him have the pilot seat in their present life. Magnify Jesus by making Him preeminent in your life. Give him control over everything—family, finances, future, etc, and trust Him. Make His agenda your agenda, His will your will, His thoughts your thoughts, His heart your heart, and His business your business. Then your joy will be fulfilled.

[Verse 31] The reason Jesus must increase and all human ministers must decrease is because Jesus Christ came from heaven and is above all. To get our attention, John said it twice in this verse. Jesus came to reveal celestial things, and His words were the words of the Father. Human ministers from the root of Adam are earthy, and their expositions, preaching, and testimonies, even when speaking by the power of the Holy Ghost, are nothing compared to the eternal word delivered by the Lord Himself. In chapter 7, the officers who were sent by the Pharisees to apprehend Jesus heard Him speak and returned empty handed and reported, *"Never man spake like this man."* Of course John wanted people to hear directly from Jesus. I too would rather you read the Bible than my commentary.

"He that cometh from above is above all"—Jesus Christ is above all teachers, preachers, pastors, prophets, priests, and popes. He is your source of truth and final authority. You need to read the

Chapter 3 – Love

Bible for yourself. This is not to say you should not listen to your church elders, but if there is a certain view, doctrine, tradition, or belief that is contrary to the Bible, then the Bible is right. Whenever the word of God disagrees with you, the smart thing to do is to agree with it, submit to it, and do what it says. The Bible says, *"It is hard for thee to kick against the pricks."* What's really sad is that some people know full well that their beliefs are contrary to the Bible, and yet they refuse to accept the testimony of Jesus Christ.

We will dive into the doctrine of baptisms next. Some readers may disagree and struggle with the biblical truth of baptisms, perhaps due to tradition or a contrary position held and taught by church elders. If so, remember that Jesus Christ is the incarnate Word from heaven and He is above all. The Bible is your final authority.

[Verses 32-36] Having presented Jesus as the Lord from heaven, who was above all, John the Baptist expressed his sadness that the majority of Jews would not receive Jesus' testimony, even though He testified of heavenly truth. However, the remnant who received Jesus' testimony set to their seal that God was true. They subscribed to the truth of God as follows:

1. *"For he whom God hath sent speaketh the words of God"*—Jesus Christ was the Sent One of God. He was God's official spokesman. Let the Bible be your final authority and not a mortal person who can be wrong. *Proverbs 8:6 Hear; for I will speak of excellent things; and the opening of my lips shall be right things. (7) For my mouth shall speak truth; and wickedness is an abomination to my lips. (8) All the words of my mouth are in righteousness; there is nothing froward or perverse in them. (9) They are all plain to him that understandeth, and right to them that find knowledge.*

2. *"For God giveth not the Spirit by measure unto him"*—Unlike the prophets and apostles who received partial communication and abilities by the Spirit, Jesus Christ received a full measure of the Spirit. According to *John 1:33*, the Spirit of God descended and remained on Jesus Christ.

3. *"The Father loveth the Son, and hath given all things into his hand"*—God entrusted everything into Jesus' hands. Human ministers are entrusted with the word of reconciliation, but it doesn't even come close to what God entrusted to Jesus. Read *Psalms 2:8, John 5:22, John 13:3, Matthew 11:27, Matthew 28:18, Ephesians 1:22, Philippians 2:9-11*.

Unfortunately today many Christians do not read their Bibles, but they consume an incredible amount of Jesus materials. Just visit a Christian bookstore and you will know what I mean. Did you know the Bible is the owner's manual for a successful life written to you by your Creator? It has everything you need on how to fix your life.

If there can be only one reason why Jesus must increase, it is the conclusion of John's speech, that is *"He that believeth on the Son hath everlasting life: and he that believeth not the Son shall not see life; but the wrath of God abideth on him."* Of course John wanted people to go to Jesus and hear from Him directly, because it could mean the difference between life and death. Don't base your hope of salvation on things you hear from someone, but search the scriptures for yourself.

Chapter 3 – Love

The doctrine of baptisms

Since this chapter touches on baptism, let's explore the doctrine of baptisms. This is needful, as virtually all Christian denominations teach and practice some form of baptism.

Baptism and the Lord's Supper are the only two ordinances given to the New Testament church to observe. Did you know there are at least six types of baptism in the Bible? *Hebrews 6:2* says *"Of the doctrine of baptisms….,"* meaning all baptisms communicate one doctrine, which is the death, burial, and resurrection of the Lord Jesus Christ.

There are physical and spiritual baptisms. Among the baptisms are:

- Baptism of Moses for the Israelites who left Egypt. *1Corinthians 10:1 Moreover, brethren, I would not that ye should be ignorant, how that all our fathers were under the cloud, and all passed through the sea; (2) And were all baptized unto Moses in the cloud and in the sea.*

- Baptism of John (or baptism of repentance) that signified a spiritual repentance in the heart of believers that prepared them to receive their Messiah. Read *Matthew 3:1-12, Mark 1:4, Luke 3:1-3, John 1:19-34, Acts 13:24, Acts 19:4. Acts 19:1-5* shows when and how this baptism ended.

- Baptism of fire is for non-believers. Read *Matthew 3:7-12.*

- Baptism of death where the wrath of God was poured out on Christ. Read *Matthew 20:20-23, Matthew 12:40.* Christians are spiritually baptized into Jesus' death, according to *Colossians 2:8-12* and *Romans 6:3-5.*

- Baptism of the Holy Ghost is for believers of Jesus Christ and takes place at the point of salvation. Read *Mark 1:8, Luke 3:16, Acts 1:5*. This is the true baptism. *Ephesians 4:4 There is one body, and one Spirit, even as ye are called in one hope of your calling; (5) One Lord, one faith, <u>one baptism</u>, (6) One God and Father of all, who is above all, and through all, and in you all.* The Holy Spirit of God baptizes Christians into Christ's death, according to *1Corinthians 12:13*.

- Believers' water baptism must be observed by all who have accepted Jesus Christ as Lord and Savior. Read *Acts 10:44-48, Matthew 28:19-20*. Water baptism is the act of immersing someone in water to depict the above mentioned spiritual truth or doctrine for the following purposes:
    1. It is a public testimony of the new convert's identification with the Lord Jesus Christ through His death, burial, and resurrection, according to *Romans 6:1-6*. As the believer is immersed under the water, it pictures the believer joining Christ in His death and burial. When the believer is raised up out of the water, it pictures the believer joining Christ in resurrection and glory. In other words, what is true of the believer spiritually is played out physically with water baptism.
    2. It identifies the believer with the church, according to *1Corinthians 12:13*.

Besides the above, water baptism gets a person wet. It does not save the person or wash away sins. Individuals get baptized because they are saved and not in order to be saved. Therefore only believers should be baptized.

The Greek word for "baptism" (βάπτισμα) means immersion or submersion. The biblical method for baptism is complete immersion. Since baptism is a picture of the death, burial, and resurrection, the proper way to bury someone is to completely cover the person. No one in the Bible was ever sprinkled. Read *Acts 8:26-39, John 3:23, Matthew 3:16*.

If you are saved and have not been baptized, then you need to do so because God commands it. Read *Matthew 28:19-20*. If your baptism is not biblical, then you need to make it right. If your baptism was from a church of unlike faith, then you should also be re-baptized because of purpose #2 above.

Baptism is the first act of obedience in service to the Lord. It marks the beginning of a believer's public ministry. Jesus set the example by submitting to baptism before He began His public ministry. Read *Matthew 3:13-17*. Baptism is not essential for salvation, but is essential for spiritual growth. Before individuals can be taught to follow Jesus Christ, they must be willing to submit to the first act of obedience. Make no mistake, if an individual refuses to obey the Lord in this first point, that individual will not obey in future points and cannot be a disciple of Jesus Christ. The Bible is not a restaurant menu where a person chooses what to obey.

Summary

God is love. *John 3:16 says, "For God so loved the world, that he gave his only begotten Son, that whosoever believeth in him should not perish, but have everlasting life."* May all readers experience the love of God and the spiritual birth by accepting the gift of God, which is eternal life through Jesus Christ. May God grant all readers the faith to believe Jesus Christ's testimony and the wisdom to receive Him as Lord and Savior for the pardoning of sins.

4 – Living Water

Historical Synopsis

We have here another famous story commonly known as "The woman at the well." It gives an account of the meeting between Jesus and the Samaritan woman by Jacob's well in the city of Sychar while Jesus was en-route to Galilee from Judea. There is a fair amount of detail on their discourse that ends with the woman's conversion. Many other Samaritans also came to believe that Jesus was the Christ, the Savior of the world, by her testimony.

The chapter concludes with the healing of a nobleman's son who was sick to the point of death at Capernaum. It was the second miracle that Jesus performed while in Cana of Galilee. The first was turning water into wine in chapter **2**.

This chapter can be outlined as such:

I. The conversion of the Samaritan woman – *John 4:1-30*
II. The counsel to behold the fields – *John 4:31-38*
III. The conversion of the people of Sychar – *John 4:39-42*
IV. The cure of a nobleman's son – *John 4:43-54*

The Book of John

JESUS' WELL

JACOB'S WELL

Chapter 4 – Living Water

Key Spiritual Lessons

God used a Samaritan woman who was thirsty for water to teach about evangelism and faith versus works-based righteousness. If you have never evangelized, you may wonder what to say, where to go, and how to overcome objections, besides experiencing fear and intimidation. But take comfort, for this chapter is a gold mine that will equip you for evangelism.

[Verses 1-4] Business was good in Jesus' camp in the rural parts of Judea. The number of baptisms and disciples grew to surpass those in John's camp. At least, that was how it was reported to the Pharisees. The report must have grieved the Pharisees even more. They now had two thorns in their side (John the Baptist and Jesus).

Knowing the Pharisees had received such a report, Jesus decided to leave Judea for Galilee. The move was by God's design— *"he must needs go through Samaria."* In Jesus' time, the land of Israel was divided into three parts: Galilee to the north, Judea to the south, and Samaria in the middle.

The Samaritans were the offspring of the colonies, which the king of Assyria planted after deporting the Israelite elite from the northern kingdom to Assyria. The poor Jews of the land were left behind and intermingled with the foreigners that were brought in from Babylon, Cuthah, Ava, Hamath, and Sepharvaim. Read *2Kings 17:24*. Because of their defective devotion to Judaism and their partly pagan ancestry, the Samaritans were despised by ordinary Jews. (The Jews thought they could not give Jesus a worse name when they said, *"Thou art a Samaritan"* in *John 8:48*.) The Jews believed they would be contaminated by passing through Samaritan territory, so they would bypass it by crossing over the Jordan River, which was a longer route.

The Book of John

Praise God that Jesus' outreach was not limited to the Jews. He made a special effort to reach outside of the commonwealth of Israel. *Romans 3:29 Is he the God of the Jews only? is he not also of the Gentiles? Yes, of the Gentiles also.*

Christians are commanded to evangelize the lost. Every believer *"must needs"* go to the lost by reaching out to neighbors, as well as to the people in the uttermost parts of the world. Read *Acts 1:8, Matthew 28:19-20*. The key word here is "go." It is needful for you to go. Do not expect lost people to come to you and say, "What must I do to be saved?" Where is your Samaria?

[Verses 5-8] In Samaria, Jesus went to the city of Sychar (known as Shechem in the Old Testament), about 34 miles from Jerusalem, and stopped at Jacob's well. It was about the Jew's 6th hour, which was high noon, and Jesus was wearied with His journey and perhaps was thirsty from the heat. In an effort to make a connection, He asked a Samaritan woman who came to draw water for a drink.

The key word here is "connect." Once you are in your Samaria, you should connect with the locals. The way Jesus reached out to the Samaritan woman was interesting in that He asked her for a favor. By so doing, He initially set Himself as the potential recipient or benefactor rather than the giver. This is the exact opposite of the method practiced by most, if not all, Christian outreach programs in that they go to minister and give rather than take. Perhaps Jesus was reaching out to the woman through her humanitarian conscience. Most people, even though they have no dealings with one another due to differences in culture or religion, will not deny humanitarian needs. And perhaps allowing the woman to show kindness first would gain Him the opportunity to return the favor. Or this could be Jesus' way of qualifying her for witnessing. After all, if the woman was so unkind to meet His basic humanitarian need and told Him to get lost, then she might not have been the right person to witness to. And then Jesus Himself had also said, *"It is more blessed to give than to receive."* Perhaps He wanted the woman to receive God's blessing.

The Samaritan woman who came to the well to draw water represents a natural person who is thirsty for God's truth, as water represents the word of God. Everyone who sojourns in this world has a spiritual thirst and will search for truth. Jesus will intercept everyone in their quest for truth, as He deliberately and purposefully intercepted the Samaritan woman in her path. Everyone will find two contrasting wells of water—Jesus' well and Jacob's well. Jesus' well is God's gift (verse 10) and is spiritual, whereas Jacob's well is man's gift (verse 12) and is physical. They are polar opposites of each other and they represent the two systems of righteousness—faith and works.

Works-based righteousness says you can work your way into heaven. Religions that teach salvation by good works include Catholicism[1], Buddhism, Taoism, Confucianism, Hinduism, Islamism, Judaism, and atheism, among others.

Faith-based righteousness says your good works will never be good enough for heaven. Helping an old lady to cross the street, giving to the poor, and doing charitable activities do not clear a person of sin.

This is what you are up against when witnessing Jesus to the lost. Many lost people are religious, faithful, and accept the concept of God. The trouble is, they subscribe to the wrong system of

---

[1] Catechism of the Catholic Church: #837 *"Fully incorporated into the society of the Church are those who, possessing the Spirit of Christ, accept all the means of salvation given to the Church together with her entire organization, and who - by the bonds constituted by the profession of faith, the sacraments, ecclesiastical government, and communion - are joined in the visible structure of the Church of Christ, who rules her through the Supreme Pontiff and the bishops. Even though incorporated into the Church, one who does not however persevere in charity is not saved. He remains indeed in the bosom of the Church, but 'in body' not 'in heart.'"*

righteousness. Be careful not to attack religion, but draw contrast to the living water. Do it in a friendly manner—in love, humility, and brokenness of spirit. Only Jesus Christ can quench a thirsty soul. Read *Exodus 17:1-6*. Nothing of this cursed earth can satisfy a thirsty soul or give everlasting life.

The name Sychar means "drunken." Don't expect God to send you to evangelize nice vacation spots. Rather, be prepared to go to a place like Sychar. (No, this is not your call to evangelize the local bars.)

[Verses 9-10] Jesus' request for water was met with racial and gender objections—*"How is it that thou, being a Jew, askest drink of me, which am a woman of Samaria? for the Jews have no dealings with the Samaritans."*

Historically, there was great enmity between Jews and Samaritans. The Samaritans were the adversaries of Judah. Read *Nehemiah 4:1-2*. To appreciate the enmity, imagine the strife between Catholics and Protestants in Northern Ireland, or the hatred between Indians and Pakistanis, between Serbs and Muslims in modern Bosnia, between Chinese and Japanese, and between Americans and the Taliban. For Jesus to ask a Samaritan woman for a drink would be as awkward as an Indian man asking a Pakistani woman for a drink inside Pakistan.

In the works-based righteousness economy, people are divided—*"The Jews have no dealings with the Samaritans."* But in the faith-based righteousness economy, Jews and Gentiles are united in Christ. Read *Ephesians 2:11-14, Colossians 3:10-11*.

The woman essentially objected by saying, "Why do you ask me for a drink when we have nothing in common?" In an effort to connect with the locals, expect to cross racial, cultural, and social barriers. In our time, people say, "We don't connect," which means we don't have much in common.

Chapter 4 – Living Water

Despite their cultural differences, Jesus tried to engage the woman in a spiritual discussion. He said, *"If thou knewest the gift of God, and who it is that saith to thee, Give me to drink; thou wouldest have asked of him, and he would have given thee living water."* So take note, even though you may not have much in common with those you witness to, understand that everyone needs a Savior because everyone is a sinner. Read *Romans 3:23, Romans 6:23.* Everyone needs to know the gift of God, which is Jesus Christ, and everyone needs the Holy Spirit of God in them, as a well of living water springing up into everlasting life.

The key word here is "engage." Engage the people in the area. Witness Jesus by sharing your testimony, offer the gift of God, be ready to handle objections, and be ready to lead them in the sinner's prayer. When someone is ready to receive Jesus, make sure they understand it is about the forgiveness of sins and not simply about going to heaven.

[Verses 11-14] Just as Nicodemus wasn't able to grasp the concept of spiritual birth and wondered how a person could crawl back into his mother's womb, the woman wasn't able to grasp Jesus' spiritual message of living water and thought He was referring to physical water from Jacob's well.

In reaction to Jesus' statement, she said, *"Sir, thou hast nothing to draw with, and the well is deep: from whence then hast thou that living water?"* The reason Jesus had nothing to draw with was because living water is spiritual and is drawn by faith and not by works of righteousness. It is a spiritual regeneration by grace through faith in Jesus Christ. *Romans 11:6 And if by grace, then is it no more of works: otherwise grace is no more grace. But if it be of works, then is it no more grace: otherwise work is no more work.* Read *Romans 3:28, Colossians 1:13-14, Colossians 2:13-15, Ephesians 1:7.* In the works-based righteousness economy, the practitioners are expected to do good works in order to gain favor with the church and with God.

Furthermore, the woman said, *"Art thou greater than our father Jacob, which gave us the well, and drank thereof himself, and his children, and his cattle?"* Works-based righteousness takes pride in physical and beggarly elements. It puts its trust in man and traditions. Works-based righteousness also:

- Is unsatisfying—*"Whosoever drinketh of this water shall thirst again."* Practitioners of works-based righteousness are never satisfied and will continue to search for truth and remain thirsty.

- Is bondage. The Samaritan woman had to return to the well daily to draw water. Practitioners of works-based righteousness go through the motion of religion in vain.

- Is burdensome. How laborious it must have been for the Samaritan woman to carry heavy buckets of water from the deep well that most likely was far from home. Imagine if she also had camels to water. Practitioners of works-based righteousness must persevere in their religious activities in order to gain favor.

- Is risky. Proponents of works-based righteousness cannot specify the amount of good works necessary to qualify a person for heaven. This is a seriously flawed system and extremely risky to subscribe to. If I promised to give you $1,000 for your good works, but did not specify how many good works you had to do to get the money, would you agree to it?

- Is powerless to wash away sins, leaving the practitioners dead in sin. Read *Hebrews 10:1-4, 11.*

In contrast, the living water from Jesus' well is satisfying—*"Whosoever drinketh of this water shall thirst again: But whosoever*

Chapter 4 – Living Water

drinketh of the water that I shall give him shall never thirst; but the water that I shall give him shall be in him a well of water springing up into everlasting life." The user has to obtain it only once to receive everlasting life. Read *1John 5:12-13*. Jesus liberates sinners from the bondage of sin. His yoke is easy and His burden is light. Read *Matthew 11:28-30*. Faith-based righteousness does not require believers to maintain their salvation because it is by grace through faith, and not by works. It is a gift, not a loan from God that one should repay. Therefore, no one can lose salvation because no one can earn it.

[Verses 15-18] The Samaritan woman jumped at Jesus' offer. She said, *"Sir, give me this water, that I thirst not, neither come hither to draw."* She was tired of repeating the same chore that gave her no satisfaction. She was a smart woman, but not so fast. Jesus was in no hurry to convert her, but asked her to call her husband. That was because He wanted to expose and deal with her sin. He knew she went through five husbands and was sleeping with a man who was not her husband.

One must come to Jesus as a sinner with full understanding of the penalty of sin and that only He can forgive. Never lead a person in the sinner's prayer if there is no confession of sin. Unfortunately, too many evangelists short-change and rush this process by asking people if they want to go to heaven and immediately lead them in the sinner's prayer when they say yes. Who wouldn't want to go to heaven? Even a dog wants to go to heaven. Please know that Jesus Christ did not die on the cross so that people can go to heaven. He died in order that their sins may be forgiven so they can have a right relationship with Him. If heaven was your motive when you prayed the sinner's prayer, you are at risk. America is full of people who think they are Christians, but God would disagree.

[Verses 19-20] Because Jesus was able to reveal the woman's sins, she perceived that He was not an ordinary man and considered Him to be a prophet. Being told of her sins, she might have been uncomfortable and tried to shift the focus off of herself by opening the controversy on the place of religious worship—*"Our fathers worshipped in this mountain; and ye say, that in Jerusalem is the place where men ought to worship."*

Naturally people become uncomfortable and ashamed when their sins are brought to light and may try to deflect the discussion with theological controversies. Questions like, "How can you believe the Bible when it was written by humans?", "Why does God allow bad things to happen to good people?", "Why did God order genocide and infanticide?", "How old is the earth?" and so on. Until the conviction comes to the point of "what must I as a rotten sinner do to be saved," the person is not ready to be saved. *Luke 5:32 I came not to call the righteous, but sinners to repentance.*

The mountain that the Samaritan woman referred to was Mt. Gerizim. God appeared to Abraham when he sojourned in Sichem (or Shechem) in the plain of Moreh, which was between Mt. Gerizim and Mt. Ebal, and promised him, *"Unto thy seed will I give this land."* There Abraham built an altar to God. Later Jacob bought a parcel of a field in Shechem, erected an altar, and called it Elelohe-Israel. Centuries later, the children of Israel carried Joseph's bones from Egypt and buried them in Shechem in a parcel of ground that Jacob bought. Read *Genesis 12:6-7, Genesis 33:18-20, Joshua 24:32*. When the Samaritan woman said, *"Our fathers worshipped in this mountain,"* she was referring to the patriarchs Abraham, Isaac, and Jacob, whose descendants the Samaritans thought themselves to be. She thought she had antiquity, tradition, and succession on her side and that leaning on those things made her okay with God. The reality couldn't be further from the truth.

It pains me to see the number of people who are in this trap. Location-based worship reminds me of the Islam religion. Mecca is regarded as the holiest city. The Muslims pray toward Mecca, and a pilgrimage to it, known as the Hajj, is obligatory for all

Chapter 4 – Living Water

able Muslims. This unfortunately does not buy the person anything with God.

The Jews also love to claim the patriarch Abraham as their father. This also does not buy them anything with God.

Jesus corrected the woman as follows:

- [Verse 21] Concerning the place of worship, Jesus said, *"Woman, believe me, the hour cometh, when ye shall neither in this mountain, nor yet at Jerusalem, worship the Father."* Location-based worship would soon be done away with and cease to matter, as a change was about to come. Now worship of the Father is not tied to a place. Worshippers who put a lot of stock in location are worshiping in vain. There is also no need of an ornate cathedral or temple to worship God. God is not impressed with man-made things. You can worship the Father anywhere and everywhere.

- [Verse 22] Concerning the object of worship, Jesus said, *"Ye worship ye know not what: we know what we worship: for salvation is of the Jews."* As mentioned at the beginning of this chapter, the Samaritans were the offspring of the colonies planted by the king of Assyria. They were a Jewish-Gentile mix. The early Gentile settlers did not fear the Lord, so He sent lions to destroy some of them. When it was reported to the king of Assyria that the Gentile settlers did not know the manner of the God of the land, he ordered a deported priest to return to Samaria to teach them. Even though the priest taught them to fear the Lord, the Gentiles made and worshipped their own gods. Read about this account in *2Kings 17:24-41*. *2Kings 17:41* explains why the Samaritans were confused regarding the true object of worship—*"So these nations feared the LORD, and served their graven images, both their children, and their children's children: as did their fathers, so do they unto this day."* People with multiple gods are like the Samaritans, worshiping gods that fit their needs, being ignorant of the true object of worship.

The Samaritans failed to understand that the means of salvation originated from the Jews. (Any nation that claims to be God's chosen people, entrusted with the knowledge of salvation is lying or is ignorant of the truth. Only to the Jews were the oracles of God committed.)

- [Verses 23-24] Concerning the manner of worship, Jesus said, *"But the hour cometh, and now is, when the true worshippers shall worship the Father in spirit and in truth: for the Father seeketh such to worship him. God is a Spirit: and they that worship him must worship him in spirit and in truth."* As God is a Spirit, He seeks true worshippers to worship Him in spirit and in truth. This is a non-negotiable requirement. The right manner of worship is for people to worship the Father in spirit with their whole heart, and in truth, which is the word of God. Read *John 17:17*. Most religions claim to worship God. Some even do it over-zealously and become radical, but they reject truth. Without truth, they worship the god of their imagination based on what is right in their own eyes. Only Christians are capable of offering up acceptable worship to the Father, because they have the word of God. If you are a Christian, you need to know the Bible, because God will accept and be well-pleased with your obedience, praises, prayers, petitions, offerings, and sacrifices when they are made according to His truth.

[Verse 25] The woman wasn't sure what to believe, so she tried to put off the conversation by saying, *"I know that Messias cometh, which is called Christ: when he is come, he will tell us all things."* She agreed to disagree and to let Christ settle it when He came.

If your salvation is based on religion rather than a personal relationship with the Lord Jesus Christ, you are an endangered creature. To Him, any denomination or religion label means nothing. Jesus Christ is not a religion. He is the living God, the Savior of those who trust in Him.

[Verse 26] Jesus bestowed incredible grace on the woman by plainly revealing Himself as the Messiah—*"I that speak unto thee am he."* In contrast, Jesus revealed Himself to the Jews in miracles. He gave them plenty of clues, but never spoke as plainly and directly as He did to the Samaritan woman. *John 10:24 Then came the Jews round about him, and said unto him, How long dost thou make us to doubt? If thou be the Christ, tell us plainly. (25) Jesus answered them, I told you, and ye believed not: the works that I do in my Father's name, they bear witness of me.*

[Verses 27-30] The disciples returned from the city with food right after Jesus revealed Himself as the Messiah to the Samaritan woman. They marveled that Jesus talked with the woman, but they didn't ask Him why or what He wanted from her. Seeing the strangers, the woman left her water pot and withdrew herself. She went into the city to bid the men to check out Jesus, whom she now called the Christ. The people responded and came to Jesus.

The woman leaving her water pot is a picture of her leaving works-based righteousness for faith-based righteousness. The living water was already springing up within her. She became a water pot or a vessel of living water and evangelized her city.

Her experience is the same for anyone who genuinely is born again. The living water will spring up and overflow, and the person can't help but to share what happened. *1Corinthians 9:16 For though I preach the gospel, I have nothing to glory of: for necessity is laid upon me; yea, woe is unto me, if I preach not the gospel!* By this definition, people who claim to be a Christian and do not share their experience (regardless of the gift of evangelism) are defective.

[Verses 31-38] While the woman was gone into the city, the disciples entreated Jesus to eat since He was wearied from His journey. But Jesus prioritized the Father's will and work over physical appetite. *Matthew 4:4 But he answered and said, It is written, Man shall not live by bread alone, but by every word that proceedeth out of the mouth of God.*

Jesus seized the teaching moment and said, "*I have meat to eat that ye know not of,*" referring to the conversion of the Samaritan woman and the souls of other Samaritans who would shortly be saved. But the disciples thought Jesus said He had some food and asked among themselves if anyone had given Him anything to eat. Then Jesus explained, "*My meat is to do the will of him that sent me, and to finish his work.*"

The lesson here is the necessity of being about God's business. It was high noon and hot, and Jesus was hungry, but to do the Father's will and to finish His work was meat to Him. It should be great excitement to you that people want to hear the word of God. The needs and wants that arise in life are no excuse for not doing the work of ministry. It is also not acceptable to be completely given to the work of ministry and neglect your personal responsibilities. Realize that to everything there is a season and a time to every purpose under the heaven. You live in the season of

Chapter 4 – Living Water

the great harvest. Now is the time to get busy and prosper in kingdom work.

- Now is the time to thrust in your sickle and reap—*"Say not ye, There are yet four months, and then cometh harvest? behold, I say unto you, Lift up your eyes, and look on the fields; for they are white already to harvest."* The harvest was four months away, but Jesus said the fields were white ready to harvest, figuratively referring to the fields of lost people who needed the Savior. The fields of lost people are ripe and are ready for you— *"The harvest truly is great, but the labourers are few: pray ye therefore the Lord of the harvest, that he would send forth labourers into his harvest."* Every farmer knows the importance of a timely harvest. Don't let this great fruitful opportunity slip by you. In vineyard terms, this is the season of the main harvest. If you miss this, the next harvest is gleanings—about the same amount of work, but much less rewarding. Now is the time to evangelize lost people.

  Do the three-L's: <u>Listen</u> to the Lord—*"behold, I say unto you,"* <u>lift</u> up your eyes, and <u>look</u> on the field. Your heart will be affected by your vision. *Lamentations 3:51 Mine eye affecteth mine heart because of all the daughters of my city.* Don't just sit there and think about a field. It is important that you go and see the field for yourself. You need to own a field. Read *Matthew 13:44*. By the way, if you look on a field and you don't see it white ready to harvest, it may be that your focus is off.

- Now is the time to be rewarded—*"And he that reapeth receiveth wages, and gathereth fruit unto life eternal: that both he that soweth and he that reapeth may rejoice together. And herein is that saying true, One soweth, and another reapeth. I sent you to reap that whereon ye bestowed no labour: other men laboured, and ye are entered into their labours."*

- o You will be rewarded for your labor. God will bless you. (You will be happy to know that the reward is according to labor and not success. God is responsible for success. Read *1Corinthians 3:6-9*.) You will also have fruit to present to the King of Kings in heaven. Your gift to Him is the souls of men, the fruit of your evangelism.
- o You will have joy. You are not alone in the field. Some sow, some water, and some reap. All will receive a reward according to their labor, but the fruit of the harvest is the joy of the whole team.
- o You only need to do half the work. Every lost soul needs Christians to sow the seed of the gospel, water, and harvest the fruit. But in the grand scheme of God's husbandry, which Jesus was referring to, the sowing had already been done by those who had died and gone on ahead. All that was left was to reap in order to enter into their labors.

[Verses 39-42] According to verse 29, when the woman went into the city to share her testimony, she said, *"Come, see a man, which told me all things that ever I did: is not this the Christ?"* Verse 39 gives the result of her evangelism—*"And many of the Samaritans of that city believed on him for the saying of the woman, which testified, He told me all that ever I did."* However some still weren't sure if Jesus was the Christ. To be sure, the Samaritans came to Jesus and asked Him to tarry with them. Jesus accommodated their request and stayed with them two days. In that time, many more believed on Jesus after hearing from Him

Chapter 4 – Living Water

directly, and they were sure that He indeed was the Christ. They said to the woman, *"Now we believe, not because of thy saying: for we have heard him ourselves, and know that this is indeed the Christ, the Saviour of the world."*

Your grasp of Jesus needs to come to the point that you are sure He is the Christ. The only way you can be sure is to hear from Him directly through reading the Bible and not simply taking someone else's word. I have unsaved relatives who also believe in Jesus, but He is not their Lord. As previously mentioned, no one believes in Jesus Christ more than the devil himself.

Notice that Jesus did not perform any miracle in Sychar, yet the people believed on Him. This is because *"faith cometh by hearing, and hearing by the word of God."*

[Verses 43-54] After spending two days with the people of Sychar, Jesus headed north and went to Cana of Galilee, where He turned water into wine. He didn't stop at Nazareth, the place where He grew up, which was south of Cana, because they treated him with disrespect and contempt. *Mark 6:4 But Jesus said unto them, A prophet is not without honour, but in his own country, and among his own kin, and in his own house.* However the Galilaeans of Cana warmly received Jesus, for they had seen the miracles that He performed at Jerusalem during the Passover feast.

At Cana, Jesus was met by a nobleman from the city of Capernaum whose son was sick to the point of death. The nobleman begged Jesus to come down to Capernaum to heal his son. He too must have seen or heard about Jesus' healing miracles. Jesus made use of the opportunity to reprove the nobleman and the Galilaeans at large concerning their unbelief despite seeing the miracles that confirmed He was the Messiah. (The nobleman addressed Jesus as Sir and not Lord.) The Bible says the Jews require a sign, but these Jews, even though they were acquainted with His former miracles, still desired to see more rather than believe.

Given the crisis at hand, the nobleman pressed Jesus even more, *"Sir, come down ere my child die."* But Jesus told him that his son would live and sent him away. The nobleman believed Jesus' words and his son was miraculously healed. Yet again, *"Faith cometh by hearing, and hearing by the word of God."* As he was returning to Capernaum, his servants met him along the way with good tidings that his son survived the fever. When the nobleman asked what hour his son began to improve, it was the same hour that Jesus pronounced the healing. As a result, the nobleman and his household believed on Jesus. This healing was the second miracle that Jesus performed outside of Judea in Galilee.

The name Capernaum means "the village of comfort," an upscale neighborhood in stark contrast to the drunken city of Sychar. Noble people from upscale neighborhoods also need Jesus. Serious sickness, such as cancer, especially when it hits home, grabs individuals' attention, changes their priorities, makes them feel helpless and hopeless, and opens their heart to Jesus. It presents an opportunity for you to minister and share the hope of the gospel and eternal life. You should reach out to families that are impacted and offer to pray for them. This is compassion-based evangelism. The Bible says, *"The effectual fervent prayer of a righteous man availeth much."* Let people see your good works. Read *Matthew 5:13-16*.

Prophecies

The end-time prophecies in this chapter reveal God's plan to take the focus off of Israel for 2,000 years while He shows Himself as the Messiah and Savior in the person of Jesus Christ to the Gentiles. When "the times of the Gentiles" is over, God will return to the Jews and find them at the point of death, because

Chapter 4 – Living Water

of the antichrist. At that time, the Jews will be happy to receive Jesus Christ as the Messiah and they will be miraculously healed.

- *John 4:4 And he must needs go through Samaria.*
  As the gospel goes to the Gentiles, the focus will be off the Jews.

- *John 4:40 So when the Samaritans were come unto him, they besought him that he would tarry with them: and he abode there two days.*
  The focus goes off the Jews for 2,000 years. (Two days = 2,000 years. Read *2Peter 3:8*.)

- *John 4:41 And many more believed because of his own word; (42) And said unto the woman, Now we believe, not because of thy saying: for we have heard him ourselves, and know that this is indeed the Christ, the Saviour of the world.*
  Many Gentiles will know for sure that Jesus is the Christ, the Savior of the world, and will by faith believe in Him according to the scripture.

- *John 4:43 Now after two days he departed thence, and went into Galilee.*
  The focus returns to the Jews after 2,000 years.

- *John 4:45 Then when he was come into Galilee, the Galilaeans received him, having seen all the things that he did at Jerusalem at the feast: for they also went unto the feast.*
  The Jews will receive Jesus Christ as Messiah at His second appearance.

- *John 4:47 When he heard that Jesus was come out of Judaea into Galilee, he went unto him, and besought him that he would come down, and heal his son: for he was at the point of death.*
 The Jews will be at the point of death from the persecution of the antichrist.

- *John 4:50 Jesus saith unto him, Go thy way; thy son liveth. And the man believed the word that Jesus had spoken unto him, and he went his way.*
 The Jews will be miraculously healed.

Summary

The phrase "living water" is unique to the Gospel of John. Twice it is used in this chapter and once in chapter 7. Consider *John 7:37-38, "In the last day, that great day of the feast, Jesus stood and cried, saying, If any man thirst, let him come unto me, and drink. He that believeth on me, as the scripture hath said, out of his belly shall flow rivers of living water."*

Religions, represented by the physical water of Jacob's well, are full of works and ceremonies that can never satisfy a thirsty soul, much less wash away sins. A person can convert from one religion to another and still not be satisfied. Jesus Christ offers the living water and He says to come and drink. This reminds me of *Revelation 22:17, "And the Spirit and the bride say, Come. And let him that heareth say, Come. And let him that is athirst come. And whosoever will, let him take the water of life freely."* I also echo the invitation—come to Jesus and drink. May God give all readers spiritual thirst for the living water.

5 – Healer

Historical Synopsis

Following His visit to Samaria and Galilee, Jesus returned to Jerusalem to celebrate a Jewish feast, which is believed to be the Passover feast. There He found many weak, sick, blind, and lame people lying under the five porches of the pool named Bethesda by the sheep gate. Nothing was able to heal their infirmities. There laid a certain man who had been impotent for 38 years. They all watched and waited for the troubling of the pool water. Apparently an angel went down into the pool at a certain season and stirred the water and would cure the first person who stepped in thereafter.

Jesus noticed the impotent man and offered to cure him. The man was immediately made whole by Jesus' word. After 38 years, he could get up, carry his bed, and walk again. The miracle was performed on a Sabbath day.

Since no one was supposed to carry a burden on the Sabbath day, the man carrying his bed in public was promptly flagged by the Jews for violating the Sabbath. The Jews reacted with rage and enmity when they learned that Jesus violated their tradition by healing the man. The Jews wanted to kill Jesus, especially when He also claimed that God was His Father. Jesus reproved the Jews and asserted Himself as God the Son by the testimony of the Father, John the Baptist, His works, and the scriptures.

The Book of John

This chapter can be outlined as such:

I. Jesus cured a man who had been impotent for 38 years – *John 5:1-16*
II. Jews sought to kill Jesus for violating the Sabbath and making Himself equal to God – *John 5:17-47*

Chapter 5 – Healer

Key Spiritual Lessons

The healing of an impotent man and the persecution of Jesus by religious unbelievers carry the important message that sinners who receive Jesus Christ as Lord and Savior are passed from death unto life, while religious unbelievers remain dead in trespasses and sins.

The need for washing in the pool of Bethesda for the healing of incurable diseases foreshadows the need for washing in Jesus' blood for the cleansing and healing of the incurable sin disease.

Following are the key spiritual lessons:

I. The cure for spiritual infirmities – *John 5:1-9*
II. The craziness and peril of having God without the Son – *John 5:10-30*
III. The certainty that Jesus was sent of God – *John 5:31-47*

The Cure for Spiritual Infirmities

[Verses 1-4] Following the events in chapter 4, Jesus went up to Jerusalem to observe a Jewish feast. At the temple by the sheep gate was a pool with five porches and a great multitude of people with incurable infirmities lying under the porches. Some were blind while others were lame, crippled, and withered. They all hoped for a miracle healing by watching and waiting for the troubling of the pool water by an angel and being the first to step into the pool.

There is potent truth in this short story. Of notable interest are the people with incurable diseases, the five porches, the angel, and the method of healing.

The Book of John

In the Bible, diseases such as leprosy, blindness, and disabilities picture sin. The multitude of people with diseases under the five porches of the pool represents all the sinners in this world. Everyone is born with the incurable sin disease. Sin is a hereditary spiritual disease that destroys life spiritually and physically. Sin brings about ungodliness in people. Read *2Timothy 3:2-5, Romans 7:14-20*. Sin also plagues people with physical illnesses. After healing the impotent man, Jesus said to him, *"Behold, thou art made whole: sin no more, lest a worse thing come unto thee,"* implying that his disease was a punishment for sin.

There was much pain, suffering, and unhappiness under the five porches. The number five in the Bible is the number of death. God paints a picture that shows a great multitude of sinners suffering through the days of their life under the cover of death. Indeed, *"the wages of sin is death."* Without intervention from the angel of the Lord (Jesus Christ), sinners have no hope of salvation. They are on a one-way path to death and hell.

The name of the pool was Bethesda, which means "house of mercy." Sinners must come out of the five porches (cover of death) and by faith step into the pool for salvation. We have established in previous chapters that water represents the word of God, and Jesus Christ is the Word. Salvation is by grace through faith according to scriptures. *1Peter 1:23 Being born again, not of corruptible seed, but of incorruptible, by the word of God, which liveth and abideth for ever.* The *"gift of God is eternal life through Jesus Christ"* only and no one can change this. I once heard a lady say, "I received Jesus in my own way." She had an imaginary plan of salvation. Read *Matthew 7:13-14*.

Observe the healing technique in verse 4, which foreshadows salvation by faith in Jesus Christ. It was a sign to the Jews that Jesus Christ was the Messiah, but unfortunately they didn't get it.

Chapter 5 – Healer

1. *"An angel went down at a certain season"*—The angel was the angel of the Lord, who was Jesus Christ. The season began about 2,000 years ago when the Word came down from heaven and was made flesh in the person of Jesus Christ.

2. *"Troubled the water"*—The troubling of the water is the troubling of Jesus Christ when He went to the cross.

3. *"Whosoever then first after the troubling of the water stepped in was made whole of whatsoever disease he had"*—After Jesus Christ was crucified, whosoever by faith steps into the pool (believes in Him) is immediately made whole from the sin disease. What about the requirement of being the first? *Romans 8:23* says the people who receive Christ as Savior are the *"firstfruits of the Spirit."*

Notice that a great multitude of impotent folks were under the five porches, but only one was healed. This is to show that a relatively small percentage of sinners will be saved. (Prophetically, this is a sign to the Jews that the majority of them will be dead in sins and only a remnant will be miraculously saved at the second appearance of Jesus Christ.) Step into Jesus' pool and be saved while the season of salvation remains open. Don't get left behind. Sadly the Bible says, *"Because strait is the gate, and narrow is the way, which leadeth unto life, and few there be that find it."*

The healing of the impotent man took place at the sheep gate. Yes, Jesus is shopping for sheep. Will you be His sheep?

[Verses 5-9] Jesus noticed the impotent man lying down and knew that he had suffered from an incurable infirmity for 38 years. He asked the man, *"Wilt thou be made whole?"* The impotent man replied that the reason he still had the infirmity was not for lack of trying, but lack of a good friend to carry him into the pool when the water was troubled. Jesus commanded the man to rise, take up his bed, and walk, and immediately the man was made whole. The healing took place on the Sabbath.

The impotent man lying down under the porches demonstrates the spiritual condition of sinners. All are beaten down and held captive by sin and death. But Jesus wants to heal and liberate every soul. He is *"not willing that any should perish, but that all should come to repentance."* Just as He took notice of the impotent man, He also sees and reaches out to all sinners. *John 1:9 That was the true Light, which lighteth every man that cometh into the world.*

"Wilt thou be made whole?" is an individual offer. The decision is personal. One does not inherit salvation from parents or relatives. Everyone needs to personally consider God's offer. Figuratively speaking, I was under the porches for 30 years before I accepted Jesus Christ as God and Savior for the pardoning of my sins. What about you? Hopefully you are not still under the porches.

The impotent man's personal best effort at racing to the pool did not gain him the much-needed healing. Having been so often disappointed, he began to despair and blamed it on the lack of a good friend. The lesson here is that human effort doesn't cut it. Thank God, salvation is not based on human effort. *Ephesians 2:8 For by grace are ye saved through faith; and that not of yourselves: it is the gift of God: (9) Not of works, lest any man should boast.* And if you need a good friend to carry you into the pool, Jesus is man's best friend. Read *John 15:13*. He will carry you into His pool of salvation.

It was a strange thing to command a man who had long been disabled to rise, take up his bed, and walk. But Jesus' word was powerful and effective when met with faith. The impotent man could have laughed at Jesus, but instead he believed and obeyed His word and was immediately made whole. You too will be made whole in an instant if you believe Jesus by faith and obey His words. All your past, present, and future sins are blotted out. The forgiveness is immediate and complete. You are declared righteous before God and your name is written in the Book of Life. Read *1Thessalonians 2:13, Romans 10:9-10, Romans 5:18-19.*

The Craziness and Peril of Having God without the Son

[Verses 10-13] In those days, a Jew carrying a burden around the temple on the Sabbath wouldn't get very far before being flagged down by those in authority, like the Pharisees. True enough, the Jews said to the man whom Jesus healed, *"It is the sabbath day: it is not lawful for thee to carry thy bed."* But the man argued that he was simply obeying the order of the person who healed him. When the Jews inquired about the healer, the man couldn't tell who He was because he didn't get a chance to know Him before Jesus slipped away from the crowd that had gathered.

Such are newly born again believers in Jesus Christ. Although immature in the knowledge of Christ, they are fully aware of the transformation in their lives, which should also be noticeable to others. The man was impotent for 38 years, and now he was walking. Has there been a noticeable change in your life since you accepted Christ as Savior? If not, perhaps the Holy Spirit of God never made it into your life, and all you have is a religious experience.

Believers must not be afraid or ashamed to openly testify of Christ and must no longer observe old religious laws and traditions. The man could have refused to carry his bed because of the Sabbath, but chose rather to obey Jesus' command. Believers should however expect persecution from religious unbelievers, as the man was challenged by the Jews.

[Verses 14-15] Jesus found the man in the temple, perhaps while he was thanking God for the great mercy bestowed on him, and warned him, *"Behold, thou art made whole: sin no more, lest a worse thing come unto thee."* The man departed from the temple and told the Jews that it was Jesus who made him whole.

Continuing on with the thought that there must be a noticeable change in a person's life after believing in Jesus Christ, believers must repent from the sins that beset them prior to meeting Jesus. For example, after forgiving the adulterous woman in chapter 8, Jesus said to her, *"Neither do I condemn thee: go, and sin no more."* What was your sin? If you were an alcoholic, a drug addict, or an idol worshipper, sin no more. You get the idea. This is not to say believers will never sin because it is impossible to live perfectly in the flesh. However, believers are to do the following things:

1. *"Behold, thou art made whole"*—Believers are to behold the new man who is regenerated by the Spirit of God and is passed from death to life. How much better and happier the new man is compared to the old man. It makes no sense to return to the old sin.

2. Bear in mind that God could send a worse disease or a sorer affliction if a believer returns to the old sin. Why? *Proverbs 3:12 For whom the LORD loveth he correcteth; even as a father the son in whom he delighteth.*

3. Bear in mind that the flesh yearns to sin and can cause the believer to backslide from God after conversion. Hence the warning from Jesus.

4. Bear witness of Jesus, as the man told the Jews that Jesus made him whole.

Chapter 5 – Healer

[Verses 15-18] The Jews were zealous of God and rested in the Law of Moses and their traditions, but did not consider Jesus to be the Messiah. Rather, they policed and persecuted people who violated tradition. They reacted with rage and enmity when they learned that Jesus had violated the Sabbath. They wanted to kill Him according to the Old Testament law—*Numbers 15:32-36*. But when Jesus defended Himself by saying, *"My Father worketh hitherto, and I work,"* it sent them over the edge because Jesus not only violated the Sabbath, He claimed God was His Father.

The Apostle Paul had this to say about the Jews: *"Romans 10:1 Brethren, my heart's desire and prayer to God for Israel is, that they might be saved. (2) For I bear them record that they have a zeal of God, but not according to knowledge. (3) For they being ignorant of God's righteousness, and going about to establish their own righteousness, have not submitted themselves unto the righteousness of God."*

The same can be said for the followers of all the world's religions. (True Christianity is not about religion, but a relationship with the Almighty God through His Son Jesus Christ.) These religious people want access to God without going through the Son. Many believe that all religions lead to the same God. They establish and improvise their own system of righteousness. Unfortunately it leads people to hell.

The truth is, there is only one way to Almighty God the Father. The way is through His Son, Jesus Christ. *1John 5:12 He that hath the Son hath life; and he that hath not the Son of God hath not life.* The reason this is unclear to natural people is because the god of this world, Satan, blinds their minds from believing the gospel of Christ. *2Corinthians 4:3 But if our gospel be hid, it is hid to them that are lost: (4) In whom the god of this world hath blinded the minds of them which believe not, lest the light of the glorious gospel of Christ, who is the image of God, should shine unto them.*

The Book of John

What follows next is Jesus' explanation of His relationship with the Father, from which we learn of the peril of having God without the Son.

1. The Son is fully integrated with the Father and cannot be decoupled from the Father. It is a Father-and-Son company.
    - Verse 19 says, *"Then answered Jesus and said unto them, Verily, verily, I say unto you, The Son can do nothing of himself, but what he seeth the Father do: for what things soever he doeth, these also doeth the Son likewise."* Jesus is the Son to whom the Father reveals the plan of His works and by whom He does all things. The Son imitates the Father according to what He sees. (Similarly, Moses built the tabernacle according to the pattern shown him by God in the mount. Read *Hebrews 8:5*.) This means the Son is with the Father, is privy to the whole plan of His works, is totally in sync with Him, and does nothing in opposition to Him. Read *Proverbs 8:22-31*. The Son implements the Father's design and is the one who gets things done. Remember *John 1:3*? *"All things were made by him; and without him was not any thing made that was made."*
    - Verse 20 says, *"For the Father loveth the Son, and sheweth him all things that himself doeth: and he will shew him greater works than these, that ye may marvel."* The Father loves the Son and has declared, *"This is my beloved Son, in whom I am well pleased; hear ye him."* It is folly to try to separate Jesus Christ from the Father.
    - [Verses 20-21] Because the Father loves the Son, He holds nothing back and reveals everything that He does to Him. The Father has greater works in store that will cause the Jews to marvel. One such work is

Chapter 5 – Healer

the resurrection of the dead. For as the Father raises the dead and gives them life, it is the Son's prerogative to give life to whom He will, according to His righteous judgment. [Verses 22-23] This is because the Father committed all judgment to the Son so that all men should honor the Son, even as they honor the Father.

2. The Son determines who gets life and death. Rejection of the Son is rejection of life. Read *John 3:36*.
    - Verses 24-26 talk about the promise of eternal life to sinners who hear Jesus' word (the gospel) and believe on the Father. *Read Isaiah 55:3*. According to verse 26, the Father has purposed that life should be in the Son. *1John 5:11 And this is the record, that God hath given to us eternal life, and this life is in his Son.*
    - Verses 27-30 talk about the promise of judgment to the dead who rejected the Son. [Verse 27] The Son has the authority and sovereignty to judge the dead who rejected Him. [Verse 28] There is an appointed hour in which all who are in their graves will hear the voice of the Son of God. [Verse 29] They will be resurrected. Every soul will return to its body and appear before the Judge, who is the Son. Read *Hebrews 9:27*. This is the Great White Throne judgment for those who died in their sins—*"They that have done good, unto the resurrection of life; and they that have done evil, unto the resurrection of damnation."* Read *Revelation 20:11-15*. (The Great White Throne judgment is not for believers. Believers participate in the Judgment Seat of Christ. See Chapter 8 for the comparison of the two judgments.) At the Great White Throne, none will

get life because *"all have sinned and come short of the glory of God."* All will die the second death, but not before they confess Jesus as Lord to the glory of God. Read *Romans 3:10-12, 23, Psalms 14:3, Psalms 53:3, Philippians 2:10-11*. [Verse 30] Jesus' judgment is just and the sentence he passes is right. He judges according to what He hears from the Father. Jesus does not seek to gratify his own will, but the will of the Father.

The Certainty that Jesus was Sent of God

Jesus produced five witnesses that testified He was sent by (or from) God.

1. The witness of John the Baptist
   [Verses 31-35] John was still alive at the time, though in prison. His testimony of Jesus was authentic and true, and he bore witness of the truth. The Jews believed John to be a prophet and looked upon him as a holy man of great integrity. John was not the Light, but he was a burning and a shining light. The Jews were willing for a season to rejoice in his light.

2. The witness of works
   [Verse 36] Jesus had a greater witness than the witness of John the Baptist. Jesus accomplished the works that the Father gave Him. Works such as the preaching of the gospel, the fulfilling of the law, and His death on the cross bore witness that the Father had sent Him. Read *John 10:25, 37-38, John 3:2, John 14:11, Isaiah 61:1-2, Luke 4:16-21*.

3. The witness of the Father

[Verses 37-38] It was the Father's pleasure to bear witness of Jesus with an audible voice from heaven at His baptism. The Father did it again at Jesus' transfiguration on the mount. Read *Matthew 3:17, Matthew 17:1-5*. These witnesses alone would have been enough, but unfortunately the Jews were ignorant of God and were not acquainted with such extraordinary revelations, even though they professed to know Him— *"Ye have neither heard his voice at any time, nor seen his shape. And ye have not his word abiding in you: for whom he hath sent, him ye believe not."* What a slap on the face! The Jews were committed with the oracles of God. They had the Old Testament, yet they couldn't recognize the Messiah. The word of God was not in them. It was in their hands, heads, eyes, and ears, but not in their hearts.

4. The witness of the scriptures
   [Verse 39] The Jews had a corrupt expectation and false hope that they should inherit eternal life because they had father Abraham, Moses, and the Old Testament law on their side. Read *Matthew 3:7-12*. Jesus challenged them to search the scriptures, not just casual reading or hearing the scriptures expounded in synagogues on the Sabbath day, but to search as someone searches for hidden treasures, and to study to rightly divide the word of truth. Read *Proverbs 2:1-9, 2Timothy 2:15*. They would find that the scriptures testify of and point to Him. By design the Old Testament law is a schoolmaster that points people to Christ. Read *Galatians 3:24*. [Verse 40] Even so, the Jews would not come to Jesus to obtain life because they were prejudiced, corrupt, perverse, stubborn, and willfully blind.

([Verse 41] In asserting His equality with the Father by producing the witnesses to the Jews, Jesus wasn't intending to receive honor and applause from them, but to vindicate Himself and glorify His Father.)

[Verse 42] The Jews, by rejecting and attempting to kill the Son, demonstrated they did not have the love of God in them. According to *1John 4:9, "In this was manifested the love of God toward us, because that God sent his only begotten Son into the world, that we might live through him."* They pretended to love God and thought they proved it by their zeal for the law, the temple, and the Sabbath.

[Verse 43] The Jews were so ignorant of God's truth that they not only rejected the Son who came in the Father's name, they would embrace someone who would come in his own name. This prophetically points to the antichrist. [Verse 44] Jesus sharply reproved their foolishness. They would believe on those who honored themselves, but would not seek after the one who was sent and honored by God. Read *John 8:54-55*. They were self-absorbed, as were the Scribes and Pharisees. They were ambitious of honor and respect from one another, doing things to be seen of men to gain their applause, and chose the uppermost rooms at feasts and chief places in the synagogues and delighted in the pompous title of Rabbi.

[Verses 45-47] Despite the Jews' rejection, Jesus did not accuse them to the Father. *John 3:17 For God sent not his Son into the world to condemn the world; but that the world through him might be saved.* Unlike the Jews who constantly looked for faults and violations of the

Chapter 5 – Healer

commandment, Jesus came not to accuse, but to advocate. Read *1John 2:1-2*. Jesus didn't need to accuse them because the Law of Moses that they trusted, rested in, and boasted of, accused them. This was because Moses wrote of Jesus. For example, the seed of the woman, the seed of Abraham, the offering of Isaac, Shiloh, the serpent on the pole, the Prophet, and the ceremonies of the law were figures of Jesus, who was to come. Read *Genesis 3:15, Genesis 13:15, Genesis 17:8, Genesis 22:18, Galatians 3:16, Genesis 22:1-14, Genesis 49:10, Numbers 21:4-9, Deuteronomy 18:15, Hebrew 9:1-12*. Therefore if they truly believed Moses, they would have believed in Jesus. This made them liars and sinners. The Law of Moses would bring charges against them, for they sinned against the law. (Sin is the transgression of the law.) The law in which they trusted for life would rise up in judgment and would be a witness against them. Read *Romans 7:7-11*.

Every religion has a set of laws, ordinances, statutes, and commandments for its believers. There are also punitive elements for its believers who fail to meet or observe its laws. But Jesus Christ is full of grace and truth, according to *John 1:14, 17*. If you trust in religion, you are under its law. Chances are you have not been able to fulfill everything that your religion expects of you, which makes you a law breaker. You are guilty under the very religion that you cling to. Why would you want to be under a law and not grace through a personal relationship with Jesus Christ?

5. Your witness
Consider *Acts 1:8, "But ye shall receive power, after that the Holy Ghost is come upon you: and ye shall be*

witnesses unto me both in Jerusalem, and in all Judaea, and in Samaria, and unto the uttermost part of the earth." You need to witness Christ. Your Jerusalem, Judea, and Samaria are the towns and cities around you. You are also commanded to testify of Jesus to the uttermost parts of the earth.

Summary

Verse 24 gives the best advice for curing the sin disease and avoiding condemnation: *"Verily, verily, I say unto you, He that heareth my word, and believeth on him that sent me, hath everlasting life, and shall not come into condemnation; but is passed from death unto life."* No one in his right mind would prefer death over life. But the path to life is obscure to many people because their minds are blinded by the devil whose motivations are to steal, kill, and destroy souls. There is an ongoing spiritual battle between light and darkness and between good and evil. May God shine the light of the glorious gospel of Christ on all readers that they might be healed of the sin disease.

6 – Bread of Life

Historical Synopsis

This chapter begins with the famous story commonly known as "the feeding of the 5,000." Following the events in chapter 5, Jesus departed from Jerusalem and went into Galilee preaching and healing people. Now, another feast of the Passover was upon them again—Jesus' third Passover since His baptism and entrance into ministry.

Many witnessed Jesus' healing miracles, and a great multitude of people followed Him. Some sought Him for healing, while others had their curiosity gratified by the novelty of the miracles. Regardless, Jesus performed yet another miracle by feeding the entire group of about 5,000 men with only five loaves of bread and two fishes.

That evening, Jesus showed His disciples that He could walk on water. The following day, Jesus taught in a synagogue and declared to the Jews that He was the bread of life from heaven.

This chapter can be outlined as such:

I. Jesus miraculously fed 5,000 men – *John 6:1-14*
II. Jesus walked on water – *John 6:15-21*
III. Jesus declared Himself as the Messiah in His discourse with the Jews – *John 6:22-59*
IV. Jesus reproved the disciples who forsook Him – *John 6:60-71*

The Book of John

5,000

104

Chapter 6 – Bread of Life

Key Spiritual Lessons

Bread, which represents the word of God, is the theme of this chapter. Jesus Christ was the personification of the bread of life who came down from heaven. Those who eat of this bread shall live forever.

To drive the message to the Jews, Jesus performed a miracle by feeding 5,000 men, besides women and children, with only five barley loaves and two small fishes. When the multitude returned to seek Him the next day, Jesus fed them again, but this time with a spiritual meal. He said, *"Labour not for the meat which perisheth, but for that meat which endureth unto everlasting life."* This set off a discourse on Jesus as the true bread from heaven, which gave life unto the world. And unless they would eat His flesh and drink His blood, they would have no life in them. Unfortunately, the Jews stumbled at the message and couldn't comprehend such spiritual things. What Jesus spoke of figuratively, they took literally. Just as Nicodemus couldn't comprehend the concept of spiritual birth and the Samaritan woman at the well couldn't grasp Jesus' spiritual message of living water, here the common Jews couldn't wrap their heads around the bread of life and spiritually eating Jesus' flesh and drinking His blood.

The miracles and the discourse in this chapter provide the following ministry insights and teach us to disseminate the bread of life to the lost.

  I. Insights into mission fields – *John 6:1-21*
  II. Insights into the mind of unbelievers – *John 6:22-59*
  III. Insights into ministry partnerships – *John 6:60-71*

Insights into Mission Fields

My relatives from Malaysia who have never been to the U.S. do not comprehend the size of the country and have no concept of time zones. As such, they have impractical ideas about travels and visits. One can drive to the northern tip of the Peninsula Malaysia from its southern tip, crossing as many as eight states in under nine hours. In the same amount of time, one will not even be able to cross the state of Kansas. Not surprising, many foreigners are shocked when they visit the U.S. for the first time.

Similarly in ministry, one who has never physically visited a mission field will not fully appreciate its size and challenges. Thankfully the first 21 verses give good insights into mission fields.

[Verse 1] The Sea of Galilee represents the sea of humanity. The first thing you need to know is that the mission field is larger than you think. The number of lost people is far greater than your forecast. Don't under estimate the size of your field. *Matthew 9:37 Then saith he unto his disciples, The harvest truly is plenteous, but the labourers are few; (38) Pray ye therefore the Lord of the harvest, that he will send forth labourers into his harvest.* There were 12 disciples against 5,000 men. You will always be begging for extra hands and help. Learn to partner with others.

Jesus going over the Sea of Galilee represents the truth of God reaching out to the sea of humanity. No one can say he is not touched by the truth of God. Read *Psalms 19:1-6*.

[Verse 2] You need something to draw a crowd. You may be tempted to use mainstream methods. Many pastors and missionaries constantly look for the next big thing to draw crowds, because the current thing is no longer cool and loses its appeal. Their next big thing may be a famous person, new electronic gadgets, games, or something cool, hip and sexy. Read the "The

Chapter 6 – Bread of Life

secrets to a big catch" section in Chapter 21 for why these mainstream methods are ineffective.

Jesus drew crowds with mercy and truth. He healed the sick and spoke truth to them. *Luke 24:19* says Jesus of Nazareth was mighty in deed and word. That is deed (mercy) before word (truth). Did you know that mercy and truth are inseparable in the Bible? Did you know that God's *"throne is upholden by mercy"*? *Read Proverbs 20:28*. What mercy or good deeds are you doing in your area for the purpose of making acquaintances and sharing the gospel? Are you able to identify, participate, and contribute to the humanitarian needs in your area? Always lead with mercy and follow with truth. Truth without mercy is cruel. Mercy without truth is social work. Churches often send people abroad to help build, repair, and paint homes. They call this missions. But if the people who go do not share the gospel, this is mercy without truth. It is social work and not missions.

You can also draw crowds through testimonies. A great multitude followed Jesus because they witnessed *"his miracles which he did on them that were diseased."* Every lost person has a sin disease that can only be cured by Jesus. A person who claims to be a Christian should have a life-transforming testimony that draws the lost to Jesus. Imagine a group of Christians with life-transforming testimonies. Surely a great multitude will follow Jesus when they see the miracle of transformation. Verse 14 says, *"Then those men, when they had seen the miracle that Jesus did, said, This is of a truth that prophet that should come into the world."* The world is tired of hypocrisy and longs for genuine, truthful, faithful, trustworthy people. Now imagine a group of name-only Christians, whose testimonies are indistinguishable from the children of the world. Unfortunately, that's not hard to do as churches are full of name-only Christians.

[Verse 3] It is important to note that Jesus sat with His disciples and not nominal believers. If you want to get things done on mission fields, partner with true disciples of Jesus Christ. See the "Lambs and sheep need to be fed" section in Chapter 21 for what it means to be a disciple of Jesus Christ. By the way, your spouse should be your ministry partner.

[Verse 5] You must serve bread (the word of God). Otherwise, your ministry might as well be a country club. When people come to see Jesus, they need spiritual food more than anything. Jesus asked Philip, *"Whence shall we buy bread, that these may eat?"* He didn't ask Philip to raise funds. Instead He asked Philip for the source of bread. Philip failed the test in two ways: 1) By looking to money as the source, and 2) By focusing on physical things.

When people come to church or Bible study, you must serve bread and not programs, entertainment, or commentaries. The only question is from whom do you buy bread? The answer is of course the Lord Jesus Christ. You must always be ready with a message, giving the truth of God. If you do not have a message, that is because you have not been praying and reading the Bible.

[Verses 6-7] Realize that the needs are far greater than your financial resources, no matter how much money you have. Like Philip, your first inclination may be to look into your bank account. If so, you will come to the same conclusion: *"Two hundred pennyworth of bread is not sufficient for them, that every one of them may take a little."* This may explain why many ministers are quick to start fundraising campaigns. However, please understand that the real need is not for physical things, but spiritual.

Money can never satisfy spiritual hunger. It would be easy if it could. Just print more money. The 5,000 men were filled with the bread that Jesus provided—*"Verily, verily, I say unto you, Ye seek me, not because ye saw the miracles, but because ye did eat of the loaves, and were filled."* Never trust in money or riches. Read *Proverbs 11:28, Matthew 6:24*. Spiritual hunger can only be satisfied

Chapter 6 – Bread of Life

by eating the bread of life, that is, a relationship with Jesus Christ by accepting Him as Lord and Savior. Read *Romans 10:9-10*.

Notice that Jesus did not use Philip's money. Instead He used the five barley loaves and two fishes from a boy. What a humble lesson for adults who think they are bigger, better, and more resourceful. Indeed, God chooses the weak things of the world to confound the things which are mighty. Read *1Corinthians 1:27*. (In Christian numerology, 5 is the number of death. Barley represents the currency of purchase. Read *Hosea 3:1-2*. The fishes represent sinners who need a Savior. The encoded message is: Jesus is the bread of life, who gave His life to purchase salvation for sinners.)

[Verses 8-9] According to *Matthew 14:15-16*, it was evening when the multitude met Jesus in the desert place. The disciples recommended that Jesus send them away into the villages to buy food. But Jesus replied, *"They need not depart; give ye them to eat."*

When people come to see Jesus, you should also address their physical needs out of compassion. You may find that their needs are far greater than your physical resources. As Andrew said, *"What are they among so many?,"* referring to the available resources. He too failed the test. He should have looked to Jesus. *2Corinthians 3:5 Not that we are sufficient of ourselves to think any thing as of ourselves; but our sufficiency is of God.*

When you enter a mission field, you will soon realize how utterly insufficient you are for the work regardless of how many resources you have. In fact, you will always be in a state of insufficiency. This is a good thing as it drives you to the Lord. The needs will always be there, but keep your eyes on Jesus and preach the word. *2Timothy 4:2 Preach the word; be instant in season, out of season; reprove, rebuke, exhort with all longsuffering and doctrine.*

If you do God's work, He will provide. God will never owe anyone. God, who spoke the universe into existence, is able and will pay for His projects.

[Verse 10] Jesus instructed His disciples to *"make the men sit down"* on a desert spot with plenty of grass. Essentially He treated the visitors as guests and wanted them to be comfortable, as grass was a better cushion than sand or rocks. Therefore receive sinners as guests and provide an environment that is conducive for the hearing of the word of God.

[Verses 11-13] Have faith in the word of God. There is an endless supply of bread and fishes as Jesus distributes them. The word of God is boundless, limitless, and all sufficient and powerful. God's word will not return void. It will accomplish God's purposes and will prosper and multiply, according to *Isaiah 55:10-11*. What's lacking is the carrier of bread—Christians who are willing to share the gospel with lost people.

The disciples gathered 12 baskets of bread fragments the crowd left on the grass after they had sufficiently eaten. (On a side note, 12 is the number of Israel. The bread of life was manifested to Israel.) The word of God was consumed by all, yet it remained over and above what was consumed. But notice that none of the fishes remained. As mentioned above, fish is a type of lost men. They either believe in Jesus and become His sheep, or are judged and burned. In the end, none will remain. Read Chapter 21 for details.

[Verses 15-21] The disciples sailed off to Capernaum (means "the village of comfort") without Jesus. Their ship was beaten by great winds and swells. They rowed hard for about 25 to 30 furlongs (about three and a half miles), but they were slower than Jesus, who came walking on the sea. When they received Him into the boat, they immediately arrived at their destination.

The story has two applications:

Chapter 6 – Bread of Life

1. It warns Christians of the danger of doing missions work without the Lord. When we engage in missions, we engage in spiritual warfare, which is foolish to do in the power of the flesh. Everything must be bathed in prayer. Otherwise, we will invest much energy, effort, and emotion, but come up empty and discouraged. *2Corinthians 10:3 For though we walk in the flesh, we do not war after the flesh: (4) (For the weapons of our warfare are not carnal, but mighty through God to the pulling down of strong holds.)* It is a good reminder that we are insufficient of ourselves and must live our lives in full dependency on the Lord. We need Jesus to help us navigate through darkness, headwinds, and turbulence, and to block and tackle our spiritual enemies. We will have a smoother sailing experience and get to our destinations faster when we rely on the Lord. This principle applies not only to missions work, but also to such personal endeavors as family, finances, and career.

2. It warns unbelievers of not having Jesus Christ in their lives. The sea represents the world. The dark hour in verse 17 represents spiritual darkness. The ship represents the body of the unbeliever. The message is clear—the world will always be a turbulent place for unbelievers. They will never be happy and peaceful until they receive Jesus Christ into their hearts.

In summary, mission fields have great needs, which can only be satisfied by the Lord and His word. Don't try to be clever and outsmart what God has set. Read *Proverbs 3:5-6*.

Insights into the Mind of Unbelievers

Just as farmers must plow their fields before sowing, missionaries must also work and engage the field before sowing the seed of the word of God into the hearts of men. Some unbelievers may receive Jesus, while others may object and reject. Verses 22-59 give insights into the mind of unbelievers, which can be categorized as follows:

- Seek material benefits – verses 22-27
- Struggle with faith – verses 28-31, 51-59
- Struggle with the identity of Jesus – verses 32-36, 41-42

Seek material benefits

[Verses 22-27] The people who were miraculously fed by Jesus the day before earnestly sought after Him again. When they realized He had left, they took advantage of the boats that came from Tiberias and went over to Capernaum. They did not seek after Jesus for the right reason. They sought Him for their bellies' sake. They were not after His doctrine as Nicodemus was. Nicodemus was convinced that Jesus was from God by the miracles He performed, but these folks were after free food. Jesus counseled them not to labor for meat that perishes, but for meat that endures to everlasting life, which He would supply.

Lost people are prone to seek after the meat that perishes, which are the things of the world, such as wealth, honor, health, food, and pleasure. They will jump through hoops and attach themselves to anyone who supplies those things for free. They try to fill spiritual hunger with worldly physical elements. Jesus gave them one free meal, but not the second. The next was a spiritual meal in which they must decide if He would be their Savior.

Chapter 6 – Bread of Life

Don't subscribe to the foolish idea that lost people will wake up one day and decide to seek after God for the right reason. The Bible is very clear. *Psalms 10:4 The wicked, through the pride of his countenance, will not seek after God: God is not in all his thoughts. Romans 3:10 As it is written, There is none righteous, no, not one: (11) There is none that understandeth, there is none that seeketh after God.* Also, verse 44 says that no man comes to Jesus except the Father draws him. Nothing inside lost people will change on its own to cause them to find Jesus attractive. Yet there are seeker-friendly churches that tone down the preaching of the word in order to cater to the lost. Those churches are run by leaders who choose worldly methods over God's prescription.

Struggle with faith

[Verses 28-29] Having been told that they must labor for the meat that endures unto everlasting life, the people wanted to know what works they might do to earn it. Their concept of righteousness was by the works of the law and not by faith. Jesus clearly defined the work of God for them: *"This is the work of God, that ye believe on him whom he hath sent."*

Lost people are fixed on good works. They think they are good with God as long as their good works outweigh their bad works. This cannot be further from the truth, but unfortunately, religions such as Catholicism[2], Buddhism, Taoism, Confucianism, Hinduism, Islamism, Judaism, and Humanism, just to name a few,

---

[2] Catechism of the Catholic Church: #837 *"Fully incorporated into the society of the Church are those who, possessing the Spirit of Christ, accept all the means of salvation given to the Church together with her entire organization, and who - by the bonds constituted by the profession of faith, the sacraments, ecclesiastical government, and communion - are joined in the visible structure of the Church of Christ, who rules her through the Supreme Pontiff and the bishops. Even though incorporated into the Church, one who does not however persevere in charity is not saved. He remains indeed in the bosom of the Church, but 'in body' not 'in heart.'"*

promote this concept. Christians do good works because they are saved, not in order to be saved.

[Verse 30-31] Still unable to comprehend faith, the people asked Jesus to produce a visible sign before they would believe in Him. Mind you, these were the people who followed Jesus after witnessing the healing miracles and were miraculously fed the day before. Yet they requested a greater sign than the miracle of manna, which to them was the benchmark for Jesus to beat. Jesus fed 5,000, but Moses fed hundreds of thousands. Jesus fed them once and reproved those who returned for another free meal, but Moses fed his followers for 40 years. Jesus fed them with barley loaves out of the earth and fishes out of the sea, but Moses fed their fathers with bread from heaven, which was angel's food. Read *Exodus 16:11-15, Psalms 78:24-25*. See the "Side Notes" section later for a comparison between bread of life and manna.

Both Jews and Gentiles are drawn to physical evidence. A young man once told me he struggled to accept Jesus because his prayers were not answered. In other words, Jesus must deliver some evidence or make something happen before he would believe.

[Verses 51-59] Seeing that the Jews struggled with understanding and murmured, Jesus once again explained that He was the living bread who came down from heaven and gave eternal life to anyone who ate the bread, which was his flesh. The concept of spiritually eating by faith was completely strange to the Jews. They could comprehend collecting physical manna from the ground and eating it, but they could not wrap their heads around spiritually eating Jesus as the bread of life. Jesus, of course, meant it metaphorically when He said *"Except ye eat the flesh of the Son of man, and drink his blood, ye have no life in you,"* for flesh and blood cannot inherit the Kingdom of God. This signified that salvation was by faith instead of works.

Chapter 6 – Bread of Life

Note:

The Hindus don't eat beef because cows are sacred to them. But Christians must spiritually eat the object of their worship, which is Jesus Christ.

Struggle with the identity of Jesus

[Verses 31-33] When the people said, *"He gave them bread from heaven to eat,"* they ascribed it to Moses. Jesus corrected their misunderstanding of scripture.

- First, Moses did not give them the bread. It was God. Read *Exodus 16:15*.
- Secondly, manna was the bread from the first heaven, not the heaven of heavens. Manna appeared after the dew was lifted up.
- Thirdly, God was offering them the true bread from the heaven of heavens of which the manna was a figure. Jesus defined for them the true bread of God—*"For the bread of God is he which cometh down from heaven, and giveth life unto the world."* The bread of God was a person who came down from the heaven of heavens with quickening virtue.

[Verses 34-36] The people responded positively by saying, *"Lord, evermore give us this bread."* Nevertheless, they did not believe Jesus was the bread of life as evident by Jesus' reply, *"I am the bread of life: he that cometh to me shall never hunger; and he that believeth on me shall never thirst. But I said unto you, That ye also have seen me, and believe not."* This is despite the fact that Jesus repeatedly telling them that He was the bread of life (verses 33, 35, 48-51), whom God sent from heaven (verses 29, 38-40, 44, 57).

The observation here is that lost people want all the heavenly blessings, including eternal life, but without Jesus Christ. A preacher went to preach in a county jail. At the end of his sermon he asked, "Who wants to go to heaven?" All raised their hands. Then the preacher followed up by asking, "Who wants to give his life to Jesus?" and only one hand remained. That's why I don't ask people if they want to go to heaven when witnessing. Only a fool would answer no. Instead I ask if they want to be right with God. I also emphasize personal sin, the penalty of sin, and who can forgive sin. Until individuals admit they are a sinner, Jesus Christ is of no use to them.

[Verses 41-42] The reason the people stumbled and did not believe that Jesus came from heaven was because they knew His parents, or at least they thought they knew. They were ignorant of the scriptures. In contrast, Andrew and his pal asked Jesus where He lived when they first met Him. The place of His residence was so important to them because the scriptures proclaimed the Messiah would be born in Bethlehem of Judea, but would arise from Nazareth of Galilee. They followed Jesus to His home and knew that He was the Messiah. Read *John 1:35-41*. Unfortunately many Jews, including the religious chief priests and Pharisees, did not know the scriptures and they struggled with Jesus' identity as the drama and rejection continued into chapter 7.

Lost people have a preconceived idea of Jesus, which they get from family, friends, culture, and religion. They have real trouble in believing that Jesus is God the Son and is the only Savior of the world because they are ignorant of scriptures. Share the word of God with them and witness Jesus with your life. What would you say to someone who asked how you know if Jesus is real?

Chapter 6 – Bread of Life

Side Notes:

- [Verses 37-40, 44-47] Not everyone will believe in Jesus Christ and receive Him as their sole God and Savior. God has to draw them. Those who believe in Jesus are secure and have eternal life. Those who die in Christ will be raised to life in the last day. (The "last day" is a period that begins with the rapture of the church and ends with the Great White Throne judgment at the end of the millennium—a period of about 1,000 years. The phrase "last day" only occurs eight times in the Bible. It is first mentioned in *Nehemiah 8:18.* All other references occur in the Gospel of John, four in this chapter alone. Don't miss the end-time significance in this chapter.)

- [Verses 48-59] Since the Jews were so proud of the manna that their fathers ate, Jesus took time to compare and contrast the breads.

Bread of Life	Manna
Jesus is the living bread, never molds, or gets old.	Manna was a dead thing. If kept but one night, it putrefied and bred worms.
Jesus is the bread of life.	All who ate manna in the wilderness died.
Jesus gives eternal life to the world.	Manna sustained the Israelites only and only temporarily.
Jesus is the true bread that came down from heaven.	Manna was a type and figure of the true bread.
Obtained by faith.	Obtained by labor.

Insights into Ministry Partnerships

[Verses 60-71] Many of Jesus' disciples found His message of eating flesh and drinking blood offensive. They said, *"This is an hard saying; who can hear it?"* and they stopped following Him. Jesus replied that if this was hard to receive and understand, then how would they process the sight of Him ascending to heaven. He clarified that His sayings were to be understood spiritually and not physically. He also exposed the root cause of their departure, which was unbelief.

When Jesus asked the twelve, if they too would leave Him, Peter said there was none other who had the words of eternal life, and that they all believed He was the Christ, the Son of the living God. However, Jesus said not all believed, because one was a devil.

Ministry needs are so great that we often have to partner with others. Ideally, the partners are mature in the Lord. In reality, this is not always the case as people are in different stages of maturity in the Lord and may have differences in their understanding of doctrines. It is okay as long as everyone can agree on the main doctrines, such as salvation, eternal life, and baptism.

Also ideally, the partners are truly born-again Christians. Time will tell, as unsaved individuals are the ones who will be offended by the truth of God, and will abandon the partnership to perhaps start a rival group. Not all disciples are believers. *1John 2:19 They went out from us, but they were not of us; for if they had been of us, they would no doubt have continued with us: but they went out, that they might be made manifest that they were not all of us.* The scary thing is that one of the partners may even be a devil. This could very well happen as it happened with Jesus.

Prophecies

The end-time prophecies in this chapter reveal that Jesus will be separated from the Jews and they will go through a severe tribulation period of about three and a half years. But Jesus will reappear to them at their moment of despair and they will receive Him as their Messiah. God will make a new covenant with the house of Israel and will put His law in their hearts. All Israel will come to Jesus.

- *John 6:9 There is a lad here, which hath <u>five barley loaves</u>, and two small fishes: but what are they among so many? (13) Therefore they gathered them together, and filled <u>twelve</u> baskets with the fragments of the five barley loaves, which remained over and above unto them that had eaten.*
  In Christian numerology, the number five is the number of death and the number 12 is the number of Israel. The barley loaves represent Jesus, who was broken and sacrificed for Israel and the world.

- *John 6:15 When Jesus therefore perceived that they would come and take him by force, to make him a king, <u>he departed</u> again into a mountain himself alone.*
  Jesus will be separated from the Jews.

- *John 6:16 And when even was now come, his disciples went down unto the sea, (17) And entered into a ship, and went over the sea toward Capernaum. And it was now dark, and Jesus was not come to them.*
  Jews will sail off on their own without the protection and blessings of their Messiah. "Dark" refers to spiritual darkness because the great Light has departed.

- *John 6:18 And the sea arose by reason of a great wind that blew.(19) So when they had rowed about five and twenty or thirty furlongs, they see Jesus walking on the sea, and drawing nigh unto the ship: and they were afraid.*

  Jews will enter into a severe tribulation period that lasts for about three and a half years. (20 to 30 furlongs is about three and a half miles.) God will give the Jews *"the bread of adversity and the water of affliction (Isaiah 30:20)"* for rejecting Jesus. However, God will be gracious to the Jews and Jesus will return to save them in their moment of despair.

- *John 6:20 But he saith unto them, It is I; be not afraid. (21) Then they willingly received him into the ship: and immediately the ship was at the land whither they went.*

  Jews will be comforted. They will gladly receive Jesus as their Messiah.

- *John 6:45 It is written in the prophets, And they shall be all taught of God. Every man therefore that hath heard, and hath learned of the Father, cometh unto me.*

  God will teach them and they will know who Jesus is. Read Isaiah 54:11-14, Jeremiah 31:33-34, Hebrews 8:10-12, Hebrews 10:16-17.

Summary

Jesus Christ is the true bread of life that came down from heaven. Unfortunately, there is false and deceitful bread, that like manna, has the appearance of heaven, but is the bread of death. May God give all readers the wisdom to discern and eat the bread of life so that they may live forever.

7 – Teacher

Historical Synopsis

Having done His works in chapter 6, Jesus went to Jerusalem in the spring to celebrate the Passover. There, the Jews still sought to kill Him for healing the impotent man on the Sabbath day and for making Himself equal to God during the previous Passover (*John 5:1, 18*). After the feast, Jesus returned to Galilee and continued His ministry there until the fall, when He needed to return to Jerusalem to celebrate the Feast of the Tabernacles.

Jesus reproved His unbelieving kinsmen because they pretended to have an interest in Him and urged Him to make a more public appearance in Jerusalem. Jesus went secretly to the Feast of the Tabernacles, but revealed Himself in the middle of the eight-day feast when He taught in the temple. The Jews marveled at His doctrine, especially given that He did not have any religious education and never sat at the feet of a rabbi. In His discourse, He gave them the key to knowing His doctrine and reproved them for their hypocritical religious practices and ignorance of scriptures. He also proclaimed His death, ascension, and second return, but the Jews didn't understand.

The Pharisees and the chief priests sent officers to apprehend Jesus, but they returned empty handed because they were taken with His words of truth, spoken with such power, grace, and authority. They found no fault in Him. This set off a

Chapter 7 – Teacher

disagreement among the Pharisees for the handling of the matter and concerning the identity of Jesus. The common Jews were also divided over His identity.

This fragmented chapter can be outlined as such:

   I.   Jesus reproved His unbelieving kinsmen – *John 7:1-9*
   II. Jesus gave the key to knowing His doctrine – *John 7:10-18*
   III. Jesus confronted hypocritical religious practices – *John 7:19-24*
   IV. Jesus reproved the Jews for not knowing the scriptures – *John 7:25-31*
   V.   Jesus prophesied of His death, ascension, and second return – *John 7:32-39*
   VI. Jesus' identity remained unresolved among the Jews – *John 7:40-44*
   VII. Jesus frustrated the Pharisees and chief priests who issued a warrant for His arrest – *John 7:45-53*

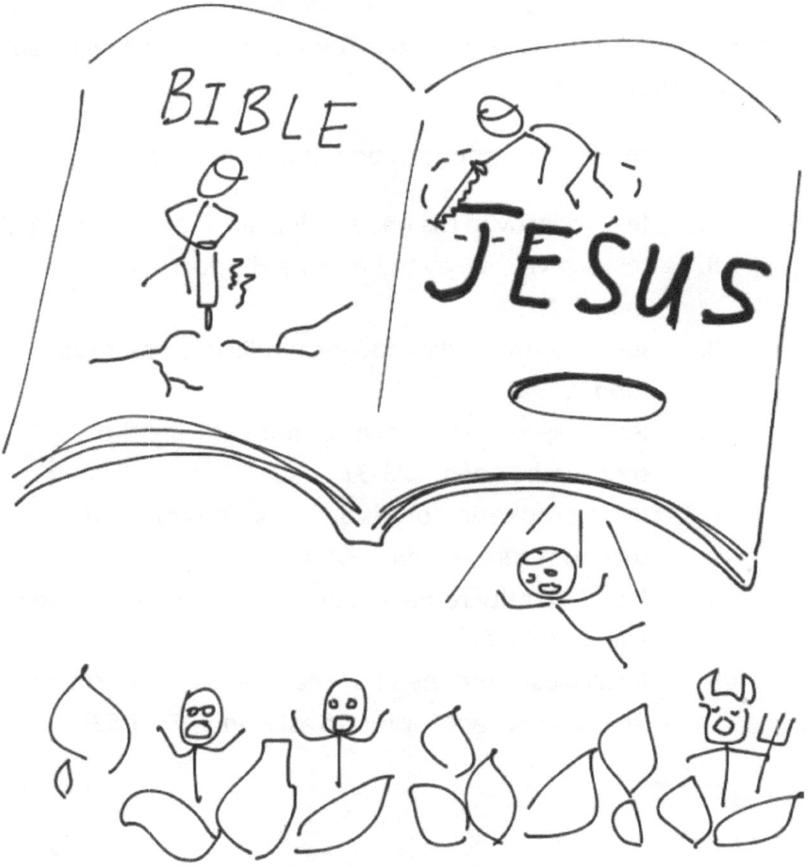
BIBLE
JESUS

Key Spiritual Lessons

Wow, what chaos, was my initial reaction to this chapter. Due to ignorance of scriptures, Jesus' kinsmen did not believe in Him; the Jews were unsure and divided over His identity; religion was observed in hypocrisy and in vain; judgment was corrupt; people trusted in false hopes; and worse, they persecuted the only one who could give them eternal life.

This mess should have been expected because, by design, faith in God is rooted in the Holy Scriptures. To know God is to know Jesus. To know Jesus is to know scriptures. To know scriptures, you need to be born again by the Holy Spirit of God because scriptures are spiritually discerned, according to *1Corinthians 2:14*. There simply is no other way. However, the unbelieving world is ignorant of scriptures and wants access to the Father while bypassing the Son. The unbelieving world subscribes to various forms of godliness that are unsubstantiated by scriptures.

Jesus' discourse with the Jews in the temple on about the fourth day of the feast offers a window into the characteristics of unbelievers.

I. Unbelievers hate truth – *John 7:1-9*
II. Unbelievers are zealous of religion – *John 7:10-13*
III. Unbelievers are stubborn – *John 7:14-18*
IV. Unbelievers judge according to man's righteousness – *John 7:19-24*
V. Unbelievers are prejudiced against truth – *John 7:25-31*
VI. Unbelievers will miss the Savior – *John 7:32-36*
VII. Unbelievers will respond to the gospel call – *John 7:37-44*
VIII. Unbelievers are ignorant of scriptures – *John 7:45-53*

The Characteristics of Unbelievers

Unbelievers hate truth

[Verses 1-9] Jesus, the Truth of God, continued His ministry in Galilee instead of in Jerusalem, because the Jerusalem Jews sought to kill Him for healing an impotent man on the Sabbath day during the previous year's Passover feast. With the Feast of Tabernacles fast approaching, Jesus needed to return to Jerusalem. The Feast of Tabernacles was one of the three great feasts, requiring that all males make a pilgrimage to the temple in Jerusalem. Read *Deuteronomy 16:16-17, Leviticus 23:33-44, Numbers 29:12-40*. Knowing this, His unbelieving kinsmen purposely gave Jesus bad advice that could have gotten Him killed under the pretense of the advancement of His name and ministry.

As much as the unbelieving world wants to present its good and kind side, its ugly side reveals itself when Jesus is the center of the matter. Nice people can turn murderers. A Christian and a Muslim man were once good friends. But during an uprise against Christianity, the Muslim man killed his friend. The truth is, there is no friendship between God and the world and no communion between light and darkness. There never was and never will be. This is why it is important for believers to not be yoked with unbelievers, especially in a marital relationship, because the two are spiritually incompatible regardless of how compatible they are in the flesh. Read *2Corinthians 6:14*. When light fellowships with darkness, light always goes out. Don't be a fool to believe that unbelievers will have the same conviction. God is the Father of one, while the devil is the father of the other. Do you think they will coexist in harmony?

The Coexist society (C☮☯✡☸✝) promotes the coexistence of Islam, Wicca, Science, Judaism, Buddhism, Taoism, and Christianity. The flawed working assumption is that everyone ultimately prays to and worships the same God, therefore the world should be able to live in peace and harmony. They are ignorant of the fact that there are only two spiritual families, fathered by two spiritual fathers. One is God the Father and the other is the devil. They both are interested in people, albeit for different reasons. One Father comes to forgive sin and give eternal life while the other comes to take and destroy life. In chapter 8, you will see the devil has many religious people in his family. Sadly, the people in the Coexist camp may long to be the children of God, but really are the devil's children, according to scriptures. See how quickly their ugly side comes out when you present that Jesus is the only way to salvation. The same applies to other religions.

The unbelieving world hates the gospel truth and does not like to face up to it. They persecuted Jesus and they will persecute His followers. Read *John 15:18-21*, *John 16:1-4*. Why is this so? Verse 7 gives the answer, *"The world cannot hate you; but me it hateth, because I testify of it, that the works thereof are evil."* Indeed, *"light is come into the world, and men loved darkness rather than light, because their deeds were evil."* Unbelievers want to do their own thing according to their lusts and are right in their own eyes, but not according to scriptures. They are ignorant of the fact that the grace of God is the only thing that holds them from falling into hell fire. By upsetting God with their actions every day, they are as smart as those who operate a jackhammer while standing on thin ice. Those who hate Jesus love death, according to *Proverbs 8:36*. Read *2Corinthians 4:3-7* for their solution. Pray for your unbelieving relatives and friends. Remember the lesson from *John 6:44* that no one can come to Jesus except the Father draws him.

Unbelievers are zealous of religion

[Verses 10-13] Jesus' unbelieving kinsmen went to Jerusalem to celebrate the Feast of Tabernacles, but Jesus went secretly because of His enemies. The religious rulers sought after

Jesus, not to learn from him, but to kill him. The common Jews were divided over the identity of Jesus. Some said He was a good man, while others thought He was a deceiver.

The Jews were devoted to fulfilling their religious obligations, although their actions amounted to nothing more than external performances because they did not accept Jesus as the Messiah. Like the Jews, the world is full of religious people who are zealous for God, but are hell bound because they do not have a personal relationship with Christ, according to scriptures. They perform religious acts in vain. There is a saying that religions send more people to hell than all their vices combined. Remember, it is not about good works or religion, but a personal relationship with the Savior.

Unbelievers are stubborn

[Verses 14-15] The Jews, who considered the scribes and Pharisees the most expert and accurate expositors of the Jewish law, marveled at Jesus' doctrine, especially because He was uneducated and never trained by a rabbi. *Matthew 7:28 And it came to pass, when Jesus had ended these sayings, the people were astonished at his doctrine: (29) For he taught them as one having authority, and not as the scribes.* In reality, the scribes and Pharisees, whom the Jews trusted, did not really know scriptures, as is evident at the end of the chapter. They were teachers who sought their own glory, who had nothing else in view but themselves and taught the traditions of men. Jesus had choice words for them. He called them hypocrites, blind fools, whited sepulchres, and serpents. Read *Matthew 23:13-33*.

Beware of Bible teachers or theologians who say the Bible cannot be trusted or that it must be understood in the way the original writer would have interpreted it. (Many original writers didn't understand what they were writing. They simply obeyed as they were moved by the Holy Spirit of God. Read *2Peter 1:20-21*.) If you have one of these as your teacher, it is time to change channels or churches.

[Verses 16-18] The Jews were also as stubborn as their forefathers. Read *Psalms 78:1-8, 1Samual 15:23*. Jesus gave them the key to confirming His doctrine in verse 17 so that they might know it was from God, but they would not do it. All they had to do was simply do the will of God, which was to believe in the Son. Read *John 6:40*.

It is interesting to see lost people marvel at the truth of God like insects are drawn to the light. What's more interesting is that God does not ask them to move a mountain, but to simply believe His Son by faith. Yet lost people would rather move a mountain than to believe scriptures.

Unbelievers judge according to man's righteousness

[Verses 19-24] The Jews, who accused Jesus for healing a man on the Sabbath day, also administered circumcision on the Sabbath. According to *Leviticus 12:1-3*, every male child must be circumcised on the eighth day.

What happened when the eighth day fell on a Sabbath? It was impossible to fulfill the conflicting laws at the same time. Similarly, what happened when the Passover fell on a Sabbath? The Jews made up their own rule and allowed for circumcision and the Passover to supersede the Sabbath because these predated the law of the Sabbath. However, consider what the Apostle Paul said in *Romans 2:25, "For circumcision verily profiteth, if thou keep the law: but if thou be a breaker of the law, thy circumcision is made uncircumcision."*

Therefore Jesus beat them in their own game. In other words, if it was okay for them to wound (circumcise) someone and violate one of the laws, then how could they blame Him for healing a person on the Sabbath? Circumcision was a bloody and painful ordinance initially practiced by Abraham, not Moses. The law inflicted pain, but Jesus made the impotent man whole and without pain.

The Jews tried to obey laws that were designed to be impossible to obey. For example, the Ten Commandments were given so that the Jews would realize there was no way anyone could fulfill them. They needed grace instead of law. *John 1:17 For the law was given by Moses, but grace and truth came by Jesus Christ. Galatians 3:24 Wherefore the law was our schoolmaster to bring us unto Christ, that we might be justified by faith.* By not knowing the scriptures, the Jews practiced religion in hypocrisy, and their judgment was not according to truth. They judged Jesus' miracle according to appearance, because on the surface, it looked as if He violated the Sabbath. But then the practices of the scribes and Pharisees were ungodly although they looked good, right, and holy to men. The unbelieving world judges according to man's righteousness instead of God's.

As previously mentioned, lost people who tend to be religious often violate numerous laws, either of their own or of God's. One has to only violate one law to be a sinner. Oh that lost people would realize that *"all have sinned and come short of the glory of God,"* and that there is no mercy, hope, or salvation in laws for law breakers. Laws are designed to protect the good, not the evil doers. *Romans 6:23 For the wages of sin is death; but the gift of God is eternal life through Jesus Christ our Lord.* Also read *Romans 13:1-10.*

Unbelievers are prejudiced against truth

[Verses 25-26] The Jerusalem Jews were the most prejudiced against Jesus. The country Jews did not know about the plot to kill Jesus, as evidenced by their response in verse 20, *"Who goeth about to kill thee?"* The Jerusalem Jews knew about the plot and were upset that the rulers didn't say anything to Jesus, allowing Him to speak boldly. They tried to infuriate the rulers into action by asking if they had changed their mind concerning Jesus. *"Do the rulers know indeed that this is the very Christ?"* In other words, "You must now believe that He is Christ, otherwise, you would have stopped Him." Clearly they did this to provoke the rulers, as none of them had changed their position concerning Jesus, according to verse 48.

[Verse 27] The Jerusalem Jews added fuel to the fire by claiming their knowledge of Jesus and of the Messiah, subjects that their rulers should have been masters of. To them it was blatantly obvious that Jesus was not the Christ because He was the son of Joseph and Mary from Nazareth of Galilee. They also said that when the real Messiah came, no one would know His origin. The message to their rulers was, "Not only have you changed your mind, you have also lost your mind and your religious authority." The tactic worked, as the Pharisees issued a warrant for Jesus' arrest in verse 32.

How much more ignorant could these Jews have been? The scriptures were very clear about how the Messiah would be conceived, where He would be born, and from where He would operate. Read *Isaiah 7:14, Micah 5:2, Isaiah 9:1-2.*

[Verses 28-30] Jesus went along with their ignorance. He reiterated their presumptuous knowledge of Him and of His origin, but pointed out a little problem with that. You can just imagine the whole room was suddenly quiet and everyone wondered, "What's that?" Then Jesus delivered the breaking news: They did not know from whom He came. He did not come of (or represent) Himself, but was sent by the Father, who they didn't know. That did not bode well with the Jews, who rested in the law and boasted of God. Read *Romans 2:17-29*. Being enraged by Jesus' claims, they sought

The Book of John

to take Him before the Sanhedrim to be tried and condemned as a blasphemer. However, no man laid hands on Jesus because His hour had not yet come, according to the predetermined counsel of God. Indeed, *"to every thing there is a season, and a time to every purpose under the heaven: A time to be born, and a time to die."*

[Verse 31] Yet many of the country Jews believed on Jesus, though they took Him as an ordinary man, the son of Joseph, and did not own Him as the Messiah. They wondered if they would see more miracles when the Christ came. This kind of testimony is troubling because *"he that cometh to God must believe that he is."* Contrast this with Peter's testimony in *John 6:69*, *"And we believe and are sure that thou art that Christ, the Son of the living God."*

The hardest people to convince are those who think they know the truth and think that they are okay with God. They trust in religion and tradition, while scriptures take a back seat. I feel it is easier to convince these people to climb Mount Everest than to read the Bible. They go through the motions like the Jews. They go full steam ahead with religious activities, but with no knowledge of the word of God. Let it be known that God does not judge a person according to religion or religious activities. Jesus said in *John 12:48b*, *"The word that I have spoken, the same shall judge him in the last day."* These people are well advised to learn what the Bible says.

Unbelievers will miss the Savior

[Verses 32-36] The Pharisees and the chief priests sent officers to arrest Jesus. When the officers came, they heard a message so perplexing that they could not fulfill their duty. Jesus told them and the surrounding unbelieving Jews that He would soon return to be with the Father who sent Him. Thereafter they would seek Him (in troublous times), but would not find Him, because where He was going they had no access. Read *Hosea 5:6, John 8:21, Proverbs 1:24-33*. The Jews were perplexed at the saying, especially

Chapter 7 - Teacher

in reference to the place where He could not be found. They wondered where He could possibly go that they would not be able to find Him. Some speculated that Jesus would go to the less fortunate Jews who were scattered abroad among the Gentiles and also teach the Gentiles. Even so, why wouldn't He be found? They could not understand the saying.

What Jesus said further underscored the fact that the Jews had no relationship with the Father, otherwise they would be able to find Him. (Contrast this with *Hebrews 4:16*, where true believers may boldly approach the throne of grace.) It didn't dawn on them that Jesus was talking about heaven above, because they never considered Him as deity. In their eyes, Jesus was lesser than Abraham and the prophets. Read *John 8:53*.

Remember the old adage, "Be careful what you wish for"? The Jews wanted so badly to get rid of Jesus, and they got their wish. Jesus left them, and they missed the Messiah.

Today Israel is left to face their enemies alone. They are surrounded by countries and people who hate them. They struggle daily with the Palestinians, and Iran is developing nuclear weapons to wipe them off the map. The U.S. is their only friend, but this relationship may end soon. These problems are just the tip of the iceberg for the Jews, because they will face the antichrist, who is many times more evil than Adolf Hitler. In their tribulation, the Jews will be knocking on Jesus' door, but He will not answer. As verse 34 says, they will seek Him, and will not find Him. *Hosea 9:12b* says, "*Yea, woe also to them when I depart from them!*"

Unbelievers who want to get rid of Jesus may also get their wish. By rejecting Jesus as their Savior, they shut off access to God the Father and heaven. Read *John 14:6*. One of these days, they too will knock on Jesus' door in their misery and calamity. It breaks my heart to think of the billions of people in the world who will die in their sins because they are trusting in false hopes.

The Book of John

Unbelievers will respond to the gospel call

[Verses 37-44] Jesus gave a gospel call on the last day of the feast.

- *"If any man thirst"*—the invitation is open to anyone who thirsts for God's righteousness.
- *"let him come unto me"*—Jesus is the righteousness of God and there is none else. Read *Romans 3:20-22, John 14:6*. It is Jesus only. You cannot come to Jesus and still hold on to your old gods, saints, or religions.
- *"and drink"*—receive Jesus by faith. *John 6:53 Then Jesus said unto them, Verily, verily, I say unto you, Except ye eat the flesh of the Son of man, and drink his blood, ye have no life in you.*

Jesus also provided validation for those who properly accepted Him.

- *"He that believeth on me"*—one must come to Jesus by belief or faith and not by works of righteousness.
- *"as the scripture hath said, out of his belly shall flow rivers of living water"*—believers will receive the Holy Spirit of God according to the promise of scripture. They will be satisfied and never again thirst for righteousness, because in them is a well of water springing up into everlasting life. Read *Ephesians 1:13, John 4:13-14*.

Many of the common Jews who heard the message believed that Jesus was the Prophet spoken of in *Deuteronomy 18:15*. Some said He was the Christ, but some doubted because according to them, the scripture said Christ should come of the seed of David and out of the town of Bethlehem. They supposed that Jesus was the son of Joseph from the town of Nazareth of Galilee. So the Jews remained divided over Jesus' identity.

As the gospel seeds are sown into the hearts of unbelievers, some seeds fall by the wayside, some fall on rocks, and some fall on good ground. The Bible says, *"The good ground are they, which in an honest and good heart, having heard the word, keep it, and bring forth fruit with patience."* Read *Luke 8:4-18*. Thank God that some unbelievers will accept Jesus as their sole God and Savior.

It is every believer's job to share and publish the gospel. *Psalms 68:11 The Lord gave the word: great was the company of those that published it.* Consider *Romans 10:14-17, "How then shall they call on him in whom they have not believed? and how shall they believe in him of whom they have not heard? and how shall they hear without a preacher? (15) And how shall they preach, except they be sent? as it is written, How beautiful are the feet of them that preach the gospel of peace, and bring glad tidings of good things! (16) But they have not all obeyed the gospel. For Esaias saith, Lord, who hath believed our report? (17) So then faith cometh by hearing, and hearing by the word of God."* What is your role in spreading the gospel of Christ? Are you sharing your faith with family and friends?

Unbelievers are ignorant of scriptures

[Verses 45-53] The chief priests and Pharisees were angry at the officers for not apprehending Jesus. The officers reported that they had never heard anyone speak like Jesus, with words of truth and with such power, grace, and authority. The Pharisees scolded the officers and questioned their judgment. They set themselves as the standard of reference for who the officers and the Jews should believe in. With great contempt, they accused Jesus' believers of not knowing the law and called them cursed people. But Nicodemus, the one who went to Jesus at night in chapter 3, could relate to the officers, because he also heard wonderful things from Jesus. He tried to defend Jesus and cautioned his fellows to not be prejudiced, but to hear what Jesus had to say for Himself and understand what His crimes were. But he was insulted by his

The Book of John

fellows. They called him a Galilean and challenged him to search the scriptures, for according to them, no prophets would ever come out of Galilee.

This section of the chapter shows how the world reacts to people who would believe in Jesus.

- Verse 45: The officers returned without apprehending Jesus—this pictures a person's repentance after hearing the marvelous gospel of Jesus.
- Verse 47: The officers were scolded and belittled—the world will steer people away from Jesus by scaring or demeaning them.
- Verse 48: The rulers set themselves up as spiritual authorities—the world will set itself up as the spiritual authority instead of Jesus and will offer a major religion that is accepted by the majority.
- Verse 49: The rulers claimed to know the law and called Jesus' followers cursed people because they were ignorant of the law. The world will call evil good and good evil. Read *Isaiah 5:20-21*.

The Pharisees revealed their ignorance of the scriptures when they claimed that no prophets would ever come out of Galilee. The prophet Jonah was from Gathhepher in Galilee. The Messiah, the great Light, also should arise in Galilee. Read *2Kings 14:25, Isaiah 9:1:2*.

It is entertaining to see unbelievers, who are spiritually blind, quote scriptures. They have a form of knowledge of the truth, enough to be puffed up and be recognized as teachers, masters, and doctors, but really are blind guides. They also have a form of godliness by professing religion, but reject truth and Jesus Christ as the only Savior of the world. Don't rely on them to teach you. The best way to learn scriptures is to believe in Jesus Christ and get your nose in the Bible. The Bible is a spiritual book; the Holy Spirit of God is the best teacher.

Prophecies

The end-time prophecies in this chapter reveal that Jesus will be rejected and separated from the Jews. However, the Jews will seek Him in their tribulation. Jesus will present Himself again to the Jews at His second coming.

- *John 7:8 Go ye up unto this feast: I go not up yet unto this feast; for my time is not yet full come. (33) Then said Jesus unto them, Yet a little while am I with you, and then I go unto him that sent me.*
  Jesus will be separated from the Jews. The Jews will be on their own without the protection and blessings of their Messiah.

- *John 7:34 Ye shall seek me, and shall not find me: and where I am, thither ye cannot come.*
  Jews will enter into a severe tribulation period in which many will be killed by the antichrist.

- *John 7:37 In the last day, that great day of the feast, Jesus stood and cried, saying, If any man thirst, let him come unto me, and drink.*
  Jesus will appear again to the Jews at His second coming. The Jews will get another chance to receive Jesus as their Messiah. See the "last day" definition in the Side Notes section in Chapter 6.

The Feast of Tabernacles is an eight-day feast with great prophetic significance. Each of the eight days represents a 1,000-year period in world history starting from *Genesis 1:2*. Collectively, they cover God's plan for the ages, which includes seven dispensational periods: Dispensation of innocence, Dispensation of conscience, Dispensation of human government, Dispensation of promise, Dispensation of law, Dispensation of grace, and Dispensation of the Kingdom. We are living in the dispensation of grace.

The Feast of Tabernacles							
Day 1	Day 2	Day 3	Day 4	Day 5	Day 6	Day 7	Day 8
1st 1000 yrs	2nd 1000 yrs	3rd 1000 yrs	4th 1000 yrs	5th 1000 yrs	6th 1000 yrs	7th 1000 yrs	The new beginning
John 7:10 Jesus was at the feast secretly, picturing the pre-incarnate Jesus in the world. Jesus has always been around. He was made flesh in the dispensation of law and manifested to Israel.				*John 7:14* Jesus, as God in the flesh, was revealed to the Jews "*about the midst of the feast*"	We are here→ The rapture of the church can happen at any moment	*John 7:37* Jesus will appear again to the Jews in the "*last day*"	*Revelation 21:1-3* God will reveal a new tabernacle, consisting of a new heaven, earth, and Jerusalem

Summary

Asure way to miss your Savior is to ignore the Holy Scriptures. If your salvation is based on an organization, church, religious figure, good works, traditions, or feelings, then I pray that God will bless you with the desire to know Jesus Christ in the Holy Scriptures. May you by faith meet the Savior of your soul in the Holy Scriptures.

8 – Forgiver

Historical Synopsis

After a full day of work in Jerusalem, Jesus retreated to the Mount of Olives, a short distance eastward of Jerusalem. He returned early the next morning to the temple to teach, and the whole town showed up. He was interrupted by the scribes and Pharisees, who architected a snare against Him. They captured an adulterous woman and presented her to Jesus for sentencing. They had reasons to accuse Him whichever way He judged. They also primed Him with the Law of Moses, that such a sinner should be stoned to death. Jesus ignored them at first, but when they pressed Him, supposedly to checkmate Him, He responded by saying, *"He that is without sin among you, let him first cast a stone at her."* The scribes and Pharisees were convicted by their conscience, because they too were sinners. They left Jesus one by one, beginning with the highest rank to the lowest. Thereafter, the adulteress accepted Jesus as Lord. He sent her away with no condemnation and told her to sin no more.

Seeing their party go down in flames, the Pharisees who remained in the crowd continued to engage Jesus. They disputed His testimony, demanding that He show His Father and identify Himself. They entrenched themselves in the law and tradition by claiming liberty and righteousness in Abraham their father.

This chapter can be outlined as such:

The Book of John

I. Pharisees laid a trap for Jesus using an adulterous woman as bait – *John 8:1-11*
II. Pharisees debated Jesus and were found to be liars – *John 8:12-59*

Key Spiritual Lessons

This chapter contrasts a sinner who was prosecuted by her own religion, but obtained mercy, forgiveness of sin, and eternal life from Jesus Christ, with religious unbelievers who died in their sins.

This chapter also exposes people who claim to know God, but really are the spiritual children of the devil.

Following are the key spiritual lessons:

I. Sinners get eternal life through saving faith in Jesus – *John 8:1-11*
II. Sincere religious unbelievers die in sins by rejecting Jesus – *John 8:12-59*

Sinners Get Eternal Life through Saving Faith in Jesus

[Verse 1] While in Jerusalem, Jesus, as His manner was, taught in the temple by day and retreated to the Mount of Olives at night, most likely in the town of Bethany.

[Verse 2] When Jesus arrived at the temple early in the morning, a multitude of people were ready to hear Him.

For me, I find it good to fellowship with God early in the morning, before the hustle and bustle of the day kicks in, and before I find myself in the boxing ring with the flesh and the devil. *Psalms 5:3 My voice shalt thou hear in the morning, O LORD; in the morning will I direct my prayer unto thee, and will look up.* Read *Psalms 63*.

[Verses 3-5] The scribes and Pharisees interrupted Jesus' teaching session by presenting a woman taken in adultery, and

The Book of John

setting her in the midst of the company to be seen by all the people. They respectfully addressed Jesus as "Master" before laying their trap. They said, *"This woman was taken in adultery, in the very act"* and wanted to know if Jesus would agree with the Law of Moses, in that such an offender should be stoned to death. *Leviticus 20:10* says, *"And the man that committeth adultery with another man's wife, even he that committeth adultery with his neighbour's wife, the adulterer and the adulteress shall surely be put to death."*

Verse 6 clearly states that the motive of the scribes and Pharisees was to accuse Jesus. If Jesus condemned the adulteress and ordered her death according to the Law of Moses, they could accuse Him for infringing upon the judicial power and privilege of the Roman governor, or accuse Him of inconsistency, because He fellowshipped with sinners. But if He cleared the adulteress, they could accuse Him for trying to destroy the Law of Moses and label Him as an enemy of the law. But Jesus stooped down and wrote something on the ground with His finger and ignored the accusers.

[Verses 7-8] When they pressed upon Him, Jesus stood up and said, *"He that is without sin among you, let him first cast a stone at her."* Then Jesus stooped down again and continued to write on the ground.

There are a number of speculations as to what Jesus wrote. According to *Leviticus 20:10* and *Deuteronomy 22:22*, both the adulterer and adulteress should be put to death. Since the woman was caught in the very act, where was the man? That man could have been one of the accusers since they devised the snare. Jesus might have written his name on the ground, among other things.

[Verses 9-11] The accusers were convicted by their conscience when they heard Jesus' words. Oh the power of the Word! One by one they left Jesus, beginning with the highest rank to the lowest. When they were all gone, Jesus asked the woman, *"Where are those thine accusers? hath no man condemned thee?"*

The woman said, *"No man, Lord."* And Jesus replied, *"Neither do I condemn thee: go, and sin no more."*

It was a bad day for the adulteress. Her party time was over when she was caught in the very act with ample witnesses for a conviction. Being shamed was the least of her problems, because she would have died that day under the Law of Moses. Thankfully, she was brought to Jesus. Her worst day turned into the best day of her life. Jesus released her with no condemnation when she received Him as Lord.

How wonderful is this! Sinners who receive Jesus Christ as Lord and Savior are clear of condemnation. Read *Romans 8:1-4*. The religious leaders who arrested the adulteress could not convict her. The law had no dominion over her. Read *Romans 7:1-6. John 8:36 If the Son therefore shall make you free, ye shall be free indeed.* (I was a rotten sinner, but now I am right with God in Jesus Christ. My sins are wiped away and I no longer carry the burden, and my conscience is clear.)

The following lessons may be gleaned from this story:

- Don't be foolish and prideful thinking you can conceal sin, such as adultery. The Bible says, *"Be sure your sin will find you out."* It is like trying to hide rust or the wind. Your sins will come to light sooner or later. Did you know that the devil reports your sins to God and accuses you before Him night and day? Read *1Timothy 5:24, Revelation 12:9-10*. You would be wise to confess them to the Lord Jesus and repent.

- There is no mercy or forgiveness in the law. With the law is the knowledge and realization of sin. The law discovers sins and prosecutes sinners. Sinners have no excuse, as all will be found guilty and will die under the law. The adulteress faced certain death for her sin.

Ezekiel 18:4 Behold, all souls are mine; as the soul of the father, so also the soul of the son is mine: the soul that sinneth, it shall die. Read *Romans 3:23, Romans 6:23*.

- God's righteousness is only obtained by faith, as it is impossible to obtain it by the works of the law. Religions that teach works-based salvation or a mix of faith and works only lead people to hell. *Romans 9:30 What shall we say then? That the Gentiles, which followed not after righteousness, have attained to righteousness, even the righteousness which is of faith. (31) But Israel, which followed after the law of righteousness, hath not attained to the law of righteousness. (32) Wherefore? Because they sought it not by faith, but as it were by the works of the law. For they stumbled at that stumblingstone; (33) As it is written, Behold, I lay in Sion a stumblingstone and rock of offence: and whosoever believeth on him shall not be ashamed.*

- Grace is better than the law because sin has dominion over people who are under the law. The indwelling sin in every human takes occasion by the prohibitions in the law of God. It stirs up all manner of evil desires and deceives the person into committing sin, which then kills the person. Read *James 1:15*. For example, the law says, *"Thou shalt not covet,"* but the indwelling sin that reigns over individuals drives them to covet, and subsequently kills them. Read *Romans 7:7-13*. Nobody can ever fulfill the law and obtain God's righteousness. *Romans 5:20 Moreover the law entered, that the offence might abound. But where sin abounded, grace did much more abound: (21) That as sin hath reigned unto death, even so might grace reign through righteousness unto eternal life by Jesus Christ our Lord.*

- The Lord Jesus Christ is a sinner's only hope for salvation. The adulteress would have been stoned to death had she not met Jesus that day. She came to the realization that Jesus was her only hope and received Him as Lord. Jesus let her go free without condemnation. Oh that all unbelievers would come to the same realization and accept Jesus as their sole Lord and Savior by faith. *John 5:24 Verily, verily, I say unto you, He that heareth my word, and believeth on him that sent me, hath everlasting life, and shall not come into condemnation; but is passed from death unto life.*

Sincere Religious Unbelievers Die in Sins by Rejecting Jesus

Jesus engaged the Pharisees, beginning with Nicodemus, in chapter 3. All was well until He healed the impotent man on the Sabbath day in chapter 5, which was viewed as a major violation of the Jewish law by the scribes and Pharisees, so much so that they wanted to kill Him. Their attempt to arrest Jesus failed in the foregoing chapter. Here, they devised a snare for Jesus by attempting to put Him in a no-win situation.

You can expect similar treatment from the religious unbelievers of the world. Everything is fine until you point out that their beloved traditions or beliefs are not according to the truth of God. Then the true colors of their spiritual DNA and lineage show. Imagine telling Hindus that bathing at the Sangam (the confluence of the Ganges, the Yamuna and the Saraswati rivers) during the Kumbh Mela festival does not by any means rid them of sins. Imagine telling Buddhists or Taoists that they are as blind, dumb, and dead as their man-made idols. Read *Psalms 115:4-8*. Imagine telling the Muslims that they are the descendants of Ishmael, whose mother was a bondwoman, but God established His covenant with Isaac, who was the son of the freewoman. Imagine telling Catholics that infant baptism does nothing for babies except get them wet and make them cry. These are all true according to the word of God, but unbelievers will despise and persecute you for telling them the truth, just as they persecuted Jesus.

I can attest to the above. I grew up in a Taoist family, and my sister was the first to receive Jesus Christ as Savior. My brothers and I tried in vain to stop her from attending church and to convince her to deny Jesus. I was furious when she led my mother to the Lord. From that time on, I was determined to persecute Christians, because Christianity violated my tradition and divided my family. Praise the Lord for His mercy, goodness, forbearance, and longsuffering that a rotten sinner like me could be forgiven and see the light of life.

Religious unbelievers attack Jesus' testimony

[Verse 12] Having delivered the adulteress from her accusers, Jesus proclaimed, *"I am the light of the world: he that followeth me shall not walk in darkness, but shall have the light of life."*

Jesus is the spiritual light and life, not only for the Jews, but for Gentiles also. By this proclamation, Jesus foretold that Jews and Gentiles would be one people, one body, and one church in Him. Read *Ephesians 2:11-22*.

The world is in darkness. It is void of spiritual light and life and is under the power of evil. Those who follow Jesus will not walk in darkness, but will have the light of life.

[Verse 13] The Pharisees didn't like the proclamation and tried to discredit Jesus by accusing Him of self-representation and

Chapter 8 - Forgiver

attacking His record. They said, *"Thou bearest record of thyself; thy record is not true."* (By the way, the devil also likes to attack God's record. He said to Eve, *"Yea, hath God said, Ye shall not eat of every tree of the garden?"*)

The Pharisees' accusation was unjust, because they purposely overlooked the witnesses that Jesus produced in chapter 5, namely the witness of John the Baptist, the witness of His miracles, the witness of the Father, and the witness of scriptures. Besides, Jesus told them in *John 7:28* that He didn't represent Himself, but the Father sent Him. Jesus fired back at the Pharisees as follows:

1. [Verse 14] You are incompetent judges because you don't know me—*"Though I bear record of myself, yet my record is true: for I know whence I came, and whither I go; but ye cannot tell whence I come, and whither I go."* The Jews were wrong about His origin (*John 7:27, 40-43, 52*) and couldn't figure out where He would go when He spoke of going away (*John 7:33, 36*).

2. [Verses 15-16] Your judgment of me is flawed, because you judge according to appearance—*"Ye judge after the flesh."* The Jews judged Jesus after the flesh or outward appearance and not according to truth. They saw a base and mean person. Therefore He could not possibly be the light of the world. But Jesus' judgment of them was true and according to the law, because He had two witnesses—Himself and the Father.

3. [Verses 17-18] Even your law says my testimony is true—*"It is also written in your law, that the testimony of two men is true."* The Law of Moses that they boasted of required two or three witnesses to establish a matter. Therefore Jesus and the Father, who was with Him

(verse 29), were enough to establish His testimony. Read *Deuteronomy 19:15, Deuteronomy 17:6, Numbers 35:30, 1John 5:6-9.*

Likewise, unbelievers don't know Jesus and are incompetent judges of His testimonies, yet they like to question the authenticity and the authority of the Bible. One of their favorite objections is that the Bible was authored by men. Read *2Peter 1:19.* Another favorite is the misapplication of scriptures in order to justify their sins and shut up Christians. For example, they like to misapply *Matthew 7:1* and say Christians are not supposed to judge. But what does the Bible say concerning judging? Read *Deuteronomy 1:16, Proverbs 31:9, John 7:24.*

Christians are to judge righteous judgment. The word of God is the standard of right and wrong. Without it, *"every way of a man is right in his own eyes."* Read *Proverbs 12:15, Proverbs 21:2, Judges 17:6.* Is the word of God the standard of righteousness in your life and your household?

Religious unbelievers will die in their sins

[Verse 19] With one black eye, the Pharisees asked Jesus to show them the Father, who He claimed to be His witness. Since they were initially wrong on Jesus' origin by supposing He was the son of Joseph, their error widened. It was absurd for them to ask *"Where is thy Father?"* because Jesus and the Father were one. Jesus was the express image of the Father and the brightness of His glory. Read *Hebrews 1:1-3.* If they truly had known the Father, they would have known Jesus. Therefore their question proved they did not know Jesus or the Father.

[Verse 20] The dialogue took place in the treasury of the temple, which was a heavily used communal place where the Pharisees made the most noise to draw attention to their giving.

Chapter 8 - Forgiver

Read *Matthew 6:1-5*. In other words, Jesus was in the open, but *"no man laid hands on him; for his hour was not yet come."*

[Verses 21-24] Jesus warned the Jews again, as He did in chapter 7, that they would seek Him after He returned to the Father, but they would die in sins, because where He was going they had no access. (One can only come to the Father by Jesus Christ. Read *John 14:6*.) The Jews couldn't figure out the place referenced by Jesus back in chapter 7. They still couldn't determine it here because of their incorrect working assumption. They assumed Jesus was the son of Joseph instead of God the Son. So, they wondered if Jesus was going to commit suicide when He said, *"Whither I go, ye cannot come."* But Jesus clarified that He was talking about heaven—that He was from above and not of this world. In contrast, the Jews were earthly beings from this world, and by not believing in Him as their Messiah, they would have no access to heaven and would thus die in their sins.

The little phrase *"whence I come"* in verse 14 is so important, because failure to grasp it gets people into a lot of trouble, with hell as a consequence. If you, like the Jews, can't figure out Jesus' origin, you may also reject Him as Savior. Your Savior had better be the incarnate Word from heaven, who was God from heaven and not from the earth, otherwise you too will have no access to heaven and will die in your sins. Think about the world's religions and their saviors—Buddha, Dalai Lama, Mohammad, Confucius, Mary, religious and political leaders, various human saints and gods, and animals—they all originated from the earth and are unable to grant you access to heaven, much less forgive your sins. Remember *John 3:31a*, *"He that cometh from above is above all: he that is of the earth is earthly."* Anyone who trusts in them will die in their sins, be eternally separated from God, and never see the light of life. The world religions refuse to accept Jesus Christ as God the Son from heaven because it makes their gods second class. They put Him in the same category as the rest of the so-called saviors. What happens when people put Jesus in the same category as other gods? Read a funny story about it in *1Samuel 5*.

Religious unbelievers have pending judgment

[Verses 25-29] In the preceding verses, Jesus called the Pharisees incompetent judges for not knowing Him and threatened them with eternal separation from God for not believing in Him. The Pharisees reacted with *"Who art thou?"* It was not a friendly question. It was more like "Who do you think you are?," or as in verse 53, *"Whom makest thou thyself?"* Jesus brilliantly responded as follows:

1. [Verse 25] I am the Truth—*"Even the same that I said unto you from the beginning."* Jesus was who He said He was in the beginning of the discourse—the light and life of the world. Nothing had changed. Read *Hebrews 13:8*.

2. [Verses 26-27] I am your Judge—*"I have many things to say and to judge of you."* Jesus had many things to say against the Pharisees and to charge them with, but He deferred judgment in obedience to the Father. As it was written in *John 5:19b*, *"The Son can do nothing of himself, but what he seeth the Father do."* In other words, if Jesus did not have the relationship that He claimed He had with the Father, He would have acted alone and would have judged them on the spot. However, the judgment was deferred because Jesus worked in concert with the Father as He said, *"But he that sent me is true; and I speak to the world those things which I have heard of him."* This doesn't mean the Jews are off the hook, because *John 5:22* says, *"For the Father judgeth no man, but hath committed all judgment unto the Son."*

Chapter 8 - Forgiver

3. [Verses 28-29] I am the Messiah—"*When ye have lifted up the Son of man, then shall ye know that I am he.*" Jesus gave them a sign for when they would know that He was the true Messiah. The Jews would be convinced when they crucified Him on the cross, as the serpent was lifted up in the wilderness. The Jews would also know that Jesus did not act alone, but was in full cooperation with the Father, and that Jesus and the Father were one. The Father was with Jesus even as He spoke.

Jesus is the Truth, the Judge, and the Messiah. Unbelievers have pending judgment because they reject Jesus as the Savior. Jesus will reckon with them at the Great White Throne judgment, as no sinner will go unpunished. *Philippians 2:10 That at the name of Jesus every knee should bow, of things in heaven, and things in earth, and things under the earth; (11) And that every tongue should confess that Jesus Christ is Lord, to the glory of God the Father.*

As a believer, you also have a pending judgment, but at the Judgment Seat of Christ. You will stand before the Lord Jesus and give an account of your life beginning from the time you received Him as your Lord and Savior.

The Judgment Seat of Christ is a judgment of reward for your service to the Lord. He expects you to be spiritually fruitful as you will see in chapter 15. What do you have to show? The Apostle Paul has this to say in *2Corinthians 5:10, "For we must all appear before the judgment seat of Christ; that every one may receive the things done in his body, according to that he hath done, whether it be good or bad. (11) Knowing therefore the terror of the Lord, we persuade men; but we are made manifest unto God; and I trust also are made manifest in your consciences."* Be forewarned, the *"terror of the Lord"* is written to Christians and should motivate you to serve Jesus and persuade others to join you. Be sure to invest for heavenly rewards instead of earthly rewards. Read *Matthew 6:19-20, 31-33, Colossians 3:1-4*.

If you are not willing to serve Christ and your Christianity is all about you, what makes you think you'll be comfortable in heaven with God who died for your sins, from whose face the earth and the heaven fled away? Think about it, wouldn't self-serving, worldly focused, me-monster Christians be more comfortable with the god of this world (the devil) than with the God of heaven? After all, they are focused on getting more of the world. They attend church only when they can find time. Bible reading, study, devotion, and fellowship—who needs that? The work of ministry—that's for pastors and missionaries. How awkward it will be for these me-monsters when they show up in heaven and the Lord of heaven is practically a stranger to them?

If you are one of these Christians who abuse the grace of God, the Judgment Seat of Christ will be a very terrifying, dreadful, shameful, and regretful time for you. Don't think that you are somehow special and deserving of service, comfort, blessings, and happiness, while your brothers and sisters in Christ are being slaughtered for their faith.

If you are born again, your life on earth is the boot camp that prepares you for life in heaven. Jesus bought you with a price and you are not your own. He is your Lord and Master. You exist to serve Him and to bring Him glory. Do not meet the King of Kings and Lord of Lords empty handed. Read *2Corinthians 5:10-11, 1Corinthians 3, 1Corinthians 6:19-20*.

Below is a comparison of the Great White Throne judgment and the Judgment Seat of Christ.

The Great White Throne judgment:

- Happens at the end of the millennium, approximately 1,000 years after the rapture of the church.

Chapter 8 - Forgiver

- Is for unbelievers only.
- Is a judgment of condemnation. All who are judged in this judgment are sinners and will be cast into the lake of fire. Read *Revelation 20:11-15*.

The Judgment Seat of Christ:

- Happens right after the rapture of the church just before Christ's second coming to earth.
- Is for believers only.
- Is a judgment of reward for obedience and service to the Lord. (Believers' sins are judged at Calvary when they accepted Jesus as Lord. Believers should never fear going to hell.) Believers will be judged for the effort, motive, and quality of service as opposed to results. Read *2Corinthians 5:10, 1Corinthians 3:13-15, 6-7, Matthew 16:24-27*.

Religious unbelievers may repent and believe in Jesus

[Verses 30-32] Many Jews believed on Jesus that day after hearing His speech. Jesus told them that they would surely be His disciples if they would abide in His word. Then they would know the truth and would be set free from ignorance and errors and from the bondage of the law and religion.

Notice the phrase *"believed on him"* in verses 30 and 31? This means to believe on a firm foundation, one based on the word of God.

Thank God for people who repent and accept Jesus Christ as their sole Lord and Savior. The best next step is to abide in the word of God. Notice that Jesus did not ask the new believers to do this or that, other than to continue or abide in His word. You will learn more about what it means to abide in His word in chapter 15. For now, don't stray away from His words. Get in the Bible daily, read it, study it, and research it as if you are searching for hidden treasures. Read *Proverbs 2, 2Timothy 2:15*. Then and only then will you know the truth, and the truth you know will deliver you from falsehoods. For example, you can spot counterfeit money by really knowing the real money. The truth will deliver you from the bondage that many religions put on their believers and from the traps of the devil and the world. According to verse 44, the devil does not abide in truth and is full of lies. The way you can spot falsehoods is by knowing the truth of God.

The Bible is your owner's manual for a successful life. It needs to be your absolute, infallible guide, like a lamp unto your feet and a light unto your path. It tells you about God and His kingdom, His will and plan for your life, how you can please Him, how to live a happy and successful life, what qualities to look for in a spouse, and how to raise children, among other things. Like Job, you need to esteem the word of God more than your necessary food. Read *Psalms 119:105, Job 23:12*. Sadly, many believers are going through the motions without knowing the truth. Make time and room for the word of God. The phrase, *"my word hath no place in you"* in verse 37 is so sad. Don't let this be true of you.

Religious unbelievers live in false hope

[Verses 33-47] The unbelieving Jews, who overheard Jesus talking with His new believers about being set free, challenged the notion. They proudly claimed to be the descendants of Abraham who were never in bondage to any man.

Unfortunately, only their claim of being Abraham's descendants was true. These Jews were incredible liars. They would lie about the most obvious things. The Roman government was in charge of them and they paid tribute to Caesar. Yet they had the audacity to say that they never were in bondage to any man. What about when Nebuchadnezzar destroyed them and hauled them off

Chapter 8 - Forgiver

to Babylon for 70 years? Or the time Tiglathpileser, the king of Assyria, carried them captive to Assyria? Even Moses reminded them of their time in Egypt, calling it the house of bondage.

Jesus masterfully took the Pharisees apart by calling out their sin in order to reveal their true spiritual father. Jesus presented four proof points to convince the Pharisees that they were the spiritual children of the devil and not of God.

1. The Pharisees were liars.
   [Verses 34-36] Concerning their boast of freedom, Jesus said, *"Whosoever committeth sin is the servant of sin."* These Pharisees just lied by claiming they were never in bondage to any man, which made them sinners and bond-servants of sin. They were not free, regardless of their tie to Abraham. As sinful servants, they would be kicked out of the house of God because they had no blood relationship with the owner of the house. The Son, however, remained in the house forever because of His relationship to the Father. Therefore, the freedom granted by the Son was the true freedom instead of the one obtained through Abraham. Read *Romans 6:16-23, Genesis 21:10, Galatians 4:21-31, Proverbs 10:30, Psalms 27:4.*

2. The Pharisees were murderers.
   [Verses 37-38] Concerning their boast of pedigree as Abraham's seed, Jesus acknowledged that they were indeed the seed of Abraham according to the flesh. However, the fact that they sought to kill Him proved that His word had no place in them. (Verse 47 describes it: *"He that is of God heareth God's words: ye therefore hear them not, because ye are not of God."*) While physically they were the seed of Abraham, spiritually they were the seed of the devil, because children imitate

The Book of John

their father. The devil was a murderer from the beginning. Jesus made a distinction between His Father and their father.

[Verses 39-41] The Pharisees quickly affirmed that Abraham was their father to make themselves look great. But Jesus shot them down by saying, *"If ye were Abraham's children, ye would do the works of Abraham."* For one, Abraham believed God by faith, and it was counted unto him for righteousness, but the Pharisees rested in the Law of Moses. Read *Genesis 15:6, Romans 4:3, Galatians 3:6*. The children of Abraham were the children of promise according to the righteousness of faith and not of the law – *Romans 4:11-13*. Therefore, the Pharisees were disqualified. Furthermore, their disbelieving and murderous hearts were in direct opposition to Abraham's, who was famous for his humanity and piety. So, neither their faith nor works resembled Abraham's.

3. The Pharisees resembled the devil, who was a murderer and liar.
   [Verses 41-44] The idiom "like father, like son" aptly applies here. The way Jesus put it was, *"Ye do the deeds of your father,"* reiterating the distinction of the fathers from verse 38. The Pharisees sensed that Jesus was talking about a spiritual father, so they switched gears and claimed that God was their spiritual Father by saying, *"We be not born of fornication; we have one Father, even God."* To this Jesus replied, *"If God were your Father, ye would love me: for I proceeded forth and came from God; neither came I of myself, but he sent me."* Not only did their faith and works not match Abraham's, their love also did not match God's. Seeing they couldn't understand His doctrines on liberty and bondage or the two spiritual families, Jesus plainly told them that they were the devil's children and they would

Chapter 8 - Forgiver

fulfill his lusts or desires, which was evident by their lies and desire to kill Him. For the devil was a murderer from the beginning, and the author and father of lies. The devil lied to and deceived Eve into eating the forbidden fruit. Adam's first-born son, Cain, murdered his brother Abel, because Cain was the seed of the devil. Read *1John 3:12*. (As you mature in the Lord, you should study the topic of "seed." *Genesis 3:15 And I will put enmity between thee and the woman, and between thy seed and her seed; it shall bruise thy head, and thou shalt bruise his heel.* So much more happened in the Garden of Eden that day beyond simply eating the forbidden fruit. The details are beyond the scope of this book.)

4. The Pharisees would not believe in truth.
   [Verses 45-47] The Pharisees would not believe in Jesus, even though they failed in every attempt to discredit His doctrine and to convict Him of sin. The root cause was simply this: *"He that is of God heareth God's words: ye therefore hear them not, because ye are not of God."*

There are two spiritual fathers—God and the devil. They both are wildly interested in people and they battle for souls. The common saying in the unbelieving world is, "We are all God's children." This is a lie because *John 8:44* is very clear about the two spiritual fathers. Read *1Peter 2:9-10*. The explanation below clarifies this misconception.

Devil's family:

- Verse 44 speaks of a group of people whose spiritual father is the devil: *"Ye are of your father the devil, and the lusts of your father ye will do. He was a murderer from the beginning, and abode not in the truth, because there is no truth in him. When he speaketh a lie, he speaketh of his own: for he is a liar, and the father of it."*

- The devil is the spiritual father of everyone who enters into this world through physical birth. Every child has the devil's spiritual DNA. It is easily observed that children are bent to do the lusts of the devil—lie, disobey, steal, hate, kill, etc.

- Adoption by Jesus Christ is the only way out of the devil's family. Read *Ephesians 1:3-6*.

God's family:

- As individuals enter into the devil's family by birth, they also enter into God's family by birth. However, this birth is not physical, but spiritual, an event known as being "born again." A natural person must be born again, because the first birth by flesh and blood is defective due to sin. Read *Genesis 5:3, Romans 5:12*. The Bible says in *John 3:3b, "Except a man be born again, he cannot see the kingdom of God,"* and in *1Corinthians 15:50a, "Flesh and blood cannot inherit the kingdom of God."*

- Believers are God's children by virtue of the new birth. They are now new creatures, according to *2Corinthians 5:17, "Therefore if any man be in Christ, he is a new creature: old things are passed away; behold, all things are become new. (18) And all things are of God, who hath reconciled us to himself by Jesus Christ, and hath given to us the ministry of reconciliation."*

- Being in God's family separates believers from the devil's family. Their bodies are now the temple of the Holy Ghost. As such, believers must be careful not to defile the body. Read *1Corinthians 3:16-17, 1Corinthians 6:18-20*.

- Believers still carry the old nature even after they are born again. The old nature remains sinful in Adam's image. The new nature is spiritual, perfect in God's image. Both natures are present constantly. The one that is fed the most is most in control. Read *Colossians 3:5-10, 2Corinthians 4:14-18*.

How can you tell if a person is a believer or a wolf in sheep's clothing—a man of God or a false prophet? Jesus said, *"Wherefore by their fruits ye shall know them."* If the person continually exhibits the traits of the devil, he probably is a child of the devil. Like they say, the apple doesn't fall far from the tree.

The unbelieving world will jump all over you for judging, but Jesus said, *"Beware of false prophets, which come to you in sheep's clothing, but inwardly they are ravening wolves."* Perhaps the greatest tell-tale sign is given in verse 47. It is when individuals refuse to hear God's words or counsel, and the Bible is not their final authority. It is typical for such individuals to profess Jesus, but advance their own unbiblical thoughts and doctrines. They blur the line between good and evil and between Christianity and other religions. Read *1John 2:18-20, Romans 9:6*.

Religious unbelievers dishonor Jesus

[Verses 48-50] Having been called the children of the devil, the Pharisees fought back, scornfully calling Jesus a devil-possessed Samaritan. The Jews had a very ill opinion of the Samaritans and would call someone a Samaritan in order to debase the person. Calling Jesus a devil-possessed Samaritan was a new low and downright reviling. But it is said of Jesus, according to *1Peter 2:23*, *"When he was reviled, reviled not again; when he suffered, he*

The Book of John

threatened not; but committed himself to him that judgeth righteously." He calmly denied having a devil, but again showed that they were the ones without God.

- "*I honour my Father, and ye do dishonour me*"—Everything that Jesus did was to the honor and glory of the Father. He said in verse 28, "*I do always those things that please him.*" When the Jews dishonored Him, they violated *John 5:22 For the Father judgeth no man, but hath committed all judgment unto the Son: (23) That all men should honour the Son, even as they honour the Father. He that honoureth not the Son honoureth not the Father which hath sent him.*

- "*And I seek not mine own glory: there is one that seeketh and judgeth*"—The Pharisees' reproach and abuse did not disturb Jesus, because He was not after their applause. He made it clear, however, that God would secure His glory and would judge them for their contempt and rejection of Him.

[Verses 51-53] Despite being reviled, Jesus still extended the scepter of grace to the Jews and offered the gift of immortality. If they would receive and observe His words, they would not experience the second or eternal death, which is everlasting separation from God. The Jews scorned this gracious offering. They continued to err on Jesus' identity. They esteemed Him lower than Abraham and the prophets. In their minds, if Abraham and the prophets, who were great men and greatly favored by God, were dead, who was this fellow to save men from death? Therefore He must be diabolical. They scornfully asked, "*Whom makest thou thyself?*"

[Verses 54-55] Jesus tried for the last time to convince the Jews that they were not of God. He answered their question by saying He didn't need to make Himself honorable, because He received His honor from God the Father, who the Jews professed to be their God, but in reality they did not know Him. Yet Jesus assured them that He knew the Father. For Him to say that He didn't know the Father would make Him a liar like them. By calling them liars, Jesus referred them back to their spiritual father, the devil.

[Verses 56-59] Finally, Jesus revealed to them that He was greater than Abraham. He told them that Abraham desired greatly to see His day, and he saw it and was glad. The Jews thought that was an absurd statement, because He was not yet 50 years old. How could He have possibly seen Abraham, who had been dead for ages? But Jesus asserted that He existed before Abraham, thus positioning Himself as the eternal God. The Jews wanted to stone Him for blasphemy, but Jesus hid Himself and left the temple.

Summary

I find two things so amazing in this chapter: the longsuffering, merciful nature of Jesus and the hardness and impenitent heart of unbelievers. Unbelievers like to argue with Jesus' doctrines, because like the Jews, they are wrong about His identity. They also like to cast Jesus as evil, because they love darkness rather than light, for their deeds are evil. They label good evil and evil good. Oh that they would realize that they are the spiritual children of the devil and that Jesus is God the Son, who would forgive their sins and deliver them from certain death.

9 – Sent One

Historical Synopsis

This chapter gives a beautiful story of the miraculous healing of a beggar man who was born blind. The condition was not a result of his sin or the sins of his parents, but it was an opportunity for Jesus to work a miracle of God and to prove that He was the Sent One. Jesus made clay of spit to anoint the eyes of the blind beggar and sent him to wash in the pool of Siloam. The man obeyed Jesus' instruction and his faith became sight, literally. The healing took place on the Sabbath day, which stirred up the Pharisees against Jesus causing a division among them regarding His identity.

The Pharisees interviewed the man who received his sight, but refused to believe his account. They summoned his parents, who confirmed the man was indeed their son, but they were too afraid to give Jesus the glory, because the Pharisees had threatened to remove anyone out of the synagogue who confessed Jesus as Christ. The Pharisees continued to grill the man, and they reviled him after failing to persuade him to accuse Jesus as a sinner.

Thereafter, the man believed Jesus was God the Son. He called Him Lord and worshipped Him. Meanwhile, Jesus pronounced the disbelieving Pharisees as blind sinners.

This chapter can be outlined as such:

Chapter 9 – Sent One

I. Man who was blind received sight by faith – *John 9:1-12*
II. Men with sight were declared blind – *John 9:13-41*

Pool of Siloam

Pharisees

Key Spiritual Lessons

This chapter brings to light a universal problem, which is spiritual blindness. The man who was born blind and received sight after washing in the pool of Siloam communicates a spiritual truth. That is, all are born spiritually blind by default, but will receive spiritual sight when they wash in the pool of Siloam, which represents Jesus Christ. The name Siloam means "Sent." Jesus Christ is the Sent One.

Did you know everyone is born with two pairs of eyes? Everyone has a physical and a spiritual pair of eyes. The spiritual eyes are blind by default because of Adam's transgression, and we are his descendants after his image and likeness. Until they are opened, we cannot see the Kingdom of God, comprehend the light of God, or receive the things of the Spirit of God. Read *John 3:3-6, John 1:5, 1Corinthians 2:14*. As such, we are beggars like the blind man when it comes to truth. It is sad when we are not able to understand what God wrote for us. What's more, we remain in spiritual darkness and cannot see the pits and snares that lie in our way that ultimately lead to destruction. Read *John 12:35*.

Once the spiritual eyes are opened, the Bible becomes alive and supernatural as we are enabled to see and understand spiritual things. We will know the hope of His calling along with the hidden treasures and secrets of God. Read *Psalms 25:14, Proverbs 3:32, Ephesians 1:18*. We will also be able to see into the future through written prophecies.

Most people need no convincing that the spiritual realm exists, as they believe in ghosts, evil spirits, the devil, angels, and God. Even the Kingdom of God is a spiritual kingdom that cannot be seen with physical eyes. Read *Romans 14:17, Luke 17:20-21*. Spiritual things can only be seen with spiritual eyes. *John 3:6 That which is born of the flesh is flesh; and that which is born of the Spirit*

Chapter 9 – Sent One

is spirit. Take the wind for example. No one has seen it, but everyone knows it exists by its effects and power. The spiritual realm is real, lively, and powerful, even though the physical eyes cannot see it.

The core message of this chapter is: people who receive Jesus Christ receive spiritual sight, while those who reject Him remain spiritually blind.

For spiritual lessons, this chapter can be outlined as such:

    I.   The cure for spiritual blindness – *John 9:1-7*
    II.   The curiosity of unbelievers – *John 9:8-34*
    III.   The confession of the blind man – *John 9:35-38*
    IV.   The condemnation of unbelievers – *John 9:39-41*

The Cure for Spiritual Blindness

[Verses 1-3] Jesus saw a man who was born blind while on His journey. His disciples were curious to know if the blindness was the result of the man's sin or his parents'. There was an expectation that the wages of sin, besides spiritual death, was also misery through affliction of the physical body by ailments and calamities. Read *John 5:14, 1Corinthians 11:28-30*. But Jesus answered, *"Neither hath this man sinned, nor his parents: but that the works of God should be made manifest in him."* In other words, God had reserved the man to teach the people about spiritual blindness and demonstrate His mercy, grace, and glory. Jesus cured blindness before, but He had never opened the eyes of a person who was born blind. It was the first of its kind.

[Verses 4-5] Right before Jesus performed the miracle, He made a couple of interesting statements: *"I must work the works of him that sent me, while it is day: the night cometh, when no man can work. As long as I am in the world, I am the light of the world."*

The Book of John

He didn't mean that He couldn't perform the miracle at night. To understand the meaning, one must recall *Genesis 1:1-5*. Day was the name of the Light of God that was manifested to counter the darkness that broke out in heaven. Night was the name of the darkness, which was spiritual wickedness in high places. Jesus was the Light that shined in darkness of whom John the Baptist testified.

Jesus meant that the window He had to complete the works that the Father had given Him was limited to the time that He was in the world. The Day or the Light left the world when Jesus returned to the Father after His resurrection from the dead.

How does this apply to us as believers? The Father has also given us a work to do—the ministry of reconciliation—that we should tell the world that God was in Christ and that sinners should be reconciled to God by the word of reconciliation, which He committed to us. We are ambassadors for Christ, and the window of opportunity to complete the work is limited to the amount of time we have in this world. Read *2Corinthians 5:17-21*. Seize the opportunity to serve God while you are able. Remember, evil days will come and the years will draw nigh, meaning one of these days, we will no longer be able to serve Him. That day will come sooner than you think.

[Verses 6-7] Having presented Himself as the Sent One to the Jews, Jesus *"spat on the ground, and made clay of the spittle, and he anointed the eyes of the blind man with the clay."* Jesus told the man to go and wash in the pool of Siloam. He did as he was commanded and received sight for the first time in his life.

Giving sight to the blind man by using clay proved that Jesus was the God who formed Adam from the same material. Adam was formed from the dust of the ground. His name means "red" or "red dust." Clay is formed by adding water (in this case, spit) to the dust of the ground. *Isaiah 64:8 But now, O LORD, thou art our father; we are the clay, and thou our potter; and we all are the work of thy hand.*

The pool of Siloam represents Jesus Christ. When the natural man, who by nature is spiritually blind, receives Jesus by faith, his sins are washed away and his spiritual eyes are opened. Only Jesus can heal spiritual blindness—not through religion, denomination, religious service, or good works. Read *Titus 3:4-5*. The world's system of religion and righteousness, represented by the religious Pharisees, is grossly incapable of curing spiritual blindness. It is troubling to see so many religious people remain spiritually blind because they only have religion without a personal relationship with the Christ of Christianity.

The healing of the blind man paints a beautiful salvation picture.

- [Verse 1] Jesus Christ is interested in everyone who is born spiritually blind. *Titus 2:11 For the grace of God that bringeth salvation hath appeared to all men.*

- [Verses 3-5] He is ready to perform the miracle.

- [Verse 7] All a person has to do is to wash in Jesus Christ according to His words. *Revelation 1:5 And from Jesus Christ, who is the faithful witness, and the first begotten of the dead, and the prince of the kings of the earth. Unto him that loved us, and washed us from our sins in his own blood.*

Salvation really is that simple, but the unbelieving world wants to complicate and corrupt God's way through philosophy and vain deceit after the traditions of men and the rudiments of the world. The Bible warns against such corruption in *Colossians 2:8*. *2Corinthians 11:3* says, "But I fear, lest by any means, as the serpent

The Book of John

beguiled Eve through his subtilty, so your minds should be corrupted from the simplicity that is in Christ."

Individuals can have their spiritual eyes opened by Jesus at any time. Read *Romans 5:8*. The Bible says in *2Corinthians 6:2b*, "Behold, now is the accepted time; behold, now is the day of salvation."

The Curiosity of Unbelievers

[Verses 8-12] The people who knew the blind beggar were awestruck by the miracle and wanted to know how he received his sight. The man told them how Jesus opened his eyes, and they wanted to meet Him.

New life is attractive. All newly born-again believers in Jesus Christ should draw the same curiosity from the people who know them. Salvation is a spiritual operation of the Holy Spirit of God. No one knows how it is done—*"by what means he now seeth, we know not."* But the change should be sudden and obvious, to the extent that people who are familiar should marvel. In verse 8, the friends of the blind beggar said, *"Is not this he that sat and begged?"* You can apply this to your case. Is not this (your name) who used to (fill in the blank)?

You are God's walking billboard. A successful billboard advertisement generates many inquiries. Likewise, people who know you should marvel at your transformation to the point that they inquire, *"How were thine eyes opened?"*

Before I believed in Jesus, I used to bar hop with my buddies. By the grace of God, I stopped that immediately after I got saved, and my drinking buddies wondered what was wrong with me. They ditched me when I told them I became a Christian. Soon after, I gave up smoking and drinking all together cold turkey.

The transformation in a new believer's life creates a golden opportunity for witnessing Jesus. Don't miss this once-in-a-lifetime opportunity. Read how the Apostle Paul witnessed Jesus in *Acts 22* and *26*. The format is simply:

- My manner of life before Jesus.
- How I met and received Jesus.
- What my life is now with Jesus.

[Verses 13-16] The beggar's friends took him to the Pharisees to be examined. The religious Pharisees also were curious to know how the man received his sight. While the man gave the same testimony, it generated a very different response. His familiar friends responded with *"Where is he"* that they might know Jesus, but there was a division among the Pharisees over who Jesus was. Some immediately condemned Him as an ungodly sinner because He restored the blind man's sight on the Sabbath day. Others struggled because no sinner could perform such a miracle.

[Verse 17] Unable to agree on who Jesus was, the Pharisees asked the man, *"What sayest thou of him, that he hath opened thine eyes."* They wanted to know his thoughts about Jesus. The man said Jesus was a prophet.

[Verses 18-23] The Pharisees refused to accept Jesus as the Prophet prophesied in *Deuteronomy 18:15* and also refused to believe that the man had been blind. So, they summoned his parents and asked them, *"Is this your son, who ye say was born blind? how then doth he now see?"* The parents confirmed their son's identity and infirmity, but they would not testify as to how and who opened his eyes. His parents were too afraid to glorify Jesus because the Pharisees had threatened to remove anyone who confessed Jesus as Christ out of the synagogue.

[Verses 24-25] This time, the Pharisees tried to coax the man into supporting their position that Jesus was a sinner. This also

The Book of John

failed as the man stood firm on his conviction and made a famous statement: *"Whether he be a sinner or no, I know not: one thing I know, that, whereas I was blind, now I see."*

The unbelieving world, even with its best theologians and professors who reject Jesus and are spiritually blind, will remain curious as to how lives are transformed when people believe in Jesus Christ. Instead of accepting Jesus by the testimonies of the works which He has began in the lives of those who believe, they make up scientific explanations that sound good. For us who believe in Jesus Christ, we all can attest, *"One thing I know, that, whereas I was blind, now I see."* The eyes of our understanding are enlightened and we can see the Kingdom of God, comprehend His divine light, and rejoice in His salvation. The Bible that previously didn't make sense, all of a sudden comes alive.

[Verses 26-30] The Pharisees then circled back to the beginning and asked the man again about what Jesus did to him and how his eyes were opened. By now, the man was rightfully frustrated. He replied, *"I have told you already, and ye did not hear: wherefore would ye hear it again?"* He also asked the Pharisees if they would be Jesus' disciples if perhaps the miracle was real. The Pharisees reviled him and affirmed that they were Moses' disciples, as Moses was a known entity, whereas they had no idea of Jesus' origin. Then the man essentially replied to the Pharisees, "Why are you so hung up on His origin when His work testifies that He is of God?" The man made the following points:

- [Verse 31] If Jesus was a sinner as the Pharisees accused Him to be, then God would not hear Him, so then how did He do the miracle?

- [Verse 32] Never in the history of the world could any person give sight to one who was born blind—not any physician by any natural means or art, nor any prophet in a miraculous way, nor even Moses himself. Jesus' miracle was wonderful beyond human capabilities.

- [Verse 33] Jesus had to be of God, otherwise He could not have performed the miracle.

[Verse 34] The Pharisees, who were masters and doctors of theology, were baffled by a man who was blind, had never read the scriptures, had no education, and was only a beggar. Unable to refute the man's reasoning, they insulted him by saying, *"Thou wast altogether born in sins, and dost thou teach us?,"* and threw him out.

It is one thing to witness to familiar friends, but it is another thing to witness to anti-Jesus religious unbelievers like the Pharisees. Below are the traits of anti-Jesus religious unbelievers.

- [Verse 15] They are curious about the power of God.
- [Verse 16] They judge Jesus' works according to their laws and traditions and speak evil of things they don't understand. Read *2Peter 2:12, Jude 1:10*.
- [Verse 17] They are curious about your thoughts of Jesus.
- [Verse 18] They will try to discredit your testimony to make you ineffective for God.
- [Verse 24] They will manipulate you into agreeing with their beliefs, which are prejudiced against Jesus.
- [Verse 28] Their hardened hearts and stance prevent them from knowing the truth.
- [Verses 30-34] They refuse to accept Jesus Christ as God the Son, regardless of any miracle or what you say or present. *John 12:37 But though he had done so many miracles before them, yet they believed not on him.* Don't waste your time on these people. Jesus didn't.

The Confession of the Blind Man

[Verses 35-38] The incredible tender care Jesus has for those who stand for Him is revealed. When Jesus heard that the man was thrown out of the synagogue by the Pharisees, He appeared to him and asked if he believed on God the Son. The man was definitely interested and wanted to know where he could find Him. When Jesus revealed Himself to the man, he said, *"Lord, I believe,"* and worshipped Jesus.

Observe the following:

- The blind man was an army of one against the scornful rulers. His parents would not stand with him because they feared the Pharisees. But not him, because he experienced the miracle. If you are born again, you too have experienced the miracle of sight. Your spiritual eyes have been opened. Will you have the courage to stand for Jesus even when others ridicule you?

- Jesus allowed the man to fight the Pharisees alone to prove him and to let him demonstrate his faith and allegiance. The man had to choose between his old religion and truth. Will you hang on to your old religion, even if the beliefs contradict the word of God? You cannot have both.

- The man lost the battle when he was thrown out, or did he? He recognized Jesus as a prophet in verse 17, but Jesus ended up as God the Son and his Lord. Not a bad deal, but a real bad deal for the Pharisees who threw him out. Will you feel bad if your religious organization throws you out for standing for truth and disagreeing with them?

- Jesus was very much against the religious scribes and Pharisees, but He was gentle and cared for those who sought Him with a pure heart. If you sincerely desire to know the truth, then pray to Jesus and search the Bible daily as if you are searching for hidden treasures. You will know the truth. Read *Job 28:12-28, Proverbs 2, Ezra 7:10, Acts 17:11*.

The Condemnation of Unbelievers

[Verses 39-41] Jesus, having comforted the man who stood for truth, condemned the spiritually blind religious rulers who fancied themselves to have great light, knowledge, and understanding of divine things, and to be guides of the blind. Read *Matthew 23* for how blind the Pharisees were.

Jesus proclaimed his design in coming into the world:

- *"That they which see not might see"*—referring to those in the realm of darkness who are spiritually blind, that they may be illuminated by the light of the glorious gospel of Christ.

- *"That they which see might be made blind"*—referring to all unbelievers, who are incapable of apprehending and receiving the truth because their minds are blinded by the devil. *2Corinthians 4:3 But if our gospel be hid, it is hid to them that are lost: (4) In whom the god of this world hath blinded the minds of them which believe not, lest the light of the glorious gospel of Christ, who is the image of God, should shine unto them.*

Imagine how dangerous it is for a blind man to drive a car. Such is the life of all unbelievers. They are spiritually blind to the truth, but they think they see clearly and know where they are going. And they criticize and persecute the believers whose eyes are opened and who clearly see and understand. Like the blind driver, all unbelievers will meet destruction.

Prophecies

The prophecy in this chapter reveals that the Jews will reap the antichrist. To understand this prophecy, we must take a trip back in time to the days of the prophet Isaiah. In those days, Israel was split into two kingdoms—the Northern Kingdom of Israel with 10 tribes, and the Southern Kingdom of Judah with two tribes. The 10 tribes of the Northern Kingdom of Israel were Asher, Dan, Gad, Issachar, Joseph (two tribes: Ephraim and Manasseh), Naphtali, Reuben, Simeon, and Zebulun. The two tribes of the Southern Kingdom of Judah were Judah and Benjamin.

God, through the prophet Isaiah, pronounced judgment on Judah as follows:

> *Isaiah 8:6 Forasmuch as this people refuseth the waters of Shiloah that go softly, and rejoice in Rezin and Remaliah's son; (7) Now therefore, behold, the Lord bringeth up upon them the waters of the river, strong and many, even the king of Assyria, and all his glory: and he shall come up over all his channels, and go over all his banks: (8) And he shall pass through Judah; he shall overflow and go over, he shall reach even to the neck; and the stretching out of his wings shall fill the breadth of thy land, O Immanuel.*

Recall that the pool of Siloam pictures Jesus Christ. The stream (*the waters of Shiloah*) that filled the pool was gentle. Jesus Christ came as the Lamb of God, meek and lowly, to Israel.

Chapter 9 – Sent One

But Judah *"refuseth the waters of Shiloah that go softly."* This is the prophecy of Israel's refusal of Jesus Christ as their Messiah.

Judah rejoiced in Rezin, who was the king of Syria, and in Pekah (Remaliah's son), who was the king of the Northern Kingdom of Israel. This is the prophecy of Israel's ties and relationships with unrighteous kings instead of with Jesus Christ. *John 19:15b The chief priests answered, We have no king but Caesar.*

God judged Judah by overwhelming them with a rapid torrent, *"the waters of the river, strong and many,"* which was the army of the king of Assyria. Prophetically, this is the antichrist, as the king of Assyria is a type of the antichrist. An extremely painful period known as the Great Tribulation awaits the Jews.

Summary

The Bible is a history book. It contains the most accurate history records as they are preserved by God. There definitely is value in learning from history. The Bible is also a book of prophecies. About a quarter of the Bible is prophetic. The Bible says, *"The testimony of Jesus is the spirit of prophecy."* You can know the future when you understand prophecies. Finally, the Bible is also a doctrinal book, which is God's instructions for how to live a successful, fruitful, and happy life in the present. Unbelievers will not be able to profit beyond the historical value of the Bible because prophecies and doctrines can only be seen and understood by believers whose spiritual eyes are opened. All in all, the Bible is a magical book!

The Lord Jesus awaits to open spiritual eyes. *"Behold, now is the accepted time; behold, now is the day of salvation."* May all readers wash their sins in the pool of the Sent One. May the eyes of their understanding be opened to behold the Kingdom of God.

10 – Good Shepherd

Historical Synopsis

Jesus continued His outreach to the Jews, this time with a discourse concerning Himself as the door of the sheepfold and the shepherd of the sheep. He began with a parable comparing Himself as the true Shepherd with thieves and robbers, who were the religious rulers of Israel. When the Jews could not understand the parable, Jesus explained its meaning. But as usual, there was division among the Jews over His identity. They demanded that Jesus end the suspense and plainly acknowledge if He was the Christ, even though He had already told them that He was. The Jews simply would not believe in His words or works.

The text places the time of this conference during the Feast of Dedication, which was in the month of Chisleu in winter.

This chapter can be outlined as such:

I. Jesus is the good shepherd – *John 10:1-18*
II. Jews are told they are not Jesus' sheep – *John 10:19-30*
III. Jews want to stone Jesus for blasphemy – *John 10:30-42*

The Book of John

Chapter 10 – Good Shepherd

Key Spiritual Lessons

We learned in chapter 8 about the two spiritual fathers—God and the devil. Here, we have the true and false shepherds who both love sheep, but with different motives. One comes to care for and give His life for the sheep, while the other comes to steal, kill, and destroy the sheep. Sheep is figurative for people. Some people are God's sheep while others belong to the devil, as Jesus said in verse 26, *"But ye believe not, because ye are not of my sheep."*

The Pharisees validated themselves as the religious leaders and rulers of Israel. Jesus was viewed as a threat to the Law of Moses. The Pharisees did their best to depose Jesus and to keep the people under the law. Jesus, on the other hand, tried to win the Jews over by showing Himself as the true Shepherd and exposing the Pharisees as the false shepherds.

For spiritual lessons, this chapter can be outlined as such:

I. Litmus tests for shepherds – *John 10:1-18*
II. Litmus tests for sheep – *John 10:19-30*
III. Litmus tests for Jesus' deity – *John 10:31-42*

Litmus Tests for Shepherds

While Jesus is the true Shepherd, the false shepherds of the world, like the Pharisees, are equally interested in shepherding people. They draw people away from the true Shepherd into their own sheepfolds, which are the various religions of the world. The litmus tests for shepherds consist of the door, voice, care, relationship, kingdom, and power.

Examine the door

[Verses 1-5] In a parable, Jesus gave the Jews the following clues for identifying the true Shepherd:

- *"He that entereth not by the door into the sheepfold, but climbeth up some other way, the same is a thief and a robber"*—Watch out for false shepherds who come to do you harm. They enter not by the door, which is Jesus Christ, according to verse 7. This carries the following warnings:
    - False shepherds such as false prophets and teachers have entered the sheepfold and are looking for victims.
    - Do not follow religious leaders who deny Jesus.

- *"He that entereth in by the door is the shepherd of the sheep"*—The real Shepherd uses the door. In this case, Jesus enters His own door as one having authority to care for the sheep. He binds the broken and strengthens the weak.

- *"To him the porter openeth"*—The porter who is in charge of the sheepfold recognizes the true Shepherd and is happy to open the door and welcome Him in. It is unclear who the porter represents. Since Jesus is the door, some think the porter is God the Father, because Jesus committed the safekeeping of the believers to Him in *John 17:11b, "Holy Father, keep through thine own name those whom thou hast given me, that they may be one, as we are."*

- *"and the sheep hear his voice"*—This means you need to know and obey the word of God, and not one of these false shepherds, who often contradict the Bible. The Bible must be your final authority.

- *"and he calleth his own sheep by name, and leadeth them out"*—Every sheep matters, and the Shepherd knows each one individually.

- *"When he putteth forth his own sheep, he goeth before them, and the sheep follow him: for they know his voice. And a stranger will they not follow, but will flee from him: for they know not the voice of strangers"*—When the Shepherd takes the sheep out from the fold to green pastures, He leads them with His familiar voice. (More on the voice later.)

[Verse 6] This is the first time the word "parable" is used in the Gospel of John, and it comes from the Greek word "παροιμία" (*par-oy-mee'-ah*), which is translated two other times as "proverb" in *John 16:25, 29*. A parable is like a proverb, which is a simple story that is impregnated with spiritual lessons or truths. A parable is designed to conceal truth from unbelievers, but reveal truth to believers. *Matthew 13:10 And the disciples came, and said unto him, Why speakest thou unto them in parables? (11) He answered and said unto them, Because it is given unto you to know the mysteries of the kingdom of heaven, but to them it is not given.*

As such, a parable is a strange story to unbelievers, because they are spiritually blind and cannot perceive the light of God. To believers, parables are exciting because of the truth and value they contain, and mining them is fun. Each time I find a nugget, it is a hallelujah moment. Read *Matthew 13:10-11*.

[Verses 7-8] Seeing the unbelieving Jews could not understand the parable, Jesus plainly declared to them that He was the door and the Shepherd of the sheep (according to verse 2 and

7). Those who came before Him were thieves and robbers, referring to the religious rulers of Israel. But His sheep knew the true Shepherd and did not give ear to the false shepherds who tried to seduce them away.

[Verse 9] Jesus further explained that He was the door to eternal life. Those who enter in His door to receive Him as Lord and Savior:

- "Shall be saved"—All sins are forgiven, and believers are saved from the judgment and wrath of God.

- "Shall go in and out"—Believers have full liberty in Christ to exercise righteousness, and sin has no dominion over them.

- "Shall find pasture"—God will satisfy believers with His goodness. *Psalms 37:25 I have been young, and now am old; yet have I not seen the righteous forsaken, nor his seed begging bread.*

[Verse 10] In contrast, those who reject Jesus Christ and elect to go with the false shepherds of the world religions will meet destruction. This is because the devil and his false shepherds have the following evil motives:

- To steal people away with heart-deceiving good words and fair speeches.

- To kill people spiritually by poisoning their mind with damnable heresies that deny the Lord Jesus Christ.

- To destroy people with their pernicious and lascivious ways. Read *2Peter 2, Jude*. They put people under the yoke of bondage with traditions, legalism, mandatory

Chapter 10 – Good Shepherd

good works, various rituals, ceremonies, and carnal ordinances.

Jesus' motive was to give abundant and eternal life to the sheep. Is your savior Jesus Christ or the thief who *"entereth not by the door into the sheepfold, but climbeth up some other way?"* The *"some other way"* is the religions, traditions, and beliefs of the world. Jesus is the way, the truth, and the life. He is the right door. Other religions' doors lead to destruction. *Matthew 7:13 Enter ye in at the strait gate: for wide is the gate, and broad is the way, that leadeth to destruction, and many there be which go in thereat: (14) Because strait is the gate, and narrow is the way, which leadeth unto life, and few there be that find it. (15) Beware of false prophets, which come to you in sheep's clothing, but inwardly they are ravening wolves.* Read *Galatians 1:6-8.*

Examine the voice

Consider all the "voice" references in the following verses:

> *John 10:3 To him the porter openeth; and <u>the sheep hear his voice</u>: and he calleth his own sheep by name, and leadeth them out. (4) And when he putteth forth his own sheep, he goeth before them, and the sheep follow him: for <u>they know his voice.</u> (5) And a stranger will they not follow, but will flee from him: for <u>they know not the voice of strangers.</u>*

> *John 10:16 And other sheep I have, which are not of this fold: them also I must bring, and <u>they shall hear my voice</u>; and there shall be one fold, and one shepherd.*

> *John 10:27 <u>My sheep hear my voice</u>, and I know them, and they follow me:*

Jesus Christ is the voice of truth. The Bible says in *John 17:17b*, *"Thy word is truth."* False religions, in order to make their lies believable, mix a dose of truth with lies. But Jesus says in verse 8, *"The sheep did not hear them."* Later in chapter 18, when He stands before Pilate, He says, *"Every one that is of the truth heareth my voice."*

Notice this is about judging the shepherd by his voice instead of by his appearance. *John 7:24* says, *"Judge not according to the appearance, but judge righteous judgment."* The Pharisees were so focused on outward appearances that they did not recognize the voice of their Messiah.

Be careful that the voice you listen to comes from word of God and not feelings or experiences. Do you know how Adam got into trouble? He hearkened to the voice of his wife instead of the voice of God. *Genesis 3:17 And unto Adam he said, Because thou hast hearkened unto the voice of thy wife, and hast eaten of the tree, of which I commanded thee, saying, Thou shalt not eat of it: cursed is the ground for thy sake; in sorrow shalt thou eat of it all the days of thy life.* But Adam clearly recognized the voice of God, according to *Genesis 3:8-10*.

It is hard to fake a voice. When I phone home, my loved ones do not need to introduce themselves, as I recognize their voices. Animals recognize voices too. Penguins sort out their young ones among thousands by their voices. Even a blind dog can differentiate his master's voice from the stranger's. If you read the Bible, you will be able to differentiate the voice of the true Shepherd from the voice of strangers. You will know the truth and be able to spot counterfeits. The truth you know will set you free from falsehood. Again, the Bible needs to be your source of truth and your final authority, and not religious leaders, teachers, Bible scholars, or commentators. Let God be true and every man a liar.

Chapter 10 – Good Shepherd

Examine the care

[Verses 11-13] Having shown Himself as the right door and the door of righteousness, Jesus presented Himself as the good Shepherd who would give His life for the sheep. This time, He contrasted Himself with a hireling.

When Jesus saw the sheep in trouble because of trespasses and sins, He gave His life for the sheep so that they might become His righteousness. *John 15:13 Greater love hath no man than this, that a man lay down his life for his friends.* Can you quote *John 3:16*?

When the hireling sees the wolf coming, he leaves the sheep to save his own skin. He lets the wolf devour and scatter the sheep. (The wolf is anything that comes upon the flock with hostile intent.)

Who is this singular "hireling" in verse 12? He is *"not the shepherd,"* so he is not the real deal. He also is not the owner of the sheep. But he wants the shepherd's position. However, verse 13 says the hireling flees because he doesn't care for the sheep. He does the job carelessly for selfish reasons.

The devil and the antichrist certainly fit the description of a hireling, as do religious leaders who are in it for the prestige, such as the Pharisees. *Matthew 23:5 But all their works they do for to be seen of men: they make broad their phylacteries, and enlarge the borders of their garments, (6) And love the uppermost rooms at feasts, and the chief seats in the synagogues, (7) And greetings in the markets, and to be called of men, Rabbi, Rabbi.*

Regardless of who the hireling is, the main point of this lesson is that only Jesus Christ died for sinners. Read *Romans 5:8*. He bore the sins of the world on the cross of Calvary. All hirelings or Jesus imposters will not give their life for your sins, neither can they, because they themselves are the descendants of Adam.

Unfortunately, billions of people look to and trust in religious leaders instead of Jesus for salvation.

Examine the relationship

The relationship between the good Shepherd and His sheep is summarized by verse 14 and 27.

(14) *I am the good shepherd, and <u>know</u> my sheep, and am <u>known</u> of mine.*

(27) *My sheep hear my voice, and I <u>know</u> them, and they follow me.*

[Verse 14] There is a fruitful relationship between the good Shepherd and His sheep. The word "know" in the Bible suggests intimacy, such as between a husband and a wife. For example, *Genesis 4:1a* says, "*Adam knew Eve his wife; and she conceived, and bare Cain.*" It is a mutual love relationship—"*know my sheep, and am known of mine.*"

Notice it is not about religion, but a relationship with the good Shepherd. The world is all about religion and religious activities, but not a relationship with the Savior.

[Verse 15] What's more important is that the good Shepherd is intimately connected with the Father—"*As the Father knoweth me, even so know I the Father.*" The good Shepherd is privy to the Father's mission and plan for the ages, is totally in sync with Him, and will only do things that please Him. This intimacy with the Father yields the following:

1. [Verse 15] A complete sacrificial life for the Father's mission. The good Shepherd lays down His life for the sheep, because He knows how much the Father loves them.

2. [Verse 16] A commitment to the Father's kingdom that includes Jewish and Gentile believers.
3. [Verse 17] A coveting for the Father's love.
4. [Verse 18] A complete obedience to the Father's commandment.

Our relationship with the good Shepherd should also yield the above.

Without access to the Father, one does not have eternal life. Access to the Father is only through the good Shepherd. Notice how the sheep in verse 14 can only connect with the Father in verse 15 through the relationship with the good Shepherd? *1Timothy 2:5 For there is one God, and one mediator between God and men, the man Christ Jesus.* But the world would have you believe that every way leads to God, and it speaks evil of Christ's claim as the way, the truth, and the life.

Examine the kingdom

[Verses 16-17] There are other sheep besides the house of Israel, referring to the Gentiles. This affirms the "Gentiles' equality with Jews in Christ" concept that the Apostle Paul mentioned in *Ephesians 2:11-17*. Some Gentiles will hear Jesus' voice and believe, and He will combine and integrate these sheep into one fold, that the Jews and Gentiles may be one, as Jesus and God are one. Read *John 17:2-23, Ephesians 2:11-22*.

Since Jesus laid down His life for both Jews and Gentiles, the salvation of the Jews and Gentiles is achieved the same way—by hearing His voice, which is the word of the gospel. Both Jews and Gentiles must accept Jesus Christ by faith, for there is no difference; for all have sinned and come short of the glory of God. Read *Ephesians 2:8-10*.

Also notice that Jesus is the one who delivers the kingdom to the Father, because He laid down His life and purchased it with His blood. Jesus Christ is the true and good Shepherd available for all people.

Examine the power

[Verses 17-18] Jesus Christ laid down His life in obedience to the Father's will and according to His determinate counsel and knowledge. No man had the power to take His life without His consent. He voluntarily surrendered to the cross so that His sheep might have life. He had the power to lay down His life and the power to raise it up again.

Of all the religious leaders people look to for salvation, name one person who has the power of Jesus. Those who are dead remain dead—Buddha, Mohammad, Confucius, and so forth. You can visit their graves because they are dead. What can a dead person do for you? If Jesus didn't rise again, there is no reason to call on Him. But Jesus Christ is alive. He is the living God. The so-called saviors who are alive today will die, because they are sinners like all of us. Why would anyone not put their trust in Jesus alone?

Litmus Tests for Sheep

[Verses 19-30] Following the above discourse, the Jews were again divided on Jesus' identity. Many said He was devil possessed while others disagreed, because He was able to open the eyes of a man who was born blind in chapter 9. So they came to Jesus and asked Him to plainly declare if He was the Christ.

Jesus had told the Jews numerous times by words and works that He was the Messiah, but they would not believe. Jesus had told them that God was His Father and He was God the Son, the light of

Chapter 10 – Good Shepherd

the world, the door to eternal life, and the good Shepherd. The works that Jesus performed in the Father's name bore witness of Him—the sick were healed, devils were disposed, lepers were cleansed, the blind received sight, the deaf received hearing, the dumb spoke, the lame walked, and the dead came to life. Read *Isaiah 35:1-6, Luke 7:19-23*. Their disbelief of Jesus' words and works was simply because they were not Jesus' sheep.

Just as there are two spiritual families, there are also two classes of sheep. A sheep either belongs to Jesus or not. The litmus tests for sheep are as follows:

- *"My sheep hear my voice"*—not just hear, but hearken to or obey. Jesus' sheep hearken to Him. Unbelievers are like the Jews in *John 8:37*. Jesus' words have no place in them. They are not at all interested in obeying His words.

- *"I know them"*—Jesus knows His sheep and calls them by name. They are those who are drawn by the Father and are given to Jesus. Read *John 6:44*. Their names are written in the Book of Life.

- *"They follow me"*—Jesus' sheep follow Him because 1) they recognize His voice, and 2) Jesus leads them, according to verses 3-4. Unbelievers turn their backs on Jesus and reject him. Refresh your memory on what it means to follow Jesus in Chapter 1.

There are advantages to becoming Jesus' sheep as follows:

- Eternal life—*"And I give unto them eternal life; and they shall never perish."* Jesus' sheep have eternal life and never have to worry about the penalty of sin, God's wrath on sinners, or hell.

- Eternal security—*"Neither shall any man pluck them out of my hand."* The sheep are eternally secure because God the Father is greater than all, and no person in the world is able to pluck them out of His hand. Read *John 17:12*. (Notice the sheep are in Jesus' hand and the Father's hand at the same time. Pay attention to the word "hand" in verse 28 and 29. This is because Jesus and the Father are one.)

Do you know anyone who will fail the litmus test for Jesus' sheep? Take a break now and pray for the person.

Litmus Tests for Jesus' Deity

[Verses 31-42] When Jesus said *"I and my Father are one,"* the Jews were infuriated and wanted to stone Him, not for His good works, but for blasphemy, according to *Leviticus 24:16*. But Jesus challenged them to look at *Psalms 82:6*, which refers to human judges as gods. Jesus' point was, if the magistrates who received a commission from God authorizing them to act in the capacity of rulers and governors, were called gods, how could they charge Him as a blasphemer who was God the Son, sanctified and sent by the Father?

Having vindicated Himself, Jesus continued to reason with the Jews that He and the Father were one. He instructed them to examine His works, because they were proof that He was deity, God's Son, and the Messiah. The works and miracles could only be done by the Father, or by one who is equal with Him. (When John the Baptist's faith in Jesus was shaken, Jesus sent messengers to him saying, *"Go your way, and tell John what things ye have seen and heard; how that the blind see, the lame walk, the lepers are cleansed, the deaf hear, the dead are raised, to the poor the gospel is preached."* That was enough to convince John the Baptist that

Chapter 10 – Good Shepherd

Jesus was the Messiah and to restore his faith.) But the Jews would not hear Jesus' reasoning and sought to capture Him. Jesus escaped out of their hand and returned to Bethabara across the Jordan River.

Many Jews believed in Jesus at Bethabara when they realized everything that John the Baptist said about Him was true.

What about you? Jesus' resurrection was the work that convinced me that He is God the Son and a living God. Jesus Christ is my Shepherd.

Other Notables

The Feast of Dedication

[Verses 22-23] The Feast of Dedication, or Hanukkah, is celebrated on the 25th day of the Jewish month Chisleu, which is partly in December, and it lasts for eight days. The Feast of Dedication is not one of the divine feasts ordered by God. It was instituted by Judas Maccabaeus and his brethren to commemorate the dedication of a new altar and the purging of the temple after it had been profaned and defiled by Seleucid king, Antiochus Epiphanes. The history is documented in the Apocryphal book of Maccabees (1Maccabees 4:52, 56, 59, 2Maccabees 10:8).

When the Israelites prevailed over their enemies and regained the temple on the 25th of the month Chisleu in 165 B.C., they found one vial of the pure and undefiled olive oil, which was enough to light the eternal flame of God for only one day. Miraculously, that oil lasted for eight days until they were able to squeeze and process new pure olive oil.

Therefore, the Jews commemorate the miracle by lighting lamps at the doors of their houses for eight nights, beginning on the 25th of Chisleu, and they are forbidden to mourn and fast. This is why the Feast of Dedication is also called the Festival of Lights.

For your edification, below are the Jewish feasts that God commanded and the significance of each to New Testament believers. Jesus fulfilled the spring feasts in His first coming. The fall feasts will be fulfilled soon.

Chapter 10 – Good Shepherd

Biblical Feasts of the Lord	Jewish Holidays	Begin on	# of days	Significance
Passover *Leviticus 23:5*	Pesach	14-Nisan	1	Jesus Christ was sacrificed as the Passover Lamb.
Unleavened Bread *Leviticus 23:6-8*	Chag HaMatzot	15-Nisan	7	Jesus Christ was the sinless (unleavened) bread of life – *John 6:35*.
Firstfruits *Leviticus 23:9-14*	Reshit Katzir	17-Nisan	1	Jesus Christ rose from the dead and became the firstfruits of them that slept – *1 Corinthians 15:20,23*
Weeks (or Pentecost, which means 50th day) *Leviticus 23:15-22*	Shavuot	50 days from the Feast of Firstfruits	1	The Holy Spirit was given to the Church on Pentecost – *Acts 2:1-4*
Trumpets *Leviticus 23:23-25*	Rosh Hashanah	01-Tishri	1	The rapture of the Church – *1 Corinthians 15:52*
Day of Atonement *Leviticus 23:26-32*	Yom Kippur	10-Tishri	1	The day of atonement for the Jews. All Israel will be saved – *Zechariah 12:8-14, Zechariah 13:1*
Tabernacles *Leviticus 23:33-44*	Sukkot	15-Tishri	7	Jesus Christ will once again dwell with His covenant people – the Jews. This also is the beginning of the Millennial reign.

The first four feasts occur in Spring; the last three in Fall.

Jan	Feb	Mar	Apr	May	Jun	Jul	Aug	Sep	Oct	Nov	Dec
Shevat	Adar	Nisan (Abib)	Iyar	Sivan	Tammuz	Av	Elul	Tishri	Cheshvan	Chislev	Tevet

193

The Book of John

Eternal security

Jesus touched on eternal security in verses 28-29. There is bad teaching in some churches that believers must work to maintain their salvation and that they can lose their salvation if they sin after being born again.

Following are some of the reasons why believers do not lose their salvation:

- *John 6:37 says "All that the Father giveth me shall come to me; and him that cometh to me I will in no wise cast out."*

- Salvation is by grace through faith and not of works. It is a gift of God and not a debt that one should repay. No one can lose salvation, because no one can earn it to begin with. Furthermore, it is God, not us, who keeps our salvation. Read *2Timothy 1:12*.

- There is absolutely nothing that can separate believers from the love of God. Even death cannot break the bond of love that God has for His children. Read *Romans 8:38*.

- Believers have a Father/child relationship with God.
    - God keeps their spiritual birth records in heaven. Read *1John 5:11*.
    - Believers are God's children no matter what they do, just like your children will always be your children, whether they make you proud or not. Read *John 1:12*.

- Believers are sealed by the Holy Spirit of God unto the day of redemption. Read *Ephesians 1:13, Ephesians 4:30*.

Summary

Whose sheep are you? I was lost in religion following false shepherds, but now am found and returned to the Shepherd of my soul. *Peter 2:25 For ye were as sheep going astray; but are now returned unto the Shepherd and Bishop of your souls.* I am now secure in Jesus Christ. May all readers perform the litmus tests on their shepherds and find Jesus Christ as the true and good Shepherd.

11 – Resurrection and Life

Historical Synopsis

The miracle of Lazarus' resurrection is exclusive to the Gospel of John. It is the zenith of all miracles—a crowning proof of Jesus' resurrection power. More than three-fourths of this chapter is devoted to the account.

Jesus did not rush to heal Lazarus in Bethany, but remained in Bethabara for two additional days when He received tidings from Mary and Martha that their brother Lazarus was very ill. Thereafter, Jesus made the journey against the advice of His disciples and at great risk to Himself, because the Jews in nearby Jerusalem sought to stone Him.

Lazarus had been dead for four days when Jesus arrived in Bethany. Martha first met Jesus and complained about His tardiness, believing that Lazarus' death could have been prevented if He had responded immediately after receiving the news. When Jesus assured her that Lazarus would rise again, Martha did not expect Jesus to raise him back to life that very day and comforted herself with the hope of seeing her brother again in the resurrection of the last day. She still didn't understand it when Jesus plainly declared to her that He was the resurrection and the life.

When Mary met Jesus, she too complained about His tardiness and wept. The sisters' distress and weakness of faith grieved Jesus so much that He wept as they led Him to Lazarus'

Chapter 11 – Resurrection and Life

grave. At the grave, Jesus commanded the stone to be removed, and after praying to the Father, brought Lazarus back to life.

Many Jews believed on Jesus after seeing the miracle. However, the ecclesiastical rulers were threatened by Jesus' success. They feared the whole nation would receive Him as the Messiah and set Him as King above Caesar, which would spell disaster for them politically and personally. The high priest Caiaphas recommended that Jesus should die for the sake of the nation. From that day forth, the religious rulers resolved to kill Jesus without a valid charge against Him.

This chapter can be outlined as such:

I. Jesus raised Lazarus to life – *John 11:1-46*
II. Jesus' life was threatened by the religious rulers of Israel – *John 11:47-57*

Key Spiritual Lessons

Physical exercise and a healthy diet are important for prolonging life, but they cannot maintain life forever, neither can they restore the dead to life. No matter how much we care for the body, it will degenerate, die, and return to dust. Death is the wages of sin. No one is exempt from physical death, not even believers in Jesus Christ, because all have sinned. *Ecclesiastes 8:8 There is no man that hath power over the spirit to retain the spirit; neither hath he power in the day of death: and there is no discharge in that war; neither shall wickedness deliver those that are given to it.*

But death is not the end. Did you know that all dead people will be resurrected to face judgment? Believers of Jesus Christ will be resurrected to face the Judgment Seat of Christ, which determines their rewards for their service to Him. Unbelievers will be resurrected to face the judgment of the Great White Throne, which condemns them to the second death and eternal torment in the lake of fire. (See Chapter 8 for the comparisons of the two events.) Depending on one's standing with the Lord Jesus, resurrection can be scarier than death, because the judgment that follows carries eternal consequences. The souls of dead unbelievers dread the resurrection and have only one wish—that they could relive the day they heard the gospel and accept Jesus Christ as their Lord and Savior. The souls of dead believers, who abused the grace of God to live a self-serving and spiritually fruitless life, dread the resurrection because of shame, but not for fear of hell. (This is because upon trusting Christ as Savior, their sins were forgiven.)

The core message of this chapter is Jesus Christ is the resurrection and the life. He has the power to resurrect and give life to the dead, as He demonstrated through Lazarus. Those who believe in Jesus, though they are dead, yet shall they live.

Chapter 11 – Resurrection and Life

For spiritual lessons, this chapter can be outlined as such:

I. Lessons from Lazarus' resurrection – *John 11:1-45*
II. Lessons from the conspiracy of the religious unbelievers – *John 11:46-57*

Lessons from Lazarus' Resurrection

Consider the sickness in Bethany

[Verses 1-2] There was sickness and death in Bethany. The name Bethany means "house of misery," and it appropriately represents the world we live in. Everyone in this world is sin sick and is in various stages of dying. This world is a miserable place. Solomon, the wisest man who ever lived, called it the vanity of vanities. It is the vanity of the worst kind, and besides hell, there is no other place more miserable than this. According to verse 18, Bethany was only about two miles away from Jerusalem, which means "double peace." The peace of God is so close to those who are miserable. The Lord Jesus visits those who are in the house of misery.

In the Bible, words such as sick, infirmity, impotent, blind, lame, disease, leprosy, and death, in all forms, are key words representing sin and the spiritual state of a person or nation. Lazarus' sickness and death represent the spiritual state of all of Adam's descendants and of the nation of Israel today.

When Jesus arrived in Bethany, Lazarus was already dead. The lesson is that Jesus finds all Adam's descendants already dead in sin, and no one has the power to overcome death. Everyone succumbs to death and loses life. No amount of religion, morality, philosophy, good works, or intellect can reclaim life from death.

The word "sick" appears five times in this chapter (verses 1-4, 6). Remember five is the number of death? Indeed, the wages of sin is death.

Consider the sisters' petition

[Verse 3] Mary and Martha sent a simple and factual prayer of intercession to Jesus.

- *"Lord"*—The sisters addressed Jesus as Lord. As Lord, He owned them and would be interested in them, including their problems.

- *"behold"*—They asked for His observation that He might behold and consider their distress. *Psalms 33:18 Behold, the eye of the LORD is upon them that fear him, upon them that hope in his mercy.*

- *"he whom thou lovest is sick"*—They presented the thing that He would care about.

The prayer was impactful because:

1. It was founded in truth. God loves and cares for His children. The sisters trusted in God's love. Read *Romans 8:38-39*.

2. It was prayed in faith. Notice the explicit desire for Lazarus to be healed was missing from the prayer request. The sisters obviously had their expectations as shown in verses 21 and 32, but they submitted the fact and the outcome to their Lord. Read about another faithful prayer request from the nobleman at Capernaum in *John 4:46-53*.

Chapter 11 – Resurrection and Life

God is well pleased when His children submit to His will and trust Him by faith. It is important for Christians to remember the lordship factor. Jesus Christ is Lord, and He loves and cares for His children and His kingdom more than anyone else in this world. Some Christians' prayers treat the Lord Jesus like a short-order cook, as they impose selfish requests, expectations and desired outcomes on Him, rather than submitting to His will and trusting Him as Lord to do what's best. Naaman is a good example. When Elisha told him to wash in Jordan seven times for his own good, he *"was wroth, and went away, and said, Behold, I thought, He will surely come out to me, and stand, and call on the name of the LORD his God, and strike his hand over the place, and recover the leper,"* according to *2Kings 5:11*.

Consider Jesus' response to the prayer request

When Jesus heard the tidings, He responded by doing nothing, which was not the typical response that most people would expect. Jesus had His reasons. Following are the lessons:

1. [Verse 4] Jesus heard the prayer.
   - Rest assured that God hears the prayers of the righteous. *Proverbs 15:29 The LORD is far from the wicked: but he heareth the prayer of the righteous.*
   - There is no need to repeat your request over and over again. It is a prayer, not a chant. *Matthew 6:7 But when ye pray, use not vain repetitions, as the heathen do: for they think that they shall be heard for their much speaking.*

2. [Verse 4] Jesus had a purpose for Lazarus' sickness— *"This sickness is not unto death, but for the glory of God, that the Son of God might be glorified thereby."*

The Book of John

- God allows needs to come into your life so that His Son may be glorified in you. Read *Psalms 50:15, Colossians 1:16*. Yes, bad things do happen to good people.
- God uses those needs to draw you to a place where He can bless you and reveal to you that your real need is the Lord Jesus Christ and His grace. Read *2Corinthians 12:7-10, 2Corinthians 3:5*.
- The most dangerous time in your life is when every single need is met and you have need of nothing, including God. Read *Revelation 3:16-17, Deuteronomy 8:6-18*.

3. [Verse 5] Jesus loved Martha, Mary, and Lazarus, even though He allowed Lazarus to die. If one of these days God does not answer your prayer and takes your loved one home to be with Him, it is not because He does not love you.

4. [Verse 6] Jesus did not rush to heal Lazarus, but remained in Bethabara for two more days. He knows what needs to be done and when to do it. God is never early, never late, and always on time.

5. [Verses 7-8] Three days after hearing about Lazarus' sickness, Jesus led His disciples into Judea to visit Lazarus against the advice of His disciples and at great risk to Himself, because the Jews there had attempted to stone Him twice. Read *John 8:59, John 10:31*. If your prayer is according to God's will, He will take action. When He moves, nothing can stop Him.

Chapter 11 – Resurrection and Life

Consider Jesus' prescription for the Christian walk

[Verses 9-10] Jesus comforted His disciples, who were concerned for His safety. He counseled them to walk in the day and not at night, so that they might avoid danger and the snares that were laid for them.

While it was practical advice, there is much more to it. As mentioned in Chapter 9, Day is the name of the Light of God and Night is the name of the spiritual darkness in high places. Read *Genesis 1:1-5, John 9:4-5, John 12:35-36*. You can avoid stumbling in your Christian walk if you walk in the Light of God, which is the word of God. Read *Galatians 5:16*. You will surely slip, stumble, and fall if you allow spiritual darkness to enter and rule your life, because you have no light of your own and cannot see in darkness. You are like the moon that receives and reflects the sunlight, but does not generate its own light. This means you cannot live a happy and successful life on your own in this dark and evil world. *Joshua 1:8 This book of the law shall not depart out of thy mouth; but thou shalt meditate therein day and night, that thou mayest observe to do according to all that is written therein: for then thou shalt make thy way prosperous, and then thou shalt have good success.*

Christians don't die, they sleep

[Verses 11-16] Jesus' disciples misunderstood Him when He said He would go to Bethany and wake Lazarus out of sleep. They couldn't understand why He would take such a big risk. To them, Lazarus should do well if he was sleeping and should be able to wake up on his own. Then Jesus made it plain to them that Lazarus had died, and He was going to raise him from the dead. Jesus was glad that He was not in Bethany earlier, because He would have prevented Lazarus' death and the disciples would miss out on the greatest miracle that would strengthen their belief in Him. (Did you realize that nobody ever died in Jesus' presence? That's because He

The Book of John

was life. The two thieves that were crucified with Jesus died only after He gave up the ghost.) But Thomas, who was convinced the journey was too risky and they would die by their enemies, stirred up his fellow disciples to go along with Jesus and die together.

The death of Christians is not an everlasting farewell. It is like sleeping, because they will rise again, rejuvenated to immortality in new and powerful spiritual bodies. Read *1Corinthians 15:35-58*. They don't feel the sting of death, they will not die the second death, and the grave is a bed and not a prison. *1Corinthians 15:55 O death, where is thy sting? O grave, where is thy victory?* For this reason, we do not sorrow as those who have no hope when we lose a loved one in Christ. Read *1Thessalonians 4:13-18*. Jesus Christ is the resurrection and the life!

Consider the sisters' faith

[Verses 17-28] Martha, as soon as she heard of Jesus' arrival, went out to meet Him, and with mixed emotions, complained about His tardiness, because Lazarus had been dead for four days. She said, *"Lord, if thou hadst been here, my brother had not died."* To her, it was an incredible missed opportunity, and Lazarus would be alive had Jesus not tarried. She regretted Jesus' timing. In her distress, disappointment, and desperation, she tapped into her head knowledge of Jesus and the scriptures. She said *"I know"* twice in verses 22 and 24.

- Martha knew Jesus was tightly connected with the Father. She petitioned Jesus to ask the Father for an intervention, even though there had been no precedent of any one raised to life that had been dead so long.

- When Jesus told her Lazarus would rise again, she said *"I know that he shall rise again in the resurrection at the*

Chapter 11 – Resurrection and Life

last day." (See the "last day" definition in the Side Notes section in Chapter 6.)

The problem with head knowledge is that it does not yield comfort in times of trial. Belief does. Jesus refocused Martha on her faith by saying, *"I am the resurrection, and the life: he that believeth in me, though he were dead, yet shall he live: And whosoever liveth and believeth in me shall never die. Believest thou this?"* Martha had to reach into her heart. She responded by saying, *"Yea, Lord: I believe that thou art the Christ, the Son of God, which should come into the world."* Thereafter, she was fine and returned home and privately told Mary that Jesus had come and called for her.

Many people have some knowledge of Jesus. I did too when I was an unbeliever. I knew He was a Christian God. But I did not believe in Him in such a way as to receive Him as my sole God and Savior. I missed Jesus by about 18 inches, the distance between my head and heart. Unfortunately, billons of people in the world will also miss Jesus by 18 inches.

[Verses 29-38] When Martha informed Mary that Jesus had called for her, she immediately left the house and hurried to Jesus. She fell down at His feet and also blamed Him for being tardy. She said, *"Lord, if thou hadst been here, my brother had not died."* Mary wept as if there was no hope, and likewise the Jews, who came to comfort her. Jesus groaned in His spirit, and was so agitated by the sisters' weak faith and hopelessness that He wept as they led Him to Lazarus' grave. But the Jews mistook His emotion for His love for Lazarus.

The sisters missed a great opportunity to demonstrate their faith in Jesus and be a witness to the Jews that came to see them. Read *1Thessalonians 4:13-14*. Do you hope in scriptures or do you cry your eyes out in hopelessness in tough times?

The Book of John

Some of the Jews began to question Jesus' authenticity. They said, *"Could not this man, which opened the eyes of the blind, have caused that even this man should not have died?"* It made sense for them that Jesus should have prevented Lazarus' death, giving joy to the family, and further proving that He was sent by God. His inability to prevent Lazarus' death, who was a believer, gave them a reason to doubt and reproach. This too caused Jesus to groan internally as He approached the grave.

Following are the key takeaways from the story:

1. Never put God in a box.
   Mary and Martha had in their minds that Jesus would cure Lazarus. Additionally, they expected Jesus would come when they called, and would be on time. When things did not happen according to their expectations, they came unglued and were upset with Jesus.

   Many Christians are like Mary and Martha. They pray to God and develop certain expectations for how He should answer their prayers. When God does not come through according to their plans, they are disappointed and become angry with Him.

   Remember, God is God. He is not an order taker. God is not obligated to answer, do, or give anything that He does not promise in His word. Make sure that you first pray according to His word (which means you have to know the Bible), and submit to His will. Never put God in a box.

2. Be prepared for evil days.
   It is easy to trust God in good times, but God uses challenging times to mature and strengthen His children's faith in Him. Don't forget to thank and praise

Chapter 11 – Resurrection and Life

God in good times. Don't come unglued and get mad at God in bad times. Your head knowledge of scriptures only serves to puff you up and is not helpful in challenging times. Martha said "I know" twice in verses 22 and 24, yet she was a mess. Your faith, belief, and hope are of little use without exercise and practice. The word of God needs to be in your heart, and you need to live it before evil days come upon you, for they will come. Bad things happen to good people, you can count on it. Always be about your Father's business, and don't be sidetracked by evil days. Read *Psalms 112:7-8, Psalms 91, Proverbs 3:21-26, Ecclesiastes 12:1, Ephesians 6:10-18*.

Christ destroyed death in Bethany

[Verses 39-45] At the grave site, Jesus commanded the stone that covered the burial cave to be removed. But Martha interjected, warning Jesus of the offensive and nauseous smell, because Lazarus had been dead for four days. Once again, Jesus had to remind Martha to exercise her faith.

When the stone was removed, Jesus looked to the heavens and thanked the Father for always hearing His prayers. He did it for the sake of the unbelievers who were present, that they might believe that He was sent by God. Thereafter, Jesus cried with a loud voice, *"Lazarus, come forth,"* so that there would be no doubt about His power and authority. He did nothing in secret or with a hocus-pocus magical whisper.

And then the miracle of miracles—Lazarus was raised to life and death was destroyed! Jesus was the resurrection and the life! Indeed, *"The hour is coming, and now is, when the dead shall hear the voice of the Son of God: and they that hear shall live."*

The Book of John

Lazarus came out of his tomb in grave clothes, which Jesus instructed the people to remove and let him go. Many of the Jews who witnessed the resurrection believed on Jesus that day.

Following are the takeaways:

1. Remove all obstacles between Jesus and the spiritually dead. The stone that was between Jesus and dead Lazarus had to be removed. Let the word of God have a direct path and a free course into the hearts of unbelievers, who are dead in trespasses and sins. They need to hear Jesus' voice (the word of God) to come alive. We don't need church programs or a priest or a saint to stand in the way of the word of God and the dead. *Romans 10:17 So then faith cometh by hearing, and hearing by the word of God.*

2. When lost people believe in Jesus, they become alive, but are still bound in grave clothes. The grave clothing represents the wrappings of the world that must be removed. The resurrected Lazarus represents a new believer in Christ. Notice that Jesus instructed others to loosen Lazarus from his grave clothing, meaning, Lazarus couldn't do it on his own. He needed help from others. Churches need to take care of new converts and remove their grave clothing through discipleship.

3. Lost people will believe in Jesus when they see the dead come to life. Many Jews believed on Jesus when they witnessed Lazarus' resurrection. If you are born again, your circle of family and friends who are lost will be influenced for Christ through your testimony. They want to see the new life and the new person in you. Read *Ephesians 4:17-21, Ephesians 5, Ephesians 6.*

Chapter 11 – Resurrection and Life

Lessons from the Conspiracy of the Religious Unbelievers

[Verses 46-57] Some of the witnesses of Lazarus' resurrection hardened their hearts in unbelief and became informers to the Pharisees. Jesus' success in drawing and converting sinners to Himself was a political threat to the Sanhedrim, the highest judicial and ecclesiastical council of the Jews. The chief priests and the Pharisees formed a council to determine the course they should take to stop Jesus. Essentially, they recognized the effectiveness of Jesus' miracles and determined that if they left Jesus alone, the people might set Him up as a new King over Caesar, and the Romans would strip them both of their civil and religious privileges.

In preserving their interests, Caiaphas, who was the high priest that year, scornfully and maliciously spoke out that Jesus *"should die for the people, and that the whole nation perish not."* Unbeknownst to him, he played straight into God's sovereign plan. Caiaphas prophesied that *"Jesus should die for that nation; And not for that nation only, but that also he should gather together in one the children of God that were scattered abroad."* The Sanhedrim unanimously supported Caiaphas, and they were resolved to put Jesus to death. Knowing the resolution of the Sanhedrim to destroy Him, Jesus removed Himself into the countryside to a city called Ephraim. His disciples followed Him there.

As the Passover feast approached, many of the country Jews went up to Jerusalem beforehand to purify themselves. (This was the fourth Passover feast from the time Jesus entered His public ministry.) The country Jews sought for Jesus at the temple in Jerusalem. They wondered if Jesus would show up since the chief priests and Pharisees had commanded the people to report Jesus' whereabouts so that they could capture Him.

The Book of John

Following are the takeaways:

1. The miracle of the resurrection of the dead is a serious threat to false religions, because they all are powerless to bring the dead back to life. Jesus Christ is the resurrection and the life, and there is none else. Thank God that a wretched Taoist sinner such as I could be forgiven and receive the light of life.

2. The world's religions desperately want to hold on to their followers. The leaders are nothing without the support and affection of their followers. Today, the various religions are disparate, but there will soon come a day when they will form a confederation, like the chief priests and Pharisees, to persecute Christians.

3. Ministry leaders beware, there is a point when the enemies of the gospel of Christ will no longer tolerate and will attack when they see many people converting to Christianity. This is not a theory. It happened in the Kandhamal district in the state of Odisha, India, in 2008. The Hindus were concerned over the number of Dalits that converted to Christianity. They launched several operations to annihilate Christians. Many who refused to deny Jesus were beaten and burned to death. The women were humiliated and their homes and churches were burned down. You can watch the gruesome videos of the persecutions on YouTube by searching for "Kandhamal violence." (The Dalits are people of the lowest social status group in the Hindu caste system. So low that they are described by the Hindus as less than humans. But Jesus Christ loves the Dalits with agape love—the highest form of love.)

Chapter 11 – Resurrection and Life

4. The world will produce the antichrist, of whom Caiaphas is a type. He will pronounce death on the Jews and Christians. (By the way, the antichrist is part Jew and is connected with the temple. Read *Psalms 55*, especially verses 12-14.)

5. I am living proof of Caiaphas' prophesy, and I hope you are too. *"Jesus should die for that nation; And not for that nation only, but that also he should gather together in one the children of God that were scattered abroad."* The true children of God are those who receive Jesus Christ by faith. Review Chapter 8 for who belongs to the devil's family.

6. Jesus Christ will remove Himself from those who want to get rid of Him. Without Jesus, they will have no light and no vision. *Proverbs 29:18 Where there is no vision, the people perish: but he that keepeth the law, happy is he.* As the saying goes, "Be careful what you wish for."

7. Jesus' disciples should always follow Him, whether to a country near the wilderness or to heaven. Read *John 12:26, John 14:3*.

Prophecies

Lazarus' sickness represents the spiritual state of the nation of Israel. Israel has sinned, because they have rejected Jesus Christ as their Messiah. As such, they are in the house of misery (Bethany) and are sick, and their sickness will degrade to the point of death.

Mary and Martha represent the people who pray for the healing of the nation of Israel. *Romans 10:1 Brethren, my heart's desire and prayer to God for Israel is, that they might be saved.*

The Lord Jesus tarried two days before visiting Lazarus. As a result, Lazarus died. The two days represents the 2,000 years of absence since Jesus' crucifixion, which is fast coming to a close. Like Lazarus, Israel will die at the hand of the antichrist. By God's mercy, a small remnant will survive. *Romans 9:27 Esaias also crieth concerning Israel, Though the number of the children of Israel be as the sand of the sea, a remnant shall be saved.*

Jesus Christ will return to visit the Jews. God is not done with them. *Romans 11:1 I say then, Hath God cast away his people? God forbid. For I also am an Israelite, of the seed of Abraham, of the tribe of Benjamin. (2) God hath not cast away his people which he foreknew. Wot ye not what the scripture saith of Elias? how he maketh intercession to God against Israel, saying, (3) Lord, they have killed thy prophets, and digged down thine altars; and I am left alone, and they seek my life. (4) But what saith the answer of God unto him? I have reserved to myself seven thousand men, who have not bowed the knee to the image of Baal. (5) Even so then at this present time also there is a remnant according to the election of grace.*

Chapter 11 – Resurrection and Life

Summary

Lazarus was not the only dead person Jesus resurrected to life. Jesus resurrected Jairus' daughter. He also resurrected the son of the widow of Nain. And don't forget that He resurrected Himself! Read *Mark 5:21-43, Luke 7:11-17, John 2:19, John 10:15-18*.

He has also spiritually resurrected me from death. And if He tarries His return, He will resurrect me from physical death. This corrupted body of sin will be raised in glory and power in a spiritual body. Read *1Corinthians 15:35-58*. Based on His track record, I trust Jesus Christ to raise me from death. Jesus Christ is the resurrection and the life. Who do you trust to resurrect you from death?

12 – King of Israel

Historical Synopsis

Six days prior to celebrating His last Passover, Jesus returned to fellowship with Mary, Martha, and Lazarus in Bethany. They made Him a supper and Mary anointed Jesus' feet with costly spikenard oil.

Five days before the Passover, as Jesus rode into Jerusalem on a young ass, He was honored by many who attended the feast as they met Him along the way waving palm branches, and crying *"Hosanna: Blessed is the King of Israel that cometh in the name of the Lord."* Jesus was also honored by certain Gentiles who came to worship at the feast and desired to see Him.

However, the majority of the Jews remained uncertain about His identity and did not believe in Him, despite the many miracles He performed before them. They said, *"Who is this Son of man?"* Their disbelief was a fulfillment of prophesies by the prophet Isaiah, particularly *Isaiah 53:1* and *Isaiah 6:10*. The words that Jesus spoke would judge these unbelievers in the last day.

This chapter can be outlined as such:

    I.   Jesus was honored in Bethany – *John 12:1-11*
    II.   Jesus was honored in Jerusalem – *John 12:12-19*
    III. Jesus was honored by Gentiles – *John 12:20-33*
    IV. Jesus was rejected by unbelieving Jews – *John 12:34-50*

Chapter 12 – King of Israel

Key Spiritual Lessons

This chapter shows a broad spectrum of the peoples' relationships (or lack thereof) with Jesus, beginning with Lazarus all the way to the unbelieving Jews. Each character represents a group of people and their standing with Jesus Christ, the King of Israel. Included in this chapter is an important lesson on fruitfulness and glory, as well as a warning to those who continue to reject Christ.

Following are the key spiritual lessons:

I. Lessons from the characters – *John 12:1-43*
II. Lessons on fruitfulness and glory – *John 12:23-28*
III. Lessons from the last call to the Jews – *John 12:29-50*

Lessons from the Characters

[Verses 1-2] Lazarus represents newly born-again believers in Jesus Christ. These adopted sons of God are given the privilege to sit and sup with the King, just as Mephibosheth was allowed to eat at David's table all the days of his life. Read *2Samuel 9*. It is important for new believers to fellowship with the King and hear from Him directly, and not get overly busy in the work of ministry right away. They need to spend a good amount of time immersing themselves in the word of God and being discipled by a mature Christian.

Martha represents Christians who are gifted and given to service. They are the unsung servants who faithfully and steadfastly do the work of ministry. They are the church cleaners, childcare providers, bus drivers, landscapers, security staff, hospitality workers, and so forth—the worker bees who keep the church operating smoothly. Like Martha, these workers may sometimes complain because the work is great and the laborers are few. I choose to paint Martha in a positive light, especially since the Apostle John did not record any fault against her as Dr. Luke did in *Luke 10:38-42*. Martha has had enough bad press over the years. Without people like Martha, churches would cease to function. That said, an out-of-balance life is not good. One cannot neglect the other aspects of the faith, such as worship, prayer, and the word. What are you gifted in? Put that to use for God.

[Verse 3] Mary represents worshippers who know the Bible. As Mary sat at Jesus' feet and prepared His body for burial, these worshippers know the word of God, understand prophecies, and spare no expense in honoring the Lord Jesus Christ. They give their best, even their glory, as Mary anointed Jesus' feet with costly spikenard oil and wiped His feet with her hair, which was her ornament, glory, and pride. Christ is the object of their ministry, and their offerings and sacrifices bring out the sweet savor that fills the house of God.

[Verses 4-8] Judas Iscariot represents fake Christians who steal from God. As Judas was closely tied to Jesus Christ, these people hitch themselves to Christian organizations and ride the Christian wave to prosperity. They call themselves Christians, but God disagrees. They really are the devil's children, just as Judas was a devil. Read *John 6:70*. They infiltrate churches and operate under the pretense of good works, such as caring for the poor and afflicted. They are active in charitable events, but really are thieves who have their hands in the treasury. They often preach a prosperity gospel to rob people of their hard-earned money and life savings. They also sell self-help programs to build up self-esteem and feelings of self-worth that are powerless to transform lives. Keep the following in mind and you will not be taken by these con artists:

1. God never promises prosperity and comfort to believers in this world. Instead, He promises the fellowship of Christ's sufferings. *2Timothy 3:12 Yea, and all that will live godly in Christ Jesus shall suffer persecution.*

2. [Verse 7] Mary cared for the Lord's body, whereas Judas pretended to care for the poor. Real worshippers care for the Lord's body, which is the church. Charlatans steal from the church.

3. [Verse 8] Charity is a good practice, but don't let these charlatans play with your emotions and talk you out of your savings to help the poor and needy. There will always be poor people in this world. Many poor people are rich in faith, which is far better than those who are rich in worldly goods. The poor may also be happier and sleep better, not being burdened with stuff.

Pause for a moment to reflect on how the King of Kings will find you when He returns. Just as Jesus returned to visit Lazarus, He will return to check on all His beloved children. Will He find you like Lazarus, as a new believer desiring the sincere milk of the word that you may grow thereby? Read *1Peter 2:1-3*. Will He find you faithfully serving the church like Martha? Will He find you a faithful worshipper like Mary? Consider how long it might have taken Mary to save up to purchase the pound of spikenard oil that she liberally used on Jesus. God forbid that He would find you like Judas—not necessarily stealing money, but wasting precious time in self-serving.

[Verse 9] The curious Jews, who came to see Jesus and the resurrected Lazarus, represent lost people who are curious about miracles. For some, God may be working in their hearts and is in the process of drawing them to Christ. They want to see evidence of spiritual birth. To them, seeing is believing. For this reason, it is

Chapter 12 – King of Israel

important for Christians to keep a good testimony. Also, don't underestimate the power of new believers in attracting people to Christ. People generally are attracted to babies.

[Verses 10-11] The chief priests represent religious zealots who are anti-Jesus and anti-Christians. Their hatred will boil over and drive them to harm Christians when they perceive many people leaving their religions to believe in Jesus Christ. In verse 19, the Pharisees said, *"Behold, the world is gone after him,"* referring to Jesus. The Pharisees had decided to kill Jesus in the foregoing chapter. Now they wanted to also kill Lazarus. Consider, what did Lazarus do? Nothing, other than resurrect to life and sit with Jesus. But his powerful testimony drew many to Christ. Verse 11 says, *"By reason of him many of the Jews went away, and believed on Jesus."* Below are the reasons why the world will persecute you:

1. Your new life in Christ is a threat to the religions of the world because they are powerless to forgive sins and raise the dead to life. Read *2Corinthians 2:14-17*. Definitely don't expect the world to congratulate and applaud you for making the right choice to follow and obey Christ.

2. Born-again believers are not of the world. *John 15:18 If the world hate you, ye know that it hated me before it hated you. (19) If ye were of the world, the world would love his own: but because ye are not of the world, but I have chosen you out of the world, therefore the world hateth you. (20) Remember the word that I said unto you, The servant is not greater than his lord. If they have persecuted me, they will also persecute you; if they have kept my saying, they will keep yours also. (21) But all these things will they do unto you for my name's sake, because they know not him that sent me.* Read *2Timothy 3:12, 1Peter 3:10-17*.

The Book of John

I cannot figure out if the highly educated chief priests and Pharisees were smart or stupid. Many Jews saw and testified that Jesus raised Lazarus from the dead. Shouldn't they run to Jesus and beg, "Even more give us this life," instead of wanting to kill Him? Also, what good is killing a dead man who was just raised to life? As many times as they kill, Jesus can still raise the person back to life. See how religion and tradition can blind people to the point they become stupid?

[Verses 12-15] The attendees of the feast who heard Jesus was coming to Jerusalem went forth to hail Him as King with palm branches and shouted, *"Hosanna: Blessed is the King of Israel that cometh in the name of the Lord."* They represent people who will receive Jesus Christ as King. Following is why it is smart to receive Him as King when you hear He is coming:

1. The Bible says Jesus is coming again. Now that you've heard He is coming, will you hail Him as King in your life? Remember the parable of the 10 virgins in *Matthew 25:1-13*? Don't be like the five foolish virgins who took lamps, but not oil to meet the Bridegroom, and they were shut out. (Oil is a type of the Holy Spirit of God.)

2. At present, Jesus wants to enter into the Jerusalem of your heart by riding a young ass colt—gently, slowly, and meekly. For those who reject Him, His next coming is on a fierce white horse, and they will face His two-edged sword. *Read Revelation 19:11-16*.

[Verse 16] The disciples were learners. They were ministers in training. (See the "Lambs and sheep need to be fed" section in Chapter 21 for what it means to be a disciple of Jesus Christ.) At first, they did not understand the prophecies of Christ riding into Jerusalem or His crucifixion. But when Christ was raised from the dead and ascended into heaven, they had their "aha" moment and understood that things happened exactly according to the scriptures.

The key phrase is *"these things were written of him, and that they had done these things unto him."* The prophecies of Christ's birth, crucifixion, burial, and resurrection were written hundreds of years before He was born, and everything happened as prophesied. *Matthew 5:18 For verily I say unto you, Till heaven and earth pass, one jot or one tittle shall in no wise pass from the law, till all be fulfilled.* Read also *Matthew 24:35*.

One of the key things that my discipler impressed upon me was that the word of God is truth and is absolutely infallible. He said, "You can take it to the bank." Now that I have a better command of the Bible, I can whole heartedly say "amen" to that. And I will pass the same on to you. I pray that God would open the eyes of your understanding that you also would enjoy the "aha" moments and know that the word of God is truth, believable, and worthy of your consecration.

If the prophecies of Jesus' first coming were fulfilled (despite the crazy and outrageous odds), what about the prophecies of His second coming? Did you know the Bible has more to say about His second coming than His first?

[Verses 17-18] The people who witnessed Lazarus' resurrection represent the evangelists. According to *John 11:45*, *"Then many of the Jews which came to Mary, and had seen the things which Jesus did, believed on him."* They became evangelists and their testimonies of the miracle drew people to Christ.

Every Christian should be an evangelist. You may not be Billy Graham, but at a minimum, you need to be able to share your testimony with the people whom God sends your way. A testimony simply consists of three parts: how life was before Jesus, how you met Jesus, and how life is since you received Jesus as Lord and

The Book of John

Savior. See the Apostle Paul's example in *Acts 26*. Remember, your testimony is powerful in introducing people to Christ. If you don't have a testimony, perhaps it is time to search your heart and face the uneasy question, "Are you truly saved?" Review "What must I do to be saved" in Chapter 3.

[Verses 20-23] The Greeks who desired to see Jesus represent Gentiles, who are drawn by God. Read *1Corinthians 1:22-24*. They asked Philip to take them to Jesus. Because Gentile seekers had no precedence, Philip consulted with his townsman, Andrew, and they both went and told Jesus. What followed was an interesting answer from Jesus. Instead of "Yes," or "No," Jesus said, *"The hour is come, that the Son of man should be glorified."* He essentially said, "It is time for me to die." This signifies that the Gentiles would know Jesus through His death and resurrection.

Also, encoded in verses 20-22 is Israel's initial failure and eventual success as a light to the Gentiles. When the Greeks requested to see Jesus, Philip did not take them directly to Jesus. This represents Israel's initial failure to fulfill her mission. Read *Romans 2:17-24*. But Philip and Andrew eventually took the Greeks' petition to Jesus. This represents Israel's eventual success in fulfilling her mission. Read *Isaiah 42:6, Isaiah 49:1-6, Isaiah 60:1-5*.

[Verses 42-43] The chief rulers who believed in Jesus, but withheld their confessions represent closet Christians. These rulers were fearful of being put out of the synagogue and losing the praise of men. Verse 43 says, *"For they loved the praise of men more than the praise of God."*

Speaking of fear, there are regions in the world where a confession of Jesus Christ (including baptism) and the outward expression of traditional conservative Christian values will certainly result in persecution. It may be from family members, villagers, or governments. Believers are vilified, treated as bigots, and driven underground in the same way that homosexuals once were.

Chapter 12 – King of Israel

Common threats include bodily harm and denial of privileges, including the right to work. The threat of persecution may cause believers in these regions to be closet Christians. This is a sensitive matter. If you belong to this category, may God grant you the wisdom to handle your situation. Following are some points to consider:

1. Fear God and not man. *Luke 12:4 And I say unto you my friends, Be not afraid of them that kill the body, and after that have no more that they can do. (5) But I will forewarn you whom ye shall fear: Fear him, which after he hath killed hath power to cast into hell; yea, I say unto you, Fear him. (6) Are not five sparrows sold for two farthings, and not one of them is forgotten before God? (7) But even the very hairs of your head are all numbered. Fear not therefore: ye are of more value than many sparrows. (8) Also I say unto you, Whosoever shall confess me before men, him shall the Son of man also confess before the angels of God: (9) But he that denieth me before men shall be denied before the angels of God.* Also read *1Corinthians 1:25*.

2. Reduce the likelihood of persecution by doing good to your persecutors. Bless them that persecute you. When the Jews wanted to stone Jesus, consider His answer in *John 10:32, "Jesus answered them, Many good works have I shewed you from my Father; for which of those works do ye stone me? (33) The Jews answered him, saying, For a good work we stone thee not; but for blasphemy; and because that thou, being a man, makest thyself God."* Also read *1Peter 3:13, Matthew 5:43-48*.

3. Consider Joseph of Arimathaea, who was an honorable counselor, a person of character and distinction, and in an office of public trust. He was also a secret disciple of

Jesus, because he feared the Jews. In the end, Joseph came forward, begged for the body of Jesus from Pilate, and provided the burial services. Read *Mark 15:42-46, John 19:38*.

4. Consider Nicodemus, who came to Jesus by night in chapter 3. He was an ecclesiastical ruler of the Jews, a member of the Sanhedrim, and a master of Israel. He too feared the Jews. He tried to defend Jesus in *John 7:50-52*, but received a backlash from his peers, the chief priests, and the Pharisees. In the end, he too came out of the closet and provided the spices for Jesus' burial. Read *John 19:39-40*. (If you are a closet Christian, you need to come out sometime.)

Lessons on Fruitfulness and Glory

[Verses 23-28] When the Greeks honored Jesus by inquiring after Him with a longing desire to see and speak with Him, He knew His appointed time to be glorified had arrived. Jesus explained His death to the disciples with a similitude, and at the same time taught them an important lesson on fruitfulness and glory.

1. You must die to self.
   - *"Except a corn of wheat"*—Like a corn of wheat, you have the capacity to be fruitful.
   - *"fall into the ground and die, it abideth alone"*— Here are three things that will prevent you from being fruitful:
     o Pride. Instead, you must fall by lowering or humbling yourself.
     o Non-commitment. You must not only fall to the ground, but *"into the ground"*— absolutely committed with no latitude; all

Chapter 12 – King of Israel

bridges are burned and there is no turning back.
- o Not dying to self.
- *"but if it die, it bringeth forth much fruit"* —Death is the doorway to fruitfulness and glory. It is a paradox, but nature shows it works. The "if" denotes a choice that you must make concerning dying to self. Something is wrong if you don't have the desire to be spiritually fruitful.

2. You must appraise your life for the cause of Christ.
    - *"He that loveth his life shall lose it"* —If you are so in love with this present temporal life and take great care to preserve and protect it, unwilling to risk it for the cause of Christ, then you are deceived. You have no power to secure your life, which is like a vapor that can go away at any moment. Then what eternal fruit do you have to show? Read *Romans 6:21, Luke 12:16-21, James 4:14.*
    - *"he that hateth his life in this world shall keep it unto life eternal"* —On the other hand, if you live your life for the cause of Christ, then you will get to keep it, for God will preserve your life and make you fruitful. This is yet another paradox, which to unbelievers is a stone of stumbling.

3. You must serve the Lord Jesus Christ.
    - *"If any man serve me, let him follow me"* —You must decide if you will serve self or the Lord Jesus Christ. To serve Christ, He must be preeminent, and you must follow His methods and prescriptions. His path goes through Calvary. It is impossible to follow Him till you die to self and resign your will to the will of

God. Read the section "What does it mean to follow Jesus?" in Chapter 1.
- *"and where I am, there shall also my servant be: if any man serve me, him will my Father honour"*—The reward of serving and following Jesus is that you will be in His presence and receive immortal honor from the Father. Because man was created to live and fellowship with God, your joy will be fulfilled when you are with the King of Kings in His glory. Even Jesus, *"For the joy that was set before him endured the cross, despising the shame, and is set down at the right hand of the throne of God,"* according to Hebrews 12:2.

4. You must fulfill your mission.
    - *"Now is my soul troubled; and what shall I say? Father, save me from this hour"*—This is where the rubber meets the road. All your wishes and talks of dying to self and serving the Lord Jesus will come down to whether or not you will fulfill the mission that God has given you, especially when under persecution. Talk is cheap, as they say. Life as a minister is not a bowl of cherries.
    - *"but for this cause came I unto this hour"*—Did you know you exist for the cause of the Kingdom of God? God gets double glory when you fulfill the mission He gave you, according to verse 28.

Lessons from the Last Call to the Jews

[Verses 29-30] Jesus, knowing the hour of His suffering had arrived, gave the Jews a last call to receive Him as Messiah. In complete submission to the Father's will, Jesus petitioned the

Chapter 12 – King of Israel

Father to glorify His name. The Father expressly answered with a voice from heaven, saying, "*I have both glorified it, and will glorify it again.*" (The name of God was glorified in the life of Jesus and would be glorified in His sufferings and death.) The voice was yet again a witness to the unbelieving Jews who were with Jesus. It was for their sakes in order that they would believe that Jesus was the Sent One of the Father. The Jews heard it, but unfortunately they didn't perceive it. Some said it thundered, while others said an angel spoke to Jesus. Compare this to the Father's witness when Jesus was transfigured on the mount. A voice out of the cloud said, "*This is my beloved Son, in whom I am well pleased; hear ye him.*" The disciples heard it and fell on their faces in fear.

[Verses 31-33] Seeing that the unbelieving Jews didn't get the message, Jesus clearly explained that He would be crucified and His death would accomplish the following two things:

1. The judgment of this world—His death on the cross is the judgment of this world, and those who refuse His salvation remain in sin and condemnation. Read *Matthew 20:28, 1Timothy 2:6*. The judgment begins with the "*prince of this world*" (Satan), who will be defeated and cast out. Satan is a squatter, who has usurped a dominion over the world and has great power and efficacy in the hearts of the children of disobedience. He destroys them with sin and death. Jesus' resurrection conquered sin and death, and those who believe in Him are passed from death to life. Sin no longer has dominion over them. Read *John 5:24, Romans 6*.

2. The expansion of God's kingdom—His crucifixion on the cross ("*if I be lifted up from the earth*") is the fulfillment of the Brazen Serpent prophecy. Read *Numbers 21:4-9*. In Moses' days, all who were bitten by the fiery serpent were required to look upon the brazen serpent on the

pole to be healed. Christ, being made sin for the world, was nailed and hung on a cross. And all who come to Him will be healed spiritually. Hence, He will draw all men (Jews and Gentiles) to Himself.

[Verses 34-36] When Jesus said, *"If I be lifted up from the earth,"* the unbelieving Jews thought they had found a discrepancy and challenged Him by saying, *"How sayest thou, The Son of man must be lifted up?"* This is because Jesus had declared Himself as the *"Son of man"* (one of the titles of the Messiah) in the context of dying in verse 23 and *John 3:14*. In their minds, this was inconsistent with scripture, as the Messiah was not supposed to die, but be *"a priest for ever after the order of Melchizedek"* and *"his dominion is an everlasting dominion, which shall not pass away, and his kingdom that which shall not be destroyed."* Read *Psalms 110:4, Psalms 21:4, Psalms 45:6, Psalms 61:6, Psalms 72:17, Psalms 89:29, 36-37, Daniel 2:44, Daniel 7:13-14*.

With that, they tauntingly asked, *"Who is this Son of man?"* In other words, "We know the real Son of man, but who is this pretender?" They were willingly ignorant of the scripture, which also speaks of the Messiah's sufferings and death. However, He was not to see corruption, and was to rise again, ascend on high, sit at the right hand of God, and rule till all his enemies become his footstool. Read *Daniel 9:26, Isaiah 53:12, Psalms 16:10, Psalms 49:9, Psalms 110:1*.

Instead of debating these fools or answering according to their folly, Jesus cautioned them of their rapidly shrinking window of opportunity for salvation, because the Light would not be with them much longer. Thereafter, Jesus departed and hid Himself from them. This action is consistent with God when He is angry. Consider *Deuteronomy 31:17, "Then my anger shall be kindled against them in that day, and I will forsake them, and I will hide my face from them, and they shall be devoured, and many evils and troubles shall*

Chapter 12 – King of Israel

befall them; so that they will say in that day, Are not these evils come upon us, because our God is not among us?"

One may continue to reject Jesus Christ, but make no mistake, there will be a point when the long-suffering God will desert a person. At that time, it is up to the person to figure out the truth and salvation, which he will not be able to find, because he is in darkness. Smart people want God to appear to them, not to depart from them. Harden not your heart toward Jesus. This may be your last call.

[Verses 37-41] Even though Jesus had done so many miracles before the Jews, they still would not believe in Him. Their disbelief and impenitence did not set aside the purposes of God. On the contrary, it fulfilled the prophecies of the prophet Isaiah, particularly *Isaiah 53:1* and *Isaiah 6:9-13*. Because of their disbelief and prevailing hardness, *"God hath given them the spirit of slumber, eyes that they should not see, and ears that they should not hear,"* until they are cut down to the nub by the antichrist (only a remnant will survive), and they mourn and repent, and call on Him whom they have pierced. Read *Romans 11:8-10, Zechariah 12:10*. The judgment is very obvious. Recently a Jewish person said to me, "We are Jews. One thing we don't do is believe in Jesus. That is the red line." At present, the Jews simply cannot believe, because previously they would not. In the mean time, the Gentiles are benefiting from the fallout, because salvation has come to them. What is so clear to the Gentiles through the eyes of faith, the Jews simply cannot see.

Israel's judgment is a pattern for all who refuse to accept Jesus Christ as Savior. One's disbelief does not thwart the purposes of God. God has nothing to lose. He gets glory from believers who worship and adore Him, as well as from unbelievers in their doom. The choice is very clear, unless one's mind is blinded by the devil. Read *2Corinthians 4:3-4*.

The Book of John

[Verses 42-43] Even though Israel as a nation did not receive Jesus as the Messiah, God will never be without witnesses. Many of the chief rulers believed in Jesus, albeit they were closet believers, primarily because they were afraid of being put out of the synagogue, and they loved the praise of men more than the praise of God. These struggled between their convictions and corruptions.

[Verses 44-50] Jesus made a last public discourse to deliver His farewell sermon. He clearly laid out the following:

- Certainty of life for believers.
    - *"He that believeth on me, believeth not on me, but on him that sent me. And he that seeth me seeth him that sent me."* Believers are connected to God through faith in Jesus Christ because:
        a) He is the Sent One of the Father.
        b) He is the only doorway to the Father – *John 14:6*.
        c) He is the only mediator between God and man – *1Timothy 2:5*.

    - *"I am come a light into the world, that whosoever believeth on me should not abide in darkness."* Believers are spiritually enlightened, are able to discern spiritual truth, and see the path of life, because Jesus is the Light of God. Unbelievers *"walketh in darkness knoweth not whither he goeth,"* according to *John 12:35*. They go through life stumbling around and falling into many foolish and hurtful lusts.

- Certainty of death for unbelievers.
    - *"He that rejecteth me, and receiveth not my words, hath one that judgeth him: the word that I have spoken, the same shall judge him in the*

last day." Let not unbelievers think they can escape the righteous judgment of God and eternal punishment by rejecting such a great offer of salvation.

Prophecies

The prophecies in this chapter reveal that Jesus will return to visit the Jews at the end of 6,000 years. The Jews will be in the house of misery (Bethany), because of the antichrist. But they will receive, serve, and worship Jesus as portrayed by Lazarus, Martha, and Mary. Jesus will reenter Jerusalem and will be welcomed as the King of Israel. The religious rulers of Israel will receive Him as their Messiah. However, this does not happen before Israel first rejects Jesus and suffers for its sins.

- *John 12:1 Then Jesus six days before the passover came to Bethany, where Lazarus was which had been dead, whom he raised from the dead.*
  The six days gives us the 6,000 years, for one day is with the Lord as a thousand years. Read *2Peter 3:8*. The name Bethany means "house of misery." The Lord Jesus will find the Jews suffering in the house of misery, being persecuted by the antichrist. The Lord Jesus will revive the Jews, just as He revived Lazarus.

- *John 12:2 There they made him a supper; and Martha served: but Lazarus was one of them that sat at the table with him. (3) Then took Mary a pound of ointment of spikenard, very costly, and anointed the feet of Jesus, and wiped his feet with her hair: and the house was filled with the odour of the ointment.*
  The Jews will receive, fellowship, serve, and worship Jesus.

The Book of John

- *John 12:12 On the next day much people that were come to the feast, when they heard that Jesus was coming to Jerusalem, (13) Took branches of palm trees, and went forth to meet him, and cried, Hosanna: Blessed is the King of Israel that cometh in the name of the Lord.*
  Jesus will be welcomed as the King of Israel when He reenters Jerusalem.

- *John 12:42 Nevertheless among the chief rulers also many believed on him.*
  The religious rulers of Israel will receive Jesus as their Messiah.

- *John 12:37 But though he had done so many miracles before them, yet they believed not on him.*
  The above will not happen before Israel first rejects Jesus as their Messiah.

- *John 12:36 While ye have light, believe in the light, that ye may be the children of light. These things spake Jesus, and departed, and did hide himself from them.*
  Because of Israel's rejection, the Lord Jesus removed Himself from them for 2,000 years. The focus shifted to the Gentiles, who in the mean time, are benefiting from the fallout.

Summary

I was amazed at how quickly Jesus went from being hailed as the King of Israel to being rejected as the Messiah and soon crucified. There was no time for Him to bask in glory. The next thing He knew, *"The hour is come, that the Son of man should be glorified."*

It reminds me of the sun in *Ecclesiastes 1:5*, which portrays the life of a person. It quickly goes from sunrise to sunset. The glory days, the days of our strength, are so short that we have no time to be idle. We must make the best use of our days so that our lives matter for the Kingdom of God. The window of opportunity for fruit bearing is narrow, and the yield is often reduced by our inability to die to self. We serve the King of Kings, therefore, let us be careful to follow Him, both in the exercise of duty and grace.

Another thing that struck me was how longsuffering Jesus was in enduring the contradiction of sinners. He told them who He was, reached out to them with good works and miracles, gave ample witnesses, and pleaded with them. Yet they wanted to kill Him. Indeed, longsuffering is the second characteristic of God, according to *Exodus 34:6-7*. Jesus Christ mirrors the longsuffering of His Father.

13 – Servant

Historical Synopsis

Jesus, having completed His public ministry, with the time of His death at hand, was not absorbed with His awful prospect, but spent His remaining days with His loved ones. He washed the disciples' feet. He also ate the Passover with the disciples and revealed who would betray Him. Thereafter, Jesus commanded the disciples to love one another as the hallmark of their discipleship.

This chapter can be outlined as such:

    I.   Jesus washed the disciples' feet – *John 13:1-17*
    II.   Jesus revealed Judas as the betrayer – *John 13:18-30*
    III. Jesus commanded brotherly love – *John 13:31-35*
    IV. Jesus foretold Peter's denial of Him – *John 13:36-38*

Chapter 13 - Servant

Key Spiritual Lessons

Beginning with this chapter, Jesus' focus shifted from convincing the unbelieving Jews to comforting and consoling His believers prior to His departure to the Father in heaven. It was necessary, because it wasn't time for believers to follow Him to heaven. Verse 36b says, *"Whither I go, thou canst not follow me now; but thou shalt follow me afterwards."* In the mean time, they would be required to do the work of ministry without the good Shepherd, who loved and protected them, cast out devils, healed the sick, opened the eyes and ears of the blind and deaf, resurrected the dead, and fed thousands.

Jesus' examples of humility, mission focus, and love in this chapter give the keys to happiness in ministry:

    I.   Overcome pride with humility – *John 13:1-17*
    II. Overcome betrayal by focusing on the mission – *John 13:18-32*
    III. Overcome infightings with love – *John 13:33-38*

There were two notable suppers at the end of Jesus' life—the supper at Simon the lepers' house in Bethany and the last supper in Jerusalem. The Apostle John did not explicitly mention which supper it was in verse 2. At first glance, the timeline in verse 1, *"before the feast of the Passover"* seems to indicate the supper was not the last supper. The cross reference to *Matthew 26:2* suggests that the supper was two days before the Passover and therefore, the washing of the disciples' feet could not have been during the last supper.

Furthermore, *John 13:2* says the devil was put in Judas' heart to betray Jesus. If this was the last supper, Judas had quite an impossible task to leave the supper to negotiate the betrayal with the religious rulers, look for the perfect opportunity to betray Jesus

Chapter 13 - Servant

(*"in the absence of the multitude"* – Luke 22:6), and execute the betrayal that same night.

To be sure which supper this is, let's compare scripture with scripture by laying out *Matthew 26, Mark 14, Luke 22,* and *John 13* as follows.

The events that we need to consider and place in the right sequence are: the religious rulers' plot to kill Jesus, the supper in Bethany, Judas' negotiation with the religious rulers over the price of Jesus, and the last supper in Jerusalem.

The plot to kill Jesus was solidified among the religious rulers two days before the Passover feast.

Matthew 26	*Mark 14*	*Luke 22*	*John 13*
1 And it came to pass, when Jesus had finished all these sayings, he said unto his disciples, 2 Ye know that after two days is the feast of the passover, and the Son of man is betrayed to be crucified. 3 Then assembled together the chief priests, and the scribes, and the elders of the people, unto the palace of the high priest, who was called Caiaphas, 4 And consulted that they might take Jesus by	1 After two days was the feast of the passover, and of unleavened bread: and the chief priests and the scribes sought how they might take him by craft, and put him to death. 2 But they said, Not on the feast day, lest there be an uproar of the people.	1 Now the feast of unleavened bread drew nigh, which is called the Passover. 2 And the chief priests and scribes sought how they might kill him; for they feared the people.	1 Now before the feast of the passover, when Jesus knew that his hour was come that he should depart out of this world unto the Father, having loved his own which were in the world, he loved them unto the end.

subtilty, and kill him. *5 But they said, Not on the feast day, lest there be an uproar among the people.*			

Next, Matthew and Mark recorded the supper at Simon the leper's house in Bethany. We know that this supper was not the last supper since it did not take place in Jerusalem, and may or may not have chronologically followed the above plot to kill Jesus. *Matthew 26:6* begins with "Now" and has a paragraph marker, which suggests a new scene. According to *John 12:1*, Jesus and His disciples arrived in Bethany six days before the Passover. It is unclear when they made Him the supper. But was this the supper at which He washed the disciple's feet?

Next, Matthew, Mark, and Luke recorded that Judas went to contract with the religious rulers to betray Jesus. It was the break the religious rulers were looking for after their unanimous decision to kill Jesus two days before the Passover.

When did Judas go to the religious rulers?

- It had to be within two days before the Passover.
- According to *Luke 22:3-8*, the devil entered into Judas, and he went to the religious rulers before the last supper and not the night of the last supper. (This makes sense, because Judas needed time to make a deal with the religious rulers and look for the perfect opportunity to betray Jesus. [*Matthew 26:16, Mark 14:11, Luke 22:6*]) But wait, *John 13:2* says the devil entered into Judas after a supper. Which supper was this and how many times did the devil enter Judas?

Chapter 13 - Servant

Matthew 26	Mark 14	Luke 22	John 13
14 ¶ Then one of the twelve, called Judas Iscariot, went unto the chief priests, 15 And said unto them, What will ye give me, and I will deliver him unto you? And they covenanted with him for thirty pieces of silver. 16 <u>And from that time he sought opportunity to betray him.</u>	10 ¶ And Judas Iscariot, one of the twelve, went unto the chief priests, to betray him unto them. 11 And when they heard it, they were glad, and promised to give him money. <u>And he sought how he might conveniently betray him.</u>	3 ¶ Then entered Satan into Judas surnamed Iscariot, being of the number of the twelve. 4 And he went his way, and communed with the chief priests and captains, how he might betray him unto them. 5 And they were glad, and covenanted to give him money. 6 <u>And he promised, and sought opportunity to betray him unto them in the absence of the multitude.</u> 7 ¶ Then came the day of unleavened bread, when the passover must be killed. 8 And he sent Peter and John, saying, Go and prepare us the passover, that we may eat...	2 And supper being ended, the devil having now put into the heart of Judas Iscariot, Simon's son, to betray him; 3 Jesus knowing that the Father had given all things into his hands, and that he was come from God, and went to God; 4 He riseth from supper, and laid aside his garments; and took a towel, and girded himself. 5 After that he poureth water into a bason, and began to wash the disciples' feet, and to wipe them with the towel wherewith he was girded.

If the supper in *John 13:2* was the supper at Simon the leper's house in Bethany, then Jesus washed the disciples' feet there, because the sentence ends in verse 4.

239

The Book of John

If the supper in *John 13:2* was the last supper in Jerusalem, then *John 13:1* must be interpreted as a foreknowledge statement, otherwise its cross reference in *Matthew 26:2* suggests that the supper in *John 13:2* was two days before the Passover and therefore couldn't be the last supper. In paraphrasing *John 13:1-2*, Jesus knew ahead of time that this Passover would be His last and that He would be betrayed, killed, and would return to the Father. And now the time had come, the last supper had ended and the devil was put into Judas' heart to execute the betrayal.

As to the number of times the devil entered into Judas, it was one time in *Luke 22:3* to drive him to negotiate the betrayal and another time in *John 13:2* to drive him to execute the betrayal.

Considering the above, I think the likelihood is that the supper at Simon the leper's house was on the day Jesus arrived in Bethany, which was six days before the Passover. (This is consistent with the culture where they treat the person on the day of arrival.) Following this was the religious rulers' decision to kill Jesus, which was two days before the Passover. Then Judas contracted with the religious rulers to betray Jesus. And finally, the last supper.

I believe the account in *John 13* is the account of the last supper and Jesus washed the disciples' feet there.

Overcome Pride with Humility

[Verses 3-5] Knowing the impending suffering and the person who would betray Him, Jesus, being Lord, Master, and God the Son, could simply have chosen not to endure the cross and straightway returned to the Father in heaven. Instead, He laid aside His garment (figure of authority – *Psalms 104:1-6*) and put on humility. He took upon Him the form of a servant, girded Himself with a towel, poured water into a basin, and washed the disciples' feet.

It is important to note that the physical washing of feet is not an ordinance commanded to be observed by the local church like baptism and the Lord's Supper. What should be observed is the example of humility and love that Jesus demonstrated when He washed the disciples' feet.

The Apostle John recorded four things that Jesus knew in verses 1-3.

- Jesus knew that He would soon depart out of this world unto the Father.
- Jesus knew the countdown had begun with His betrayal, which was set in motion the moment the devil entered Judas' heart.
- Jesus knew *"the Father had given all things into his hands, and that he was come from God, and went to God."*

Believers can draw parallels to the things that Jesus knew in verses 1-3. We know that we will be with God in heaven when we depart out of this world—absent from the body and present with the Lord. What an incredible promise and comfort. The countdown for us to leave this world has begun and our time is ticking away. We should also know that God has blessed us with all spiritual blessings in heavenly places in Christ. Wow, should we be lifted up with pride? No, the right thing to do is to emulate Jesus. We should put on humility and be servants. This concept is foreign nowadays in the entitlement culture that we have degraded into. It is always, "What do I get?" instead of, "How do I serve?"

Consider the acts of the Lord:

- *"He riseth from supper"*—A master would sit down and dine while being served, but Jesus rose up to serve. *Luke*

The Book of John

22:27 For whether is greater, he that sitteth at meat, or he that serveth? is not he that sitteth at meat? but I am among you as he that serveth. We should be given to serving.

- *"and laid aside his garments"*—We need to lay aside our garments of pride. Put on humility and be meek and lowly in heart like the Lord. *1Peter 5:5b Yea, all of you be subject one to another, and be clothed with humility: for God resisteth the proud, and giveth grace to the humble. (6) Humble yourselves therefore under the mighty hand of God, that he may exalt you in due time."* Read *James 4:10, Philippians 2:5-11*.

- *"and took a towel, and girded himself"*—We need to gird ourselves with a towel and serve, just as *"the Son of man came not to be ministered unto, but to minister, and to give his life a ransom for many."* Jesus wiped the disciples' feet with the towel that was attached to His body, essentially transferring their dirt to His body. We must do the work of ministry, including the work of the lowliest servant, and not be afraid of getting dirty. (The word "towel" appears in the Bible only twice, both are in this chapter.)

- *"After that he poureth water into a bason, and began to wash the disciples' feet"*— What does it mean to pour water into a basin and wash others' feet? We are not walking on the dusty streets of Palestine in sandals. The common application is being helpful and doing acts of kindness to our brethren. But the true meaning is much more than that. Water represents the word of God and the basin represents us. It is sharing the word of God with fellow servants who are active in ministry, whose

Chapter 13 - Servant

beautiful feet take them places to preach the gospel of peace, so that they may be refreshed. Read *Romans 15:30-32, 1Timothy 1:16-18*. It is important for ministers to refresh each other often. Before we can wash others' feet, we must put on humility, be willing to serve, and be filled with the word of God.

[Verses 6-11] When Jesus was about to wash Peter's feet, Peter was surprised and astonished that the Son of the living God would offer to do such a thing for him. Peter did not understand the purpose and protested by saying, *"Thou shalt never wash my feet."* But when Jesus answered, *"If I wash thee not, thou hast no part with me,"* Peter was worried that he would lose his communion with Christ and was glad to submit, not only his feet, but also his hands and head. Then Jesus had to explain that the washing of the feet was not for salvation, and assured Peter that he had already been cleansed, and need not to be washed again, except for his feet. However, Jesus noted that not all the disciples were clean, referring to Judas, who would betray Him.

We must first be washed by Jesus (salvation) before we can wash others' feet (minister the word of God). It is pointless for the unsaved to share the word of God. The Bible says in *Proverbs 26:7* that a parable in the mouth of fools is like the legs of the lame, which are not equal. Salvation is a one-time event, but sanctification is on-going until we are eventually glorified. We should routinely wash our brethrens' feet. Read *1Timothy 5:10*. Those who are washed by Jesus must not refuse to be washed by the brethren.

[Verses 12-17] When Jesus had washed the disciples' feet, He put on His garment and sat down to reveal the mystery of His action and what they should learn from it. As Master and Lord, He had set an example of humility and love, so that they should practice the same on their brethren, and that no one should be too lofty for the task, because *"the servant is not greater than his lord."*

And since the Lord had done it, no one should be exempted from it either.

Jesus gives us the essential principles of leadership in *Matthew 20:25-28*. Ungodly leaders exercise dominion and lordly power over their subjects. In contrast, godly leaders minister to and serve their flock, and lead by example. *Mark 9:35 And he sat down, and called the twelve, and saith unto them, If any man desire to be first, the same shall be last of all, and servant of all.* A good leader is a servant-leader, like a good shepherd who takes good care of his sheep. Nothing is too low, difficult, or dirty for the leader to do. A leader who washes his subjects' feet is an awesome leader. I heard of an airline CEO who helped his baggage handlers load luggage into planes. A good husband is a servant-husband; a good wife is a servant-wife; a good manager is a servant-manager; a good president is a servant-president; a good pastor is a servant-pastor, and so forth. But a carnal ambitious leader uses and abuses others instead of serving them.

The best way to develop or groom someone, at home or at work, is to lead by example. This definitely applies to discipleship. Hypocrite leaders would say, "Do as I say and not as I do."

It is not enough to just know about servant-leadership. The benefit is reserved for the practitioners—*"happy are ye if ye do them."* To be happy or blessed in ministry, we must serve in lowliness and meekness, and forbear one another with longsuffering in love.

Side observations:

- [Verse 1] Jesus loved His own to the end. Do you know that the bond of the love of God is so strong that nothing can separate us from His love, which is in Christ Jesus? *Romans 8:38 For I am persuaded, that neither death, nor life, nor angels, nor principalities, nor powers, nor things present, nor things to come, (39) Nor height, nor depth, nor any other creature, shall be able to separate us from the love of God, which is in Christ Jesus our Lord.*

- [Verse 3] Jesus' deity is unquestionable, as He *"was come from God."* Jesus Christ is God the Son.

- [Verse 4, 12] Notice that Jesus put off His garment to serve and then put it back on after He was finished. This shows Jesus' first coming was as a servant, but He will return as the Lord of Lords.

Overcome Betrayal by Focusing on the Mission

Jesus conquered betrayal and secured eternal salvation for His believers by being humble and in full submission and obedience to the Father's will, without deviating from His design and commandments. Jesus spared nothing, even His life, in order to complete His mission.

We must be completely focused on fulfilling the ministry of reconciliation that God has committed to us, for which He sent us into the world as ambassadors for Christ. We must not be sidetracked by betrayals and backstabs that unfortunately happen in ministry. A pastor once told me, "You need a thick hide to be in ministry."

Verses 18-32 can be outlined as such:

- Betrayal prophesied – verses 18-20
- Betrayer revealed – verses 21-30
- Betrayal conquered – verses 31-32

[Verses 18-20] During the Passover supper, Jesus prophesied of His betrayal and offered the following purposes:

1. For the fulfillment of scripture. *Psalms 41:9 Yea, mine own familiar friend, in whom I trusted, which did eat of my bread, hath lifted up his heel against me.* Some scriptures have multiple fulfillments, and this is one of them. It applies not only to Judas, but also to the antichrist, who is soon to come. The antichrist is a complex person with ties to the core leadership of Israel. Read *Psalms 55*, especially verses 12-14. Like Judas in verse 29, no one will suspect that the antichrist's actions will result in a horrible betrayal of the Jews. The devil will also enter into the antichrist's body. Read *Revelation 13:1-8*.

2. For the strengthening of the disciples' faith. Verse 19 says, *"Now I tell you before it come, that, when it is come to pass, ye may believe that I am he."* When Christ's betrayal happened, the disciples were not to freak out, but know that Jesus was the Messiah and His word was truth. For us today, we have the privilege of knowing that it all happened according to the scriptures, and not a jot failed. The word of God is truth and Jesus Christ is God the Son. We are also seeing the unfolding of Bible prophecies in our generation, which should strengthen our faith.

Jesus also said, *"I know whom I have chosen"* in verse 18. According to *John 6:70*, He chose Judas, even though he was a devil—*"Have not I chosen you twelve, and one of you is a devil?"* Judas ministered with the real disciples. He looked and sounded like a Christian, and he was busy in ministry, but he was not a Christian. The wolf in sheep's clothing was with the sheep, and the Shepherd allowed it so that scripture might be fulfilled.

The lesson is that all who eat bread with Christ are not necessarily His. Are you sure you are a Christian? If God were to ask

Chapter 13 - Servant

you why He should let you into heaven, what would you say? Hint: there is only one right answer. Review "What must I do to be saved" in Chapter 3. A large group of people who flatter themselves to be Christians is in for a nightmare. *Matthew 7:21 Not every one that saith unto me, Lord, Lord, shall enter into the kingdom of heaven; but he that doeth the will of my Father which is in heaven. (22) Many will say to me in that day, Lord, Lord, have we not prophesied in thy name? and in thy name have cast out devils? and in thy name done many wonderful works? (23) And then will I profess unto them, I never knew you: depart from me, ye that work iniquity.* I pray you are not in this group. However, this scripture will be fulfilled, so sadly, there are people who will realize this nightmare. The number of people who claim to be Christians, but are not, could be so vast that I would not be surprised if church services go on like gangbusters after the rapture.

What about the people who believed in Jesus by the preaching of Judas? Verse 20 says, "*He that receiveth whomsoever I send receiveth me; and he that receiveth me receiveth him that sent me.*" If they believed in Jesus according to the word of God, their salvation was secure. Jesus would honor His word. I personally have sat under the teaching and preaching of a pastor who turned out to be a crook. The word of God is steadfast, even if it is delivered by a crook.

[Verses 21-30] Seeing the disciples didn't quite get His message in verse 18, Jesus made it plain to them by saying, "*One of you shall betray me.*" Then Jesus was troubled in His spirit. He was visibly distressed and emotional, perhaps even choked up when He said it, which showed His humanity. That got the disciples' attention. They were dumbfounded and looked at each other, wondering who among them would commit such a horrible iniquity. Then as the Apostle John leaned toward Jesus, he saw Peter motioning him to ask Jesus to reveal the traitor. When the inquiry was made, Jesus said, "*He it is, to whom I shall give a sop, when I have dipped it,"* and He gave it to Judas, who sat at arm's length from Him. Thereafter, Satan possessed Judas and filled his mind. Jesus basically gave him the green light to pursue his wicked design by saying, *"That thou doest, do quickly."* But the disciples weren't sure why Jesus sent Judas away. They thought that since he was in charge of the finances, Jesus might have asked him to get provisions for the feast, or to give something to the poor. It was night when Judas left the supper.

Following are the lessons:

1. A sop is a morsel of bread. It represents the word of God. It was probably dipped in oil, which is a type of the Holy Spirit of God.
    a. That little morsel of bread revealed Judas as the traitor. It doesn't take much truth to reveal sin and the sinner. All it takes is one verse. *Romans 3:23 For all have sinned, and come short of the glory of God.*
    b. Jesus knew His traitors from the beginning. He saw the end from the beginning. Nothing is hid from truth. Read *Isaiah 46:10, Psalms 19:1-6*. Don't even think you can betray God and get away with it. God is not mocked. Read *Galatians 6:7*.

2. God is supreme. He was in control of what Judas and the devil could or couldn't do. Nothing in the entire universe happens by chance. Everything goes according to His sovereign design and plan. God is in control, even when things seem to be out of control. Relax, God is still on the throne.

3. The devil possessed Judas, but he cannot possess born-again believers, because their bodies are the temple of

Chapter 13 - Servant

the Holy Ghost. Read *1Corinthians 3:16-17, 1Corinthians 6:19*. The bodies of unbelievers, however, are fair game for the devil.

[Verses 30-32] When Judas the traitor left the supper to execute the betrayal, Jesus could smell the victory and see the glory. His betrayal was literally hours away, when He would be tortured and killed. This may not sound right, but remember the paradox in Chapter 12, that death is the doorway to fruitfulness and glory? So, Jesus proclaimed *"Now is the Son of man glorified, and God is glorified in him. If God be glorified in him, God shall also glorify him in himself, and shall straightway glorify him."*

Following are the lessons:

1. As a man, Jesus Christ endured the cross, despised the shame, and went through the most horrific time in His life to secure the victory for the Kingdom of God by focusing on the joy and glory that He would have with the Father. Read *Hebrews 12:2, John 17:5*. What is preventing you from completing the mission that God has for you?

2. God the Father is glorified in Jesus Christ. In other words, God is not glorified outside of Jesus Christ. One who wishes to glorify God must worship Jesus Christ.

3. God the Father and the Son of man are inseparable. *"If God be glorified in him (Jesus Christ), God shall also glorify him (Jesus Christ) in himself."*

4. The word "glorify" is repeated five times in verses 30-31. Five is the number of death. The common saying, "No pain, no glory" should be modified to "No death, no glory." You must die to self before you can experience glory.

Overcome Infightings with Love

[Verses 33-38] With the affection of a good father, Jesus called His disciples *"little children."* The disciples knew and acknowledged Him as Lord and Master up to this point. But now, Jesus as a good Father, was about to embark on a long journey to prepare a better place for His children. To prepare them to face life without Him, He explained the following:

1. *"Yet a little while I am with you"*—In just a few days, Jesus would rise from death and ascend into heaven to be with the Father, and the disciples would see Him no more.

2. *"Ye shall seek me"*—After His departure, the disciples would miss Jesus for various reasons, such as guidance and protection.

3. *"Whither I go, ye cannot come"*—The disciples would want to be with Jesus, but they would not be able to follow Him to heaven right away. They would, however, eventually be with Him.

The message Jesus gave to the disciples was similar to the message He gave to the unbelieving Jews in *John 7:34-36*, but with one major difference. To the unbelieving Jews, He said, *"Ye shall seek me, and shall not find me."* Jesus did not say *"ye shall not find me"* to the disciples. He would be absent in body, but always present and available in spirit.

Again, as a good Father, who was about to die and leave His children behind, Jesus laid down His dying commandment that was based on an age-old commandment in *Leviticus 19:18b*, *"Thou shalt love thy neighbour as thyself."* The new, or rather renewed, commandment was, *"That ye love one another; as I have loved you, that ye also love one another."* Read *1John 2:7-11, 1John 3:23, 1Peter 1:22, Romans 13:8, Romans 12:10*.

- *"That ye love one another"*—The Greek word for love in this verse is "agapao" (ἀγαπάω), which is the same type of sacrificial love in *John 3:16, "For God so loved the world, that he gave his only begotten Son..."* We are commanded to sacrificially love one another.

- *"As I have loved you, that ye also love one another"*
    - The scale and depth of our love towards the brethren should be according to the love of Christ. This is a tall order. The key to living it is in *Romans 12:1-2*. Needless to say, we cannot fulfill this commandment if we do not die to self. Infightings among Christians destroy the unity that Christ bled to unite.
    - We also should not just love in word, but in deed and in truth. Read *1John 3:16-18*. We must not be big talkers like Peter, who chickened out and denied Jesus three times that night before the cock crowed.

Our sacrificial love for the brethren is the evidence of the work of grace that began in our hearts after salvation. It is a window by which lost people get a glimpse of the Kingdom of God—*"By this shall all men know that ye are my disciples, if ye have love one to another."* Brotherly love is the badge of Christ's disciples and the hallmark of discipleship. Read *1John 3:14, 1John 4:7-21*. In contrast, the way of the world is self-love where everyone is for himself. Read *2Timothy 3:1-5*. The world is tired of selfishness and is looking for love. I personally know of a student from France who accepted Jesus Christ as Savior because she witnessed the brotherly love among her Christian friends. She wanted the love that she knew she couldn't get from the world.

Summary

To be happy in ministry, we must serve with humility. We overcome betrayal in ministry by being completely focused on our mission as ambassadors for Christ and sacrificially loving the brethren.

14 – Way, Truth, Life

Historical Synopsis

In the foregoing chapter, Jesus gave His disciples three prophecies that rattled them to their core. He foretold His betrayal, His glorification (death), and Peter's denial in *John 13:18-19, 31-32, 36-38*. The disciples were troubled by the bad news, which they had to process in a short amount of time.

The disciples had abandoned everything and went all in with Jesus when they believed He was the Messiah. It had worked out well for them. They were on the famous and winning team. Their Chief performed one-of-a-kind miracles, cast out devils, defeated the Pharisees in debates, and so forth. They might have expected Him to deliver Israel from the Romans and set up a powerful and glorious kingdom. Suddenly, they were about to lose their Chief. Not surprisingly, they were troubled—shocked, confused, disappointed, saddened, feared, shamed, and doubted. They must have asked, "Did we make a bad decision in following Jesus? Is this really Him in whom we should believe? Why can't we follow Him to wherever He is going? What are we going to do without Him?"

Seeing that the disciples were traumatized, Jesus continued to comfort and prepare them for life without Him. He exhorted them to steadfastly believe in Him. He assured them of their eternal future and that He would return to receive them to heaven. He also bid them to keep His commandments, for in so doing, they would be comforted by His spiritual manifestation and by the Father. He would also send another Comforter, which was the Spirit of Truth, who would indwell them and abide with them forever. Finally, He promised them His peace, by which they might endure persecution and tribulation.

The general scope of this chapter is Jesus comforting His disciples before His crucifixion.

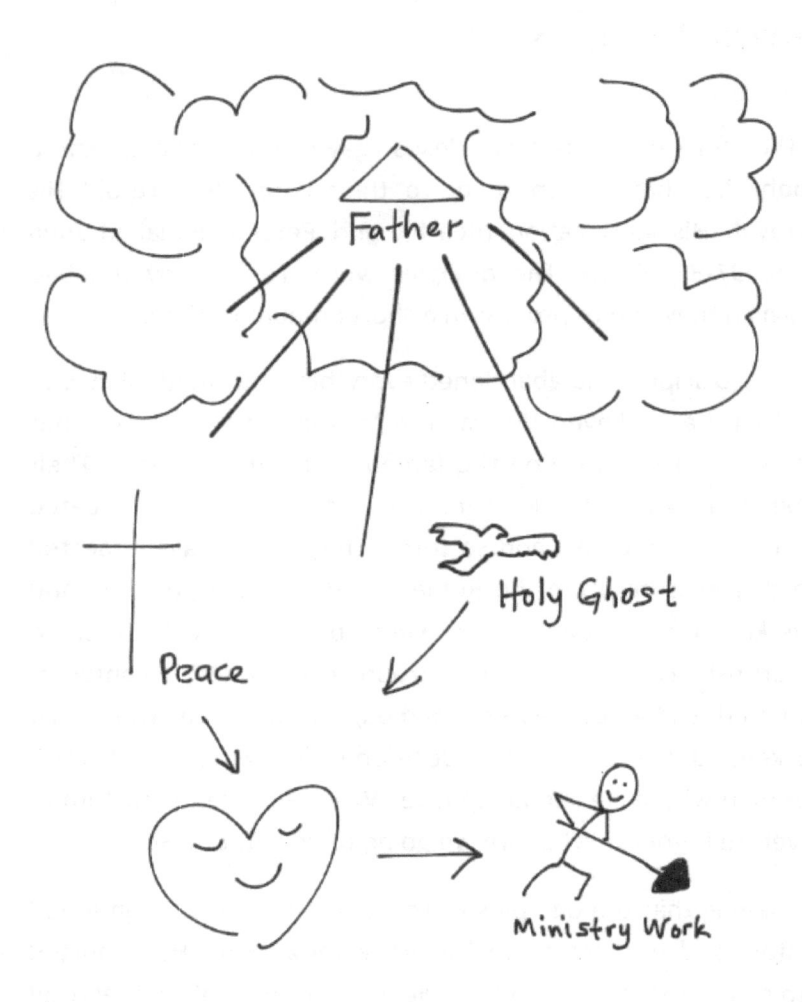

Chapter 14 – Way, Truth, Life

Key Spiritual Lessons

Jesus' return to heaven to be with the Father was not a retreat in defeat, but was according to design. It was a two-step grand strategy to win over the entire nation of Israel: 1) To provoke Israel to jealousy. Due to their disbelief, salvation would go to the Gentiles, according to *Romans 10:19-21, Romans 11:11*. 2) To let Israel experience the Great Tribulation because of their rejection, and to wait for their confession of sin and acceptance of Jesus Christ as their Messiah – *Hosea 5:15*.

What do we as believers do while waiting for Israel to get its act together? We must do the work of ministry without the bodily presence of the Lord Jesus Christ. Ministry is not only laborious, it is also dangerous work, especially in places that are hostile to Christianity. The world in general is anti-Christian, so there is no real safe place for ministry. But we must not be overcome by fear. This chapter teaches us how to overcome fear in ministry.

I. Check our belief – *John 14:1-14*
II. Check our love – *John 14:15-26*
III. Check our peace – *John 14:27-31*

Check Our Belief

[Verse 1] Jesus prescribed belief as the antidote for a troubled heart. He exhorted the disciples to exercise equal faith in God and in Him—*"ye believe in God, believe also in me."*

While doing the work of ministry, we may come across people, things, or events that trouble our hearts and threaten our lives. Even in these stormy circumstances, we may still experience the joy of faith, if we have a proper belief in God and in Jesus Christ as follows: (The word "believe" is used seven times in this chapter. Seven is the number of perfection.)

1. Believe that Jesus is equal to God – verse 1. Read *John 1:1-2,14, Romans 9:5, Colossians 2:9, 1Timothy 3:16, Hebrew 1:8, 1John 5:20*.
2. Believe that Jesus is in the Father, and the Father is in Jesus – verses 10-11.
3. Believe that Jesus went to the Father and will come again – verses 28-29.

If our belief is right, we can do the work of ministry with the following comforts:

1. Comfort of an eternal future with Jesus Christ in heaven.
2. Comfort of access to the Father.
3. Comfort of knowing the Father.
4. Comfort of an audience and help from heaven.

Comfort of an eternal future with Jesus Christ in heaven

[Verses 2-4] Mansions and streets of gold are some of the things many Christians hope for when they go to heaven. Songs and hymns are written of this hope. The chorus of "Mansion over the hilltop" goes like this:

> I've got a mansion just over the hilltop
> In that bright land where we'll never grow old
> And some day yonder we will never more wander
> But walk on streets that are purest gold

Bible believers debate whether or not there are mansions (as in large residential estates) in heaven. While both sides have compelling arguments, I don't think we can be dogmatic about this one way or the other. My bias, however, is toward no large residential estates. Following are my reasons:

Chapter 14 – Way, Truth, Life

1. The phrase *"Father's house"* refers to the nation of Israel (*Hosea 5:1*), which sets the context. This passage is not written to the church. Believers are not called Christians until *Acts 11:26*. Jesus had not died, so technically this is still Old Testament.

2. Mansions are not mentioned in the new heaven and new earth in *Revelation 21* and *22*.

3. In verse 3, Jesus said, *"And if I go and prepare a place for you, I will come again, and receive you unto myself"* instead of into their own place.

4. The Greek word for mansion, "μονή" (mon-ay'), is also translated as "abode" in verse 23. The best way to understand this is to swap the word "abode" with "mansion" as such: *"...we will come unto him, and make our abode* [mansion] *with him."* The mansions in heaven are not large residential estates. We are the mansions! Just as now, the body of our flesh is the temple of the Holy Ghost (*1Corinthians 6:19*), in the future, our glorified bodies are the mansions in which the Godhead will indwell. Another helpful reference is *2Corinthians 5:1*, *"For we know that if our earthly house of this tabernacle* [flesh body] *were dissolved, we have a building of God,* [glorified body] *an house not made with hands, eternal in the heavens."* Notice the *"building of God, an house not made with hands"* is not a piece of real estate in heaven, but the glorified body of the believer.

Since your glorified body does not require physical food or sleep, why would you need a large residential estate in heaven? Is it so that you can claim, "This is my piece of heaven and this is my mansion"? Or, do you plan to compare your lot size with the Joneses?

So, if there are no large residential estates in heaven, why did Jesus say *"I go to prepare a place for you"*? This is because heaven will not be a place for born-again believers if Jesus is not there. Remember, born-again believers are in Christ. By going to prepare a place, He obtains the admission and opens the way into the Holiest of all (for He is the way).

The main message here is not mansions, but the assurance of an eternal future with Jesus Christ in heaven. (In the text, the disciples weren't concerned at all about their mansions. They didn't ask about the address, the neighborhood, the lot size, or who their neighbors would be. Instead they wanted to know where Jesus was going, the way to get there, and they wanted to see the Father. Sadly, Christians nowadays make mansions the main prize.)

The assurance is as follows:

1. Our eternal future with Jesus is secure—*"where I am, there ye may be also."*
2. Jesus will receive us.
3. We know the place and the way—*"whither I go ye know, and the way ye know."*

Comfort of access to the Father

[Verses 5-6] Thomas wasn't sure about where Jesus was going and spoke out for the rest of the disciples, saying, *"Lord, we know not whither thou goest; and how can we know the way?"* To that, Jesus replied, *"I am the way, the truth, and the life: no man cometh unto the Father, but by me,"* which has become one of the most quoted verses in the Bible along with *John 3:16*.

John 14:6 is so simple; it is self-explanatory.

Chapter 14 – Way, Truth, Life

- *"I am the way"*—Jesus Christ is the way of salvation and there is none else. If you add anything to this, such as Jesus Christ plus church, religion, or good works, you are on your own. *1Timothy 2:5 For there is one God, and one mediator between God and men, the man Christ Jesus.*

- *"the truth"*—Jesus Christ is not only true, but truth itself.

- *"the life"*—Jesus Christ is the author and source of all life forms, physical and spiritual. *John 1:4 In him was life; and the life was the light of men.*

- And what part of *"no man cometh unto the Father, but by me"* do people not understand? Still, the religions of the world want access to the Father, but deny the Son. Please be forewarned, people who deny Jesus will die in their sins.
    - *1John 2:23 Whosoever denieth the Son, the same hath not the Father: (but) he that acknowledgeth the Son hath the Father also.*
    - *1John 5:12 He that hath the Son hath life; and he that hath not the Son of God hath not life.*

How comforting it is to know that if we have Jesus Christ, we have access to God. There is no need to wait until we die, for Jesus Christ has made it possible for us to boldly approach the throne of grace by prayer. *Hebrews 4:16 Let us therefore come boldly unto the throne of grace, that we may obtain mercy, and find grace to help in time of need.* How cool is that! Both mercy and grace are available anytime we need them. We should be encouraged in the work of ministry.

Comfort of knowing the Father

[Verses 7-11] Having mentioned the way to the Father, Jesus reinforced the concept that the unbelieving Jews rejected as blasphemy, which was He and the Father were one. The disciples knew Jesus as Lord, the Messiah, the Christ, the Son of the Living God, and the King of Israel (*John 1:41, 49, John 6:69*), but they might not have known Him as the Father. So, Jesus essentially said, "Oh by the way, you also know the Father and have seen Him," which piqued Philip's interest.

Philip, out of weakness of faith and ignorance, asked to see the physical manifestation of the Father, saying, *"Lord, shew us the Father, and it sufficeth us."* Philip thought it would be a treat to see the Father to satisfy all his doubts. But to his shame, Philip, who was able to identify Jesus as the Messiah from day one (*John 1:43-45*), failed to realize the Father was in Jesus, even though he had been with Jesus for over three years. Jesus reproved him, *"Have I been so long time with you, and yet hast thou not known me, Philip? he that hath seen me hath seen the Father; and how sayest thou then, Shew us the Father?"*

Philip's syndrome is typical of people who struggle with faith and who will only believe when they see the physical manifestation of God. Following are the reasons why people who do not know Jesus Christ should not want to meet God:

1. No one can see God and live to tell. *Exodus 33:20 And he said, Thou canst not see my face: for there shall no man see me, and live.*

2. In God's presence, people will immediately realize how sinful they are and how holy God is, and they will die instantly.
    a. *Isaiah 6:5 Then said I, Woe is me! for I am undone; because I am a man of unclean lips, and*

> *I dwell in the midst of a people of unclean lips: for mine eyes have seen the King, the LORD of hosts.* Isaiah had to be revived by an angel. His iniquity and sin were purged by a live coal from the altar of God before he could speak to God.
>   b. The only safe way to know and see God is in Jesus Christ. *John 1:18 No man hath seen God at any time; the only begotten Son, which is in the bosom of the Father, he hath declared him.*

Seeing Philip's struggle with the concept of the Father in Jesus, perhaps through his furrowed brows, Jesus asked him, "Believest thou not that I am in the Father, and the Father in me?," and gave him two reasons to believe:

> 1. Examine the doctrines. *"The words that I speak unto you I speak not of myself: but the Father that dwelleth in me, he doeth the works."* Jesus never received any religious education or sat at a rabbi's feet, yet He spoke the wisdom and mind of God, and people marveled at His doctrines. *John 7:14 Now about the midst of the feast Jesus went up into the temple, and taught. (15) And the Jews marvelled, saying, How knoweth this man letters, having never learned? (16) Jesus answered them, and said, My doctrine is not mine, but his that sent me.*
>
> 2. Examine the works. *"Believe me that I am in the Father, and the Father in me: or else believe me for the very works' sake."* Philip should have taken Jesus at His word, or else believed that the Father was in Jesus by the miracles that He performed. (Jesus gave the same advice to the unbelieving Jews in *John 10:37-38*.)

The assurance of verse 7 is very comforting—*"If ye had known me, ye should have known my Father also: and from henceforth ye know him, and have seen him."* We now know and see Jesus by faith, therefore, we also know and see the Father by faith. One of these days, our faith will become sight, and we will safely see the Father and Jesus Christ, and will observe how they are alike.

Comfort of audience and help from heaven

[Verses 12-14] To further calm the disciples' fears, Jesus assured them of His continued involvement and support for their ministry. Jesus would only be absent bodily, but would always be present in spirit and accessible through prayer. He expected them to replicate His works—*"to seek and to save that which was lost"* and *"to make fishers of men"*, representing evangelism and discipleship. Jesus said, *"Verily, verily, I say unto you, He that believeth on me, the works that I do shall he do also; and greater works than these shall he do; because I go unto my Father."*

We also are expected to replicate Jesus' works (evangelism and discipleship) in greater number. Trust God for *"greater works"* by being equipped and engaged. Equip yourself with the knowledge of God—learn the Bible, get discipled, and live His truth. Engage unbelievers with the good news of Jesus Christ.

There is much work to be done while many souls still live in darkness. The Lord has commissioned us to go and make disciples, and He expects fruit as we will see in chapter 15. *Matthew 28:19 Go ye therefore, and teach all nations, baptizing them in the name of the Father, and of the Son, and of the Holy Ghost: (20) Teaching them to observe all things whatsoever I have commanded you: and, lo, I am with you alway, even unto the end of the world. Amen.*

We are in a co-mission with the Lord Jesus. We are laborers together with God (*1Corinthians 3:9)*. There are many great needs in ministry that require much prayer. How comforting it is to know

Chapter 14 – Way, Truth, Life

the Lord Jesus will hear and assist from heaven, if we properly petition as follows:

1. *"And whatsoever ye shall ask in my name, that will I do"* —We are to ask in Jesus' powerful name; the name above all names. This is very important as it is repeated in verse 14, *"If ye shall ask any thing in my name, I will do it."*

2. *"That the Father may be glorified in the Son"* —This should be the focus of our prayers. Remember, the context of verse 13 and 14 is ministry works as set by verse 12.

Check Our Love

[Verses 15-26] To further impress upon His disciples, Jesus essentially offered them a three-for-one deal, which was the Godhead or the Trinity for His replacement. Upon Jesus' departure, He promised that the Comforter, who was the third person in the Godhead, would indwell them. Moreover, the Father and Jesus would also abide with them spiritually.

Verse 15, *"If ye love me, keep my commandments"* is a good checkpoint. Just as good works are the evidence of our faith in Jesus Christ, and brotherly love is the evidence of discipleship, our love for Jesus is real when we obey His commandments. According to verse 21a, *"He that hath my commandments, and keepeth them, he it is that loveth me."* Consider verse 23:

- *"If a man love me, he will keep my words"* —Our love for Jesus Christ must not be in words only, but must translate to obedience. Obedience is the fruit of our love for Christ. *Luke 6:46 And why call ye me, Lord, Lord, and do not the things which I say?*

- *"and my Father will love him, and we will come unto him, and make our abode with him"*—True love for Jesus Christ will result in a reciprocal manifestation of the Godhead in the believer. Those who are obedient to the word of God know this comfort intimately. It is a state of fulfillment and contentment that is better than the high from any substance. Unbelievers will never experience this manifestation and comfort, according to verse 22.

Later in verse 31a, Jesus said, *"But that the world may know that I love the Father; and as the Father gave me commandment, even so I do."* Jesus demonstrated His love for the Father by His obedience to the Father's commandments and was obedient unto death, even the death of the cross. *John 10:17 Therefore doth my Father love me, because I lay down my life, that I might take it again. (18) No man taketh it from me, but I lay it down of myself. I have power to lay it down, and I have power to take it again. This commandment have I received of my Father.*

Just as Jesus loved and obeyed the Father, so must we love Jesus and obey Him. The phonies are those who say they love God, but their lives and actions do not match the word of God—*"He that loveth me not keepeth not my sayings."* Again, a genuine love results in obedience to the word of God and righteous choices, but love in word only is dysfunctional. (By the way, you can serve the Lord without loving Him, but you cannot love Him without serving Him. The first instance demonstrates carnality.)

Are there areas in your life that you should submit to the word of God? *Psalms 139:23 Search me, O God, and know my heart: try me, and know my thoughts.*

Chapter 14 – Way, Truth, Life

Besides being obedient to God's words, verse 28 states that we should rejoice or celebrate if we love Jesus. The disciples preferred to have Jesus present with them bodily, but Jesus went away to accomplish a larger purpose for the Kingdom of God. His salvation was to be extended to the Gentiles, and the Jews would eventually repent of their disbelief. Therefore, Jesus said to the disciples, *"If ye loved me, ye would rejoice, because I said, I go unto the Father: for my Father is greater than I."* In other words, if we love Jesus, we should have a kingdom mindset and we should rejoice, because Jesus is now at the right hand of the Father.

Side Notes:

[Verses 16-17] Jesus introduced the Comforter, who is the Spirit of truth and the Holy Ghost, according to verses 17 and 26. He is the third person of the Trinity and is 100% God. Read *1John 4:12, 15, Romans 8:9, 2Corinthians 3:17*.

- The Holy Spirit indwells believers the moment of salvation and takes up permanent residence. (In the Old Testament, the Holy Spirit did not take permanent residence in the bodies of believers.) Believers' bodies are the temple of the Holy Ghost. Read *Galatians 4:6, Ephesians 2:19-22, 1John 3:24, 1Corinthians 6:19*. Believers get 100% of the Holy Spirit, and not in installments.

- The Holy Spirit has specific functions. Below are some examples:
    - He is the Comforter who comforts believers in time of need – verse 16, *2Corinthians 1:3-4*.
    - He is the Spirit of Truth who teaches, guides, and reminds believers of the word of God – verse 26, *John 16:13, 1John 2:27*.

- He bears witness of believers' salvation and is the seal of their salvation – *Romans 8:16, Ephesians 1:13-14, Ephesians 4:30.*
- He intercedes in prayer for believers – *Romans 8:26-27.*

- The Holy Spirit produces nine character qualities in believers, known as the fruit of the Spirit, as they obey the word of God. According to *Galatians 5:22-23*, they are love, joy, peace, longsuffering, gentleness, goodness, faith, meekness, and temperance.

[Verse 18] When Jesus says He will not leave us comfortless, this does not mean we will have a comfortable life. It bears repeating that God never promises prosperity and comfort in this world. Instead, He promises the fellowship of Christ's sufferings. Read *2Timothy 3:12*. What this means is the Godhead will accompany us in tribulation. This is why our obedience to the word of God is critical. Evil days will come. The question is, who would we have to accompany, comfort, and strengthen us through evil days?

Check Our Peace

[Verse 27] Jesus' will for the disciples before He left the world was not silver and gold, but His peace—*"Peace I leave with you, my peace I give unto you."* He left His peace with them, as in something for them to manage—for example, the gospel of peace. He also bequeathed peace to them, as in to help them in ministry.

Jesus made clear that His peace was not the world's peace, which is external, unsubstantial, ineffective, and mostly words of insincere people based on false hope. Jesus gave the peace of God that was internal and that surpassed all understanding, to keep their hearts and minds as they performed the work of ministry. It was the kind of peace that would carry them through difficulties and tribulations. With that, Jesus said to them, *"Let not your heart be troubled, neither let it be afraid."*

We are comforted by the same promise. *Philippians 4:6 Be careful for nothing; but in every thing by prayer and supplication with thanksgiving let your requests be made known unto God. (7) And the peace of God, which passeth all understanding, shall keep your hearts and minds through Christ Jesus.* We can find strength in Jesus' peace (for He is the Prince of Peace) to do the work of ministry and endure trials and tribulations.

Prophecies

The phrase *"that day"* in verse 20 is the unmistakable sign that end-time messages are encoded in this chapter. *"That day"* or *"The day of the Lord"* is often used to speak of the Messiah coming in judgment and establishing His literal kingdom on earth—the period beginning from the Great Tribulation (following the rapture of the church) to the end of the millennium. Examples include *Zechariah 12* to *14*, *Isaiah 2*, and *1Thessalonians 5:1-5*. It is the most dramatic time!

The message *"I will come again"* is stated three times in verse 3, 18, and 28. When God repeats a message three times, we better pay attention. Rest assured, Jesus Christ will come again.

The phrases *"I will come to you"* and *"come again unto you"* in verse 18 and 28 respectively, refer to Israel as a nation. For now, the Jews are cast away because of their unbelief, but Jesus will return to reconcile and receive them in the future. Read *Romans 11:15*. However, Jesus had to first leave the world and return to the Father until the Jews acknowledge their offence and call upon Him, according to the prophecy in *Hosea 5:15*. As mentioned in the beginning of this chapter, this is a two-step grand strategy to win over the entire nation of Israel.

[Verse 29] Jesus prophesied of His betrayal, death, and resurrection, and they happened. Jesus also prophesied of His return to the Father, and He is now with the Father. Jesus said, the Comforter would be given, and He was. All genuine born-again believers can testify of the indwelling of the Holy Ghost. Jesus promised to come again, and He will. Jesus Christ is absolutely believable. Who is Jesus Christ to you?

Summary

What an incredible assurance and comfort Jesus has bestowed upon His believers to help and encourage them in the work of ministry. This is the best guarantee any worker can expect. By this, our faith in Jesus Christ should be solidified, our love for Him should translate to obedience and celebration, and the peace of God should drive us to perform the work of ministry with joy. Shame on us if we are not involved in kingdom work. This chapter concludes with *"Arise, let us go hence."* That is to say, "let's roll." Come on, let's roll!

15 – True Vine

Historical Synopsis

This chapter features a one-way, uninterrupted discourse from Jesus to the disciples at the close of the last supper. He wanted them to know and maintain His joy after His departure. He showed them that their joy was linked to fruitfulness and gave them the secret. He also reiterated the commandment to love one another so that they might be comforted in the midst of the world's hatred and persecution.

This chapter can be outlined as such:

I. Prescription for joyfulness – *John 15:1-17*
II. Promise of persecution – *John 15:18-27*

The Book of John

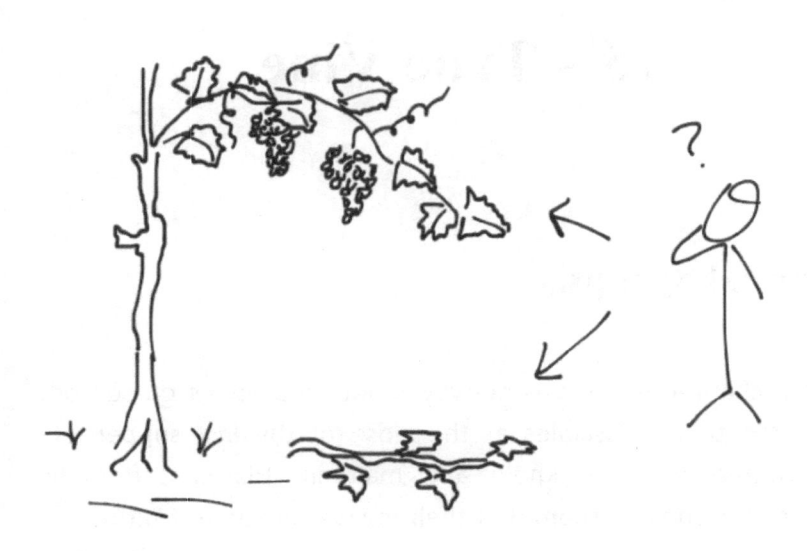

270

Key Spiritual Lessons

One should not miss the glaring message in this chapter. The Greek work "μένω" (men'-o) is repeated 12 times—nine times as "abide," twice as "remain," and once as "continue." When God repeats His word, we need to pay attention and apply the principles to our lives, especially when He says it 12 times.

The word "love" is repeated 10 times—five times as "ἀγαπάω" (ag-ap-ah'-o), four times as "αγαπη" (ag-ah'-pay), and once as "φιλέω" (fil-eh'-o). (Refer to Chapter 3 verse 16 for the definition of these terms.)

The three words that define this chapter—"abide," "love," and "endure"—form the foundation for the Lord's expectations for His believers.

    I.   Jesus expects believers to be fruitful – *John 15:1-8*
    II.   Jesus expects believers to continue in His love – *John 15:9-17*
    III.   Jesus expects believers to endure persecution – *John 15:18-27*

Jesus Expects Believers to be Fruitful

[Verse 1] Jesus began His discourse on spiritual fruitfulness by positioning Himself as God, the great I AM. *Exodus 3:14 And God said unto Moses, I AM THAT I AM: and he said, Thus shalt thou say unto the children of Israel, I AM hath sent me unto you.*

Jesus portrayed Himself as the true vine. The vine similitude puts the discourse in Jewish context, as Israel was a vine that came out of Egypt. *Psalms 80:8 Thou hast brought a vine out of Egypt: thou hast cast out the heathen, and planted it. (9) Thou preparedst room before it, and didst cause it to take deep root, and it filled the land.* While Israel was a vine, Jesus was the true vine.

Jesus also portrayed the Father as the husbandman, who planted the true vine. (A husbandman is one who cultivates the land. The relationship is a beautiful picture of the great sacrifice of God for mankind.) Jesus Christ was the seed (*Luke 8:11*) that was planted (buried and died), and brought forth much fruit (*John 12:24*). He rose again from the dead and became the firstfruits of them that slept (died), according to *1Corinthians 15:20*.

[Verse 2] Every husbandman expects fruit from the things he grows. The Father expects the fruits of righteousness and holiness from the true vine, and the true vine expects the same from its branches. The branches are believers in Jesus Christ as defined in verse 5.

Does fruit-bearing mean having lots of physical children? No. While some Christian factions promote this, the context here is spiritual fruitfulness. Spiritual fruit includes the nine character qualities of the fruit of the Spirit in *Galatians 5:22-23*, the seven additions to faith (virtue, knowledge, temperance, patience, godliness, brotherly kindness, and charity) in *2Peter 1:5-8*, and fruit from ministry (the souls of men and disciples).

Please note that the Father inspects every branch (believer). Consider His method for maximizing fruit.

- *"Every branch in me that beareth not fruit he taketh away."*
  God wastes no time. Believers who are spiritually fruitless will be cut off. This does not mean they will go to hell, but they will suffer the severity of God. There is a sin unto death, according to *1John 5:16*. God has been known to punch the time cards of His disobedient and unfruitful children and take them home early. If your

Chapter 15 – True Vine

Christianity does not go beyond your profession of faith in Jesus Christ, then you are spiritually barren and are at risk. If your Christianity is limited to making an honest living, providing for your family, and raising good children, then you don't understand your role in the Kingdom of God. God bought you with a price and He expects you to be fruitful. Did you know that an unfruitful believer is an unfaithful believer? How long have you been a Christian? God forbid He should find you fruitless when it is high time for you to be fruitful. Read *Luke 13:6-9*.

Israel is also a branch that is cut off. The Jews are supposed to be the light to the Gentiles and bring glory to God. Instead, they rebelled and established their own righteousness, which is based on the law and not on faith, and as a result they are barren. Read *Romans 10:1-6, Romans 11:17. Hosea 10:1 Israel is an empty vine, he bringeth forth fruit unto himself: according to the multitude of his fruit he hath increased the altars; according to the goodness of his land they have made goodly images. (2) Their heart is divided; now shall they be found faulty: he shall break down their altars, he shall spoil their images. (3) For now they shall say, We have no king, because we feared not the LORD; what then should a king do to us?*

- *"Every branch that beareth fruit, he purgeth it, that it may bring forth more fruit."*
  In natural husbandry, pruning is necessary to promote proper growth, form, and fruit. Pruning means cutting back as opposed to cutting off a branch. One suffers setback, but the other is dead. Both are not fun and are grievous, but one will eventually experience fullness of

joy. The Father prunes the fruitful branches to maximize yield. Persecutions and afflictions are some of the means of pruning. This can happen to individuals or churches.

The expectation of spiritual fruitfulness is not negotiable. It is not an option for believers who are washed by the precious blood of Jesus Christ to be spiritually barren. All believers are chosen and ordained to go and bring forth fruit, and that their fruit should remain. Trust me, you do not want to appear empty handed before the King of Kings and Lord of Lords who died for your sins. What fruit do you have in your life that glorifies the Father? Do not be like Israel according to *Isaiah 5:1 Now will I sing to my wellbeloved a song of my beloved touching his vineyard. My wellbeloved hath a vineyard in a very fruitful hill: (2) And he fenced it, and gathered out the stones thereof, and planted it with the choicest vine, and built a tower in the midst of it, and also made a winepress therein: and he looked that it should bring forth grapes, and it brought forth wild grapes.*

[Verse 3] Being clean is the prerequisite of fruit bearing, as no unholy branches can abide in the true vine. *Matthew 7:18 A good tree cannot bring forth evil fruit, neither can a corrupt tree bring forth good fruit.* Unbelievers are like corrupt trees. It is impossible for unbelievers to bring forth holy and acceptable fruit to God, no matter what or how much they do, because their unpardoned sins. The Holy God will not accept offerings from sinners who have not accepted Christ. Read *Proverbs 15:8*. Believers are declared clean through the word of Christ and have the capacity to bring forth good fruit. Notice that believers are not cleansed through various physical washings or sacraments. Believers are cleansed and sanctified with the washing of water by the word. Read *Ephesians 5:26-27, Titus 3:5*.

Verses 4-8 give the principles for fruit bearing. The message is loud and clear. We must abide in Jesus Christ and His word must

Chapter 15 – True Vine

abide in us—*"Abide in me, and I in you."* The key word for spiritual fruitfulness is "abide," which is repeated nine times in this chapter. In Christian numerology, nine is the number of fruitfulness.

To help us understand the necessity of mutual inhabitation, Jesus uses the example of the relationship between the vine and the branches. Branches cannot bear fruit independently of the vine. They need a vital connection with the vine and the sap from the vine. Therefore it is said, *"As the branch cannot bear fruit of itself, except it abide in the vine; no more can ye, except ye abide in me."*

In case we are slow to understand, verse 5 defines who the vine and the branches are. Hereby is the precept, *"He that abideth in me, and I in him, the same bringeth forth much fruit: for without me ye can do nothing."* Let's break this down.

- *"He that abideth in me"*—Abiding in Jesus means continuing in the exercise of faith and observing His commandments. *1John 3:24 And he that keepeth his commandments dwelleth in him, and he in him. And hereby we know that he abideth in us, by the Spirit which he hath given us.* Do not be like the Galatians who began in faith, but wanted to be made perfect by the flesh – *Galatians 3:1-3*.

- *"and I in him"*—Jesus abides in us through His word and the Holy Ghost. Our heart must be sensitive to the Spirit and fertile for the word of God. *Matthew 13:23 But he that received seed into the good ground is he that heareth the word, and understandeth it; which also beareth fruit, and bringeth forth, some an hundredfold, some sixty, some thirty.* Make room for the scriptures and not for weak Christian publications that compete for the same space. That's like eating junk food, which will make us unhealthy. We must esteem the word of God more than our necessary food and read, study, and memorize the Bible. Read *Proverbs 23:26, Proverbs 6:20-22, Psalms 19:7-14*.

- *"the same bringeth forth much fruit"*—When the above is true, we are guaranteed to be fruitful.

- *"for without me ye can do nothing"*—Every believer must never forget this. This truth is not limited to fruit bearing only, but to every aspect of a believer's spiritual and physical life. The Bible says, *"For in Him we live, and move, and have our being."* We can never be joyful and successful without the Lord Jesus Christ.

[Verse 6] Those who abide not in Jesus, either through disbelief, disobedience, or by departing from faith, are cast forth as a branch by the Husbandman. They will soon realize the fatal consequence of their decision. This is because without Christ's spiritual life support, they will dry up spiritually and fall into the reproach and snare of the devil. Imagine how quickly leaves wither when the branch is severed from the vine. Dead branches are only good for one thing—fuel for fire. How awful and what a shame it is for a son of God, who is chosen and ordained to be fruitful and who should be presented to the Father as a fruitful bouquet, to be gathered up as a stick as fuel for fire! It is inconceivable for one who professes Jesus Christ as Lord to be spiritually barren! Read *Ezekiel 15:1-5*. Consider your life. What fruit do you have to glorify the Father? Don't be a Christian in name only. God will get His glory one way or another—either from you as a fruitful branch or as a stick.

What types of people are likely to depart from Jesus Christ and be spiritually barren?

1. People who think they are Christians, but are not. Judas Iscariot is an example. Read *1John 2:19, Hebrews 6:4-8*.

2. People who do not study the Bible. These people are initially happy to receive the word of God, but their faith is not deeply rooted in the word. They will be the casualty of tribulation and persecution. Read *Matthew 13:20-21, Mark 4:16-17, Luke 8:13*. Nowadays, many Christians measure their spiritual wellbeing by how they feel. This is contrary to the advice in *Colossians 3:16* and *2Timothy 2:15, "Study to shew thyself approved unto God, a workman that needeth not to be ashamed, rightly dividing the word of truth."* Bible study is hard work, but it is extremely rewarding. Feelings-based Christians have a shallow understanding of the Bible, and as such, their anchor does not hold in stormy times. Many blame God for their adversities.

3. People who are choked with the cares, riches, and pleasures of life. Read *Matthew 13:22, Mark 4:18-19, Luke 8:14*.

[Verse 7] If we abide in Jesus and His words abide in us, we can confidently pray for fruit and know that our prayers are heard. (Notice the shift from the phrase *"I in him"* in verse 5 to *"my words abide in you"* in verse 7. This is because Jesus Christ is the Word of God.) *1John 5:14* says, *"And this is the confidence that we have in him, that, if we ask any thing according to his will, he heareth us."* God's will is for us to be spiritually fruitful, according to verses 8 and 16. Our prayers and desire for fruit should be as intense as Rachel's desire for children in *Genesis 30:1b, "Give me children, or else I die."* That said, some believers try too hard to be fruitful. Fruitfulness is the byproduct of the mutual inhabitation and will occur in due season.

- *"He that abideth in me, and I in him"*—This condition must be true.

- *"the same bringeth forth much fruit"* —This is the byproduct. Live and obey the word and fruitfulness will come naturally. Read *Psalms 1:1-3*.

[Verse 8] Just as a husbandman is pleased with branches that are loaded with fruit, the Father is glorified when believers bear much fruit. A little fruit is not good enough. Notice the progression. Verse 2: *"...that it may bring forth more fruit."* Verse 5: *"...the same bringeth forth much fruit."* Verse 16: *"...your fruit should remain."* Believers, both young and old, must bear fruit. Old age is no excuse for cutting back or stopping production. *Psalms 92:12 The righteous shall flourish like the palm tree: he shall grow like a cedar in Lebanon. (13) Those that be planted in the house of the LORD shall flourish in the courts of our God. (14) They shall still bring forth fruit in old age; they shall be fat and flourishing.*

In Chapter 13, we learned brotherly love is a hallmark of discipleship. Here, the evidence of discipleship is extended to include spiritual fruitfulness.

Jesus Expects Believers to Continue in His Love

[Verse 9] Besides the prescription for spiritual fruitfulness in the preceding verses, Jesus further prescribes the continuance in His love. Since the word "love" is repeated 10 times, let us slow down and pay careful attention.

- *"As the Father hath loved me, so have I loved you"* — Here, the love of God is received and communicated. The same is commanded of us in verse 12. The Greek word for love is "ἀγαπάω" (ag-ap-ah'-o), which is the verb form of the noun "αγαπη" (ag-ah'-pay). It means "beloved" or "to love dearly." We can paraphrase this as

Chapter 15 – True Vine

"As the Father has dearly loved me, so I have dearly loved you."

- *"continue ye in my love"*—In consideration of the love of God that Jesus bestowed upon us, we have an actionable commandment to continue in it. In other words, to live it. (The word "continue" and "abide" in verse 10 are from the same Greek word "μένω" [men'-o].)

The proofs of those who continue or abide in the love of God are as follows:

1. Keeping Jesus' commandments—Verse 10 shows how we can continue in Jesus' love and that is by keeping His commandments. *John 14:15 If ye love me, keep my commandments.* Thus, we prove and adorn our love for God by our obedience to His commandments, and not by mere words only. Jesus set the example for abiding in the Father's love by keeping His commandments. *John 14:31a But that the world may know that I love the Father; and as the Father gave me commandment, even so I do.*

2. Being full of joy—Verse 11 shows why we should continue in Jesus' love. Jesus' prescriptions for fruitfulness and continuance in His love are centered on joy. It is designed in such a way that the Lord will rejoice in us and we will be full of joy when we bear fruit and continue in His love. (The Bible also says, "*The joy of the LORD is your strength,*" which the disciples would desperately need to face the world without Jesus.)

3. Loving one another—[Verses 12-13] We are commanded to love the brethren according to Jesus'

love for us—*"as I have loved you."* This is a tall order. And there is no greater proof of love than for a man to lay down his life for his friends as Jesus did.

Who are Jesus' friends? Jesus distinguishes friends from servants in verses 14-15. His friends are those who obey whatsoever He commands in the same way servants respond promptly and simply do as they are told without question. The difference is, servants have no idea of the larger picture and purpose, but Jesus reveals to His friends all things that He heard of the Father. A friend of God is therefore privy to the Father's innermost thoughts, counsels, purposes, and mysteries. In human relationships, it would be like a friend who is in on all the juicy secrets.

[Verse 16] In wrapping up His discourse for this section, Jesus reiterated His commandment for fruit bearing more forcefully, that believers are chosen and ordained to not only bear fruit, but that their fruit should remain. He said:

- *"Ye have not chosen me, but I have chosen you, and ordained you"*—We have been drafted with power and authority from above to replenish the Kingdom of God. It is a responsibility and not an option. Remember Adam and Eve's mission?

- *"that ye should go and bring forth fruit"*—Where should we go to sow the seeds of truth, water, fertilize, and eventually harvest the fruit? Consider *Acts 1:8,* "But ye shall receive power, after that the Holy Ghost is come upon you: and ye shall be witnesses unto me both in Jerusalem, and in all Judaea, and in Samaria, and unto the uttermost part of the earth." We should evangelize our Jerusalem, which is the area we live in. Judaea represents the neighboring cities, while Samaria represents the distant cities. We should even evangelize the uttermost parts of the earth. *Proverbs 11:30 The fruit of the righteous is a tree of life; and he that winneth souls is wise.* Are you able to deliver the gospel of salvation?

- *"and that your fruit should remain"*—In order for fruit to remain, we must disciple new converts. Teach them to observe all things whatsoever the Lord has commanded. But we will not have anyone to disciple if we do not evangelize. Therefore, evangelism and discipleship are two sides of the same coin.

- *"that whatsoever ye shall ask of the Father in my name, he may give it you"*—Don't forget that this is a spiritual operation that must be bathed in prayer in Jesus' name. The phrase *"in my name"* appears six other times in *John 14* and *John 16*.

[Verse 17] Jesus capped His commandments for fruitfulness and continuance in His love with the command to love one another. The issue of brotherly love laid heavily on His heart, so much so that He mentioned it twice in chapter 13 and twice in this chapter. It was perhaps due to the strife among the disciples regarding who should be the greatest, as documented in *Luke 22:24-30*.

Ministry runs much better on the rails of relationships that are built on love.

Jesus Expects Believers to Endure Persecution

Perhaps the reason the commandment to love one another is reiterated in verse 17 is because it is absolutely essential for

The Book of John

believers who live in a world that hates and persecutes them. Love provides relief from persecutions that can arise even from immediate family members and relatives.

The children of the world do not confess Jesus as God the Son. They have the spirit of the antichrist, according to *1John 4:3*. The devil is their spiritual father. While they come from various religious backgrounds that disagree with each other, one thing they have in common is the hatred for practicing believers in Jesus Christ.

We shouldn't be shocked that the world hates us. *1John 3:13* says, *"Marvel not, my brethren, if the world hate you."* Why?

1. [Verse 18] The world hates the Lord Jesus Christ. We should not expect the world to congratulate and applaud us for following Christ.

2. [Verse 19] We are not of the world. To them, we are intolerant and problematic and the world would be a better place without us. We should win them over, but we should not emulate or be like them, because *"whosoever therefore will be a friend of the world is the enemy of God."*

3. [Verse 20] They persecuted the Lord Jesus Christ, therefore, don't think it is a strange thing when they persecute us. *2Timothy 3:12 Yea, and all that will live godly in Christ Jesus shall suffer persecution.* Read *1Peter 4:12-14*.

4. [Verse 21] They do not know the Father. The only way to know the Father is through Jesus Christ. If they knew the Father, they would not persecute us. They also would not remove prayer from schools, teach evolution, or take down the Ten Commandments from court houses.

Chapter 15 – True Vine

[Verses 22-27] The Jews had no excuse for their sins, because Jesus Christ revealed Himself to them, provided ample witness, pleaded with them, and performed supernatural miracles that proved He was the Messiah. Yet they hated Him and killed Him. Unbeknownst to them, their unreasonable hatred was prophesied in their very own law. Thus they fulfilled the scripture, *"They hated me without a cause."* Read *Psalms 69:4, Psalms 109:3, Psalms 119:78,161*.

But Christians will bear witness of Jesus Christ, even under persecution, because the indwelling Comforter, the Spirit of truth, testifies of Jesus' deity and son-ship. Jesus Christ is the real deal!

Prophecies

The Greek work "μένω" (men'-o), translated as "abide," "remain," and "continue," is repeated 12 times. In numerology, 12 is the number of Israel. It is a clear message to Israel to remain in the Messiah vine. However, because of disbelief, Israel's branches are broken off, and blindness in part has befallen them. Read *Romans 9, 10, 11*.

Today, Israel is blind to the truth. They see, but perceive not; they hear, but understand not, according to *Isaiah 6:9-10, Jeremiah 5:20-21, Ezekiel 12:1-2*. I have witnessed to Jewish people and there seemed to be an invisible veil in front of them that the truth of Jesus Christ just couldn't penetrate. It was like water off a duck's back. And they are still looking and waiting for the Messiah.

The good news is that Israel will eventually get its act together and be fruitful. Read *Jeremiah 24:4-7*.

Summary

Fruitfulness is not an option for believers. God the Father expects fruit. Don't come into His presence with an empty basket. The parable of the sower in *Matthew 13* is a good companion to this chapter. Your fruitfulness is tied to the amount of seed (the word of God) you sow.

Following are the three P's of the philosophy of fruitfulness. May God give you the understanding to know the hope of His calling and bless you with abundant fruit for your labor in ministry.

- Pillars of fruitfulness
    - Abide in Jesus Christ
    - Abide in Jesus' love
    - Adore (love) one another
- Prize of fruitfulness—is the joy of the Lord.
- Price of fruitfulness—is persecution.

16 – Advisor

Historical Synopsis

This chapter concludes Jesus' farewell sermon to His disciples. The topic of persecution bleeds over from the previous chapter and is expounded here to prepare the disciples for inevitable hardship.

This chapter can be outlined as such:

    I.   Readiness through warning – *John 16:1-6*
    II.   Readiness through understanding – *John 16:7-15*
    III.   Readiness through the hope of reunion – *John 16:16-22*
    IV.   Readiness through clarity and peace in Jesus Christ – *John 16:23-33*

The Book of John

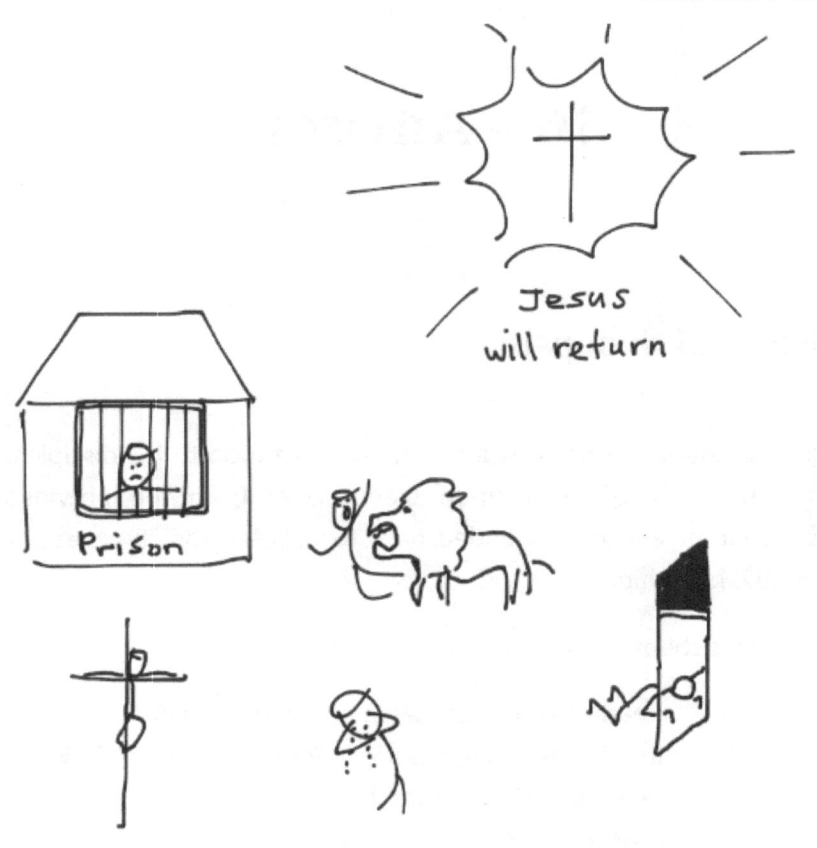

Jesus will return

Prison

Tribulation & sorrow

Key Spiritual Lessons

People who live in coastal areas and flood zones should expect and prepare for flooding. Likewise, those who live around fault lines should expect and prepare for earthquakes. Similarly, Christians should prepare their hearts for the persecution of the world, which is addressed in this chapter. Let's use the same outline as in the Historical Synopsis section above.

Readiness through Warning

[Verses 1-6] Heads up, *"These things have I spoken unto you, that ye should not be offended."* Meaning, when persecution arises, it should not cause you to distrust, lose faith in God, or blame Him for the hardship, because you have been forewarned. Believers who miss this memo are those who do not read the Bible. Verse 4a says, *"But these things have I told you, that when the time shall come, ye may remember that I told you of them."* Well, if they don't read the Bible, they will not know that the Lord already warned them and so, persecution will take them by surprise.

What can be expected?

- Expect excommunication—*"They shall put you out of the synagogues."* If the Lord Jesus Christ has chosen you out of the world, there is no point in hiding the fact that you are a Christian. The world will figure you out, single you out, and kick you out. The world will excommunicate and persecute you, because you are not of the world. Remember the blind man who was born blind in chapter 9, whom Jesus opened his eyes? He was cast out of the synagogue after he testified of Jesus' miracle work in him. You should be happy if you suffer for righteousness' sake. *Luke 6:22 Blessed are ye, when men shall hate you, and when they shall separate you from their company, and shall reproach you, and cast out your name as evil, for the Son of man's sake.*

- Expect cruelty—*"Yea, the time cometh, that whosoever killeth you will think that he doeth God service."* Yes, the religious unbelievers of the world will exercise cruelty, because they do not know the Father or His Sent One. Their spiritual father is the devil.
    - Prior to meeting Jesus, Saul (the Apostle Paul) zealously persecuted the church. He also consented to the stoning of Stephen. Read *Galatians 1:13-14, Philippians 3:6, Acts 7:54-Acts 8:3, Acts 9:1-2*.
    - All but one of the 12 apostles were martyred for their faith. The Apostle John, who remained, was exiled to the Island of Patmos. Read *Matthew 23:34-35*.

All who will live godly in Christ Jesus will suffer persecution, according to *2Timothy 3:12*. It is not a matter of "if," but "when." The phrase in verse 4 says, *"The time shall come."* The only way to avoid persecution is to be totally ineffective for God. Don't claim to be a Christian; don't share your testimony; don't witness Jesus to the lost; set your affection on the world; and focus on self. Live a good life that is spiritually barren and the devil will leave you alone. If you do this, you are deceiving yourself. You will be unhappy and unfulfilled.

Don't think for a moment that Christian persecution is a thing of the past. More Christians are being slaughtered today than ever before. Christians are singled out and massacred everywhere in the world, and churches in America are keeping silent. Christians

Chapter 16 - Advisor

in the Middle East and Africa are being kidnapped, tortured, raped, and beheaded. The ISIS (Islamic State of Iraq and Syria) militant group is killing Christians in northern Iraq and Syria. The list goes on and it will only get worse. Wait till the antichrist comes to power. *Revelation 20:4 And I saw thrones, and they sat upon them, and judgment was given unto them: and I saw the souls of them that were beheaded for the witness of Jesus, and for the word of God, and which had not worshipped the beast, neither his image, neither had received his mark upon their foreheads, or in their hands; and they lived and reigned with Christ a thousand years.*

I highly recommend everyone read "Foxe's Book of Martyrs." It contains tragic yet triumphant stories of men and women who stood for their faith in the Lord Jesus Christ, while enduring torture and martyrdom. For current events, I invite everyone to check out "The Voice of the Martyrs" at www.persecution.com. (You can sign up for news alerts in the "Newsroom" section.) I salute these brave brothers and sisters in Christ. They are the heroes of the faith. May God have mercy on their souls.

How should one prepare for persecution?

- Don't be consumed by sorrow at the prospect of persecution. Sorrow filled the disciples' hearts when they learned about the things that would befall them, so much so that they neglected to ask Jesus where He was going. (Persecution is the fertilizer for faith. In many persecuted areas, faith in God increases tremendously.)

- Don't build bunkers to hide in. Safety is of the Lord, according to *Proverbs 21:31*. Read *2Timothy* to find out what instructions the Apostle Paul gave to Timothy on handling persecutions.

- Do good works and continue to preach the gospel. Implement mercy and truth. *Matthew 5:44 But I say unto you, Love your enemies, bless them that curse you, do good to them that hate you, and pray for them which despitefully use you, and persecute you.*

- Most important of all, be fully persuaded that Jesus Christ is able to keep that which you have committed unto Him against that day. It is this persuasion that allowed Shadrach, Meshach, and Abednego to submit to the fiery furnace, Daniel to the lion's den, and the disciples, Stephen, and the Apostle Paul to martyrdom. Until this persuasion is settled in your life, persecution will run you over like a freight train. *2Timothy 1:11 Whereunto I am appointed a preacher, and an apostle, and a teacher of the Gentiles. (12) For the which cause I also suffer these things: nevertheless I am not ashamed: for I <u>know whom I have believed</u>, and <u>am persuaded</u> that he is able to keep that which I have committed unto him against that day.*

Readiness through Understanding

[Verses 7-15] Jesus helped the disciples understand that they would be better off with the Comforter, whom He would send when He returned to the Father. For it was agreed in heaven that the Comforter (Holy Spirit) would not come unless He departed.

How is the Comforter better for believers than the bodily presence of Jesus? While both Jesus and the Comforter are 100% God (*John 1:1-2,14, 2Corinthians 3:17*), in the flesh, Jesus could only be in one place at one time, but the Comforter is an omnipresent Spirit. As such, the Holy Spirit is more efficient at reproving (convincing) the world and in instructing and comforting believers.

Chapter 16 - Advisor

The ministry of the Holy Spirit with reference to unbelievers is as follows:

1. To convince the world of sin—"*Of sin, because they believe not on me.*" Ministers may present the gospel, but the ultimate convincing is done by the Holy Spirit, because He has the supernatural ability and power to touch and open sinners' hearts. It takes the Holy Spirit to convince sinners that it is a sin to reject Jesus Christ and His salvation.

2. To convince the world of righteousness—"*Of righteousness, because I go to my Father, and ye see me no more.*" The Holy Spirit convinces sinners that Jesus Christ is the righteousness of God. Read *Romans 3:22, 2Corinthians 5:21, 1John 2:1*. He was the only begotten of the Father. He came forth from the Father, and returned to sit at His right hand. Verse 28 summarizes it, "*I came forth from the Father, and am come into the world: again, I leave the world, and go to the Father.*" His ascension to heaven was witnessed by many. Read *John 7:33, John 13:1-3, John 16:16, Mark 16:19, 1Corinthians 15:1-6*.

3. To convince the world of judgment—"*Of judgment, because the prince of this world is judged.*" The devil is the prince of this world, who has usurped dominion over the world and is destroying it with sin and death. But the death of Jesus Christ the righteous judged him and cast him out of his usurped dominion. *John 12:31 Now is the judgment of this world: now shall the prince of this world be cast out. 1John 3:8a For this purpose the Son of God was manifested, that he might destroy the works of the devil.* The Holy Spirit convinces sinners that those who believe in Jesus Christ are liberated from the fetters of

the devil to become the sons of God. Those who do not believe in Jesus Christ are judged with the devil, and will spend eternity in the lake of fire.

The above gives us a good framework for how we should pray for our lost family and friends. We should ask the Holy Spirit to convince them of sin, of righteousness, and of judgment while we share the good news of the gospel with them.

The ministry of the Comforter with reference to believers is as follows:

1. He guides believers into all truth. Jesus had yet many things to say to the disciples, but they were not ready to bear or receive them, especially concerning things to come. The Comforter, who is also known as the Spirit of truth, would give them revelations of things to come. In other words, they would have the complete Bible (all truth). And like the Lord Jesus, the Spirit of truth does not speak of Himself, but communicates what He hears from the Father.

2. He glorifies Christ on earth by showing the riches of His glory, according to verses 14-15, *"He shall glorify me: for he shall receive of mine, and shall shew it unto you. All things that the Father hath are mine: therefore said I, that he shall take of mine, and shall shew it unto you."* All that the Father has is Christ's. Read *John 3:35, Colossians 1:16.*

Readiness through the Hope of Reunion

[Verses 16-22] When the disciples couldn't comprehend the statement that Jesus made in verse 16, He explained it using the example of a woman in travail.

- *"A little while, and ye shall not see me"*—Jesus would be taken away from them by death.

- *"And again, a little while,"*—Some commentators take this as the resurrection of Jesus Christ, which soon followed His death and burial. However, the reference to the woman in travail in verse 21 points to the seven-year period of great tribulation that the Jews will suffer. During this time, they will weep, lament, and be sorrowful, while the world rejoices. Their sorrow, however, will turn to joy when Jesus reappears to them at His second coming.

- *"And ye shall see me, because I go to the Father"*—Jesus is now at the right hand of the Father, but He will return for the nation of Israel. Verse 22a says, *"I will see you again, and your heart shall rejoice, and your joy no man taketh from you."*

Ministry carries great risk. Many faithful servants of God minister in areas known as "hot beds" and some do it in underground churches. The worst thing the enemy of Christ can do to believers is to kill them. But that's not true, because martyrs are united with the Lord. The hope of reunion with the Lord should settle the fear of persecution. In reality, the worst thing the enemy of Christ can do to believers is to cause them to sin against God. Read *Nehemiah 6:10-14*.

Readiness through Clarity and Peace in Jesus Christ

[Verses 23-24] Having clarified what He said in verse 16, Jesus told the disciples that there would come a day when things concerning Him would be clear, and they would not be raising questions like students. *Hebrews 8:10 For this is the covenant that I will make with the house of Israel after those days, saith the Lord; I will put my laws into their mind, and write them in their hearts: and I will be to them a God, and they shall be to me a people: (11) And they shall not teach every man his neighbour, and every man his brother, saying, Know the Lord: for all shall know me, from the least to the greatest.*

In the mean time, they were encouraged by a sure promise to pray to the Father in Jesus' name for understanding, and the Spirit of truth would give revelation. Up to that point, the disciples hadn't prayed anything in Jesus' name because He was with them. Going forward, the Spirit would reveal the mystery of God to them (verses 14-15) to the intent that their joy might be full. The joy of faith is based on the understanding of scriptures and not on feelings.

Did you know that we have the same promise? *James 1:5 If any of you lack wisdom, let him ask of God, that giveth to all men liberally, and upbraideth not; and it shall be given him. (6) But let him ask in faith, nothing wavering. For he that wavereth is like a wave of the sea driven with the wind and tossed.* With help from the Holy Spirit of God, any child of God with a prayerful attitude can understand the Bible. Read *1John 2:27*. Don't buy the lie that the Bible can only be interpreted by priests or learned men. The Bible is a supernatural book and the Holy Spirit is the best teacher.

The understanding of scriptures helps us cope with the persecution of the world. The best thing is, we know how things will end, and in the scope of eternity, our times of trials in this world will not even be a blip on the radar screen.

Chapter 16 - Advisor

[Verses 25-27] Many things that Jesus said to the disciples after chapter 13 were spoken as proverbs or dark sayings. Things like, *"Whither I go, thou canst not follow me now; but thou shalt follow me afterwards"*; the mansions in His Father's house, and the way to get there; how He would manifest Himself to the disciples and not to the world; the vine and the branches; his departure from them and His return to them; and the woman in travail. But there will come a time (*"at that day"*) when proverbs and prophecies will be obsolete, because Jesus will show them plainly of the Father. At that day, they will pray in Jesus' name, and the Father will answer their prayers, because the Father loves them for loving Jesus and believing that He came from God.

In this present life, we live by faith and not by sight. When this life is over, our faith will become sight, because absent from the body is to be present with the Lord. We will see God face to face. For now, we see God darkly (in an enigma, riddles, or dark sayings) through a lens, but one of these days the lens will be removed and we will see God clearly. Read *2Corinthians 5:6-8, 1Corinthians 13:12*. Remember the story of the man who was born blind in chapter 9? Didn't his faith turn into sight?

[Verses 28-30] Finally, Jesus plainly declared to the disciples that He proceeded from the Father, was sent to the world, and was about to return to the Father. Then the disciples were satisfied and said, *"Lo, now speakest thou plainly, and speakest no proverb."* More importantly, they were impressed, because the declaration addressed the burning question in their hearts concerning His identity, without them asking. They were sure that Jesus was a discerner of the thoughts and intents of the heart and that He knew all things and prevented their question. By this, the disciples said they believed Jesus came from God.

[Verses 31-32] As soon as they said that, Jesus asked *"Do ye now believe?"* In other words, "Do you really believe?," because their test was just hours away and they would fail miserably, for they would all forsake Jesus that very night.

Let us not have faith that is full of hot air. All Christians will say they believe and love Jesus, but persecution will separate the faithful from the talkers. Unfortunately, there are more talkers than faithful believers.

Our faith in Jesus Christ comes with a package that contains benefits and adversities. We cannot pick out the good and leave the bad. The good news is Jesus shows us how to endure persecutions in the next verse.

[Verse 33] Jesus concluded His sermons to the disciples with the following advice:

- *"In me ye might have peace"*—The secret for enduring persecution is to remain steadfast in Jesus Christ. The flames of persecution could not consume and destroy Shadrach, Meshach, and Abednego in *Daniel 3*. In *Acts 7*, Stephen saw the heavens opened and the Son of man standing on the right hand of God before he kneeled down to pray for his persecutors who stoned him to death.

- *"In the world ye shall have tribulation"*—There is just no escaping persecution in the world, but we can embrace it with good cheer, because the Lord Jesus has overcome the world.

Prophecies

The phrase *"that day"* appears five times in the Gospel of John, and the last two times are in this chapter. See the Prophecies section of Chapter 14 for the definition of "that day." Phrases and words like *"that day," "woman in travail," "weep," "lament," "sorrow,"* and *"joy"* confirm that end-time messages are encoded in this chapter.

"A little while, and ye shall not see me"—this already happened. Jesus is presently seated at the right hand of the Father. The next big event for the nation of Israel is the awful great tribulation, which is depicted by the woman in travail and the reference to sorrow in verses 20-21. Many Jews will die in this great tribulation that will last for seven years, with the highest toll in the second half. *Matthew 24:21 For then shall be great tribulation, such as was not since the beginning of the world to this time, no, nor ever shall be.*

As awful as the great tribulation is, there is hope for the nation of Israel. They will come to the realization that Jesus Christ is the Messiah and will accept Him. Their sorrow will turn to joy when the Lord Jesus Christ returns for them.

Summary

This world is not getting better for faithful believers of Jesus Christ. The closer we get to the end time, the worse it will get. The transition of power will not happen smoothly. The devil, who is the god of this world, will not give up without a fight. *Revelation 12:12a Woe to the inhabiters of the earth and of the sea! for the devil is come down unto you, having great wrath, because he knoweth that he hath but a short time.*

Always remember the first four verses of this chapter and always be about the Father's business with the limited time we have. *Ephesians 5:15 See then that ye walk circumspectly, not as fools, but as wise, (16) Redeeming the time, because the days are evil. (17) Wherefore be ye not unwise, but understanding what the will of the Lord is.*

17 – Advocate

Historical Synopsis

Jesus ended His sermons, which began after Judas left the supper in *John 13:31*, with a prayer. This is the true Lord's Prayer. (The prayer in *Matthew 6:9-13* is a model prayer and is often mislabeled, taught, and recited as the Lord's Prayer.)

This prayer was for Him and His believers, but not for the world. Jesus uttered a short prayer for the Father to honor Him. Then at length, He asked the Father to protect, sanctify, unite, and glorify the disciples and future believers. In the prayer, Jesus spoke from an eternal perspective. He said things like "*I have finished the work which thou gavest me to do*" when He hadn't gone to the cross, and "*I am no more in the world*" when He was still there.

This chapter can be outlined as such:

I. Jesus prayed for glorification – *John 17:1-5*
II. Jesus prayed for His believers – *John 17:6-26*

The Book of John

300

Chapter 17 - Advocate

Key Spiritual Lessons

Jesus was returning to the Father, but His will for the disciples was for them to remain and accomplish greater things in the world that hated them. Therefore, He covered them with a prayer. We are very fortunate to have an extensive prayer of Jesus recorded and preserved, not just for the historical value, but that we may know the things that were important to Him; things that were on His mind and in His heart in His final hours on earth. The prayer also serves as a model for us to pray for other believers.

Since Jesus prayed for us, we should find out what He asked, because the Father would surely grant those things. Following are the key spiritual lessons:

    I.   Our goals as Christians – *John 17:1-5*
    II.   Our mission as Christians – *John 17:6-10*
    III. Our support as Christians – *John 17:11-26*

Our goals as Christians

[Verses 1-5] As when He raised Lazarus from the dead in *John 11:41*, Jesus lifted His eyes to heaven to pray. He did not have to do this, because the Father was in Him, according to *John 14:11*. This outward expression teaches that *"every good gift and every perfect gift is from above, and cometh down from the Father of lights."*

Jesus said, *"The hour is come,"* and asked the Father to honor Him, so that He too might honor the Father by His accomplished work on earth.

The Father gave Jesus sovereign power over all flesh (the fallen race), to the intent that He should give eternal life to as many as the Father gave Him. (Eternal life is a gift, not owing to the merits of men.) This could only be accomplished with His death on the cross. Knowing His crucifixion was just hours away, Jesus claimed to have finished the work that the Father gave Him to do, and as such He had honored the Father on earth.

Our goals as Christians should mimic Jesus' as follows:

1. To give the message of eternal life to as many as God gives us.
   This is evangelism. It is a must for all believers. It is a responsibility that will be accounted for at the Judgment Seat of Christ. Your gifts or the lack of them is no excuse. Every child of God must *"be ready always to give an answer to every man that asketh you a reason of the hope that is in you with meekness and fear,"* according to *1Peter 3:15*. It is not so much skill as it is obedience that matters.

2. To honor the Father on earth.
   Like the Lord Jesus, we should also honor the Father on earth by doing and finishing the work that He gives us to do. This is evangelism and discipleship.
   - Verse 6: *"I have manifested thy name unto the men which thou gavest me out of the world."*
   - Verse 8: *"I have given unto them the words which thou gavest me."*

3. To finish the course.
   "The hour is come"—everyone has an appointed hour. When that time comes, will we be able to say with the Apostle Paul, *"I have fought a good fight, I have finished my course, I have kept the faith"*? Imagine what a regret it would be if we couldn't say that. Frankly, at that time,

Chapter 17 - Advocate

regret may be the least of our problems. Read *2Corinthians 5:10-11*.

4. To be glorified by the Father.
   Verses 1 and 5 are the bookend prayer requests for honor. Of all the things that Jesus could ask, why did He ask to be honored with the *"glory which I had with thee before the world was"*? This is because *"all have sinned, and come short of the glory of God."* When Adam sinned, he lost the glory of God that clothed him. When Jesus took on the sins of the world, He too was without God's glory. So, of all the things that we could ask, we should ask for the glory of the Father.

Our Mission as Christians

[Verses 6-10] Having uttered a short prayer for Himself, Jesus now prayed for the disciples. He recommended them to the Father as follows:

1. I have invested in them—*"I have manifested thy name unto the men,"* *"I have given unto them the words which thou gavest me."*
2. They are yours—*"thine they were."*
3. They are mine—*"thou gavest them me."*
4. They are profitable—*"they have kept thy word."*
5. I am glorified in them.

Jesus' recommendations of the disciples form the basis of our mission as Christians, which is evangelism and discipleship. Consider verses 6 and 7:

- *"I have manifested thy name unto the men which thou gavest me out of the world: thine they were, and thou*

303

gavest them me..."—This is evangelism. In order to manifest the Father's name to the children of the world, we must share Christ with them. In so doing, we should pray in Jesus' name that the Father would lead us to those with whom He has been working.

- *"...and they have kept thy word. Now they have known that all things whatsoever thou hast given me are of thee."*—This is discipleship. In discipleship, we aim to reproduce ourselves in faithful men and women in the Lord. Read *2Timothy 2:2*. This concept is reinforced in verse 8:
    - *"For I have given unto them the words which thou gavest me"*—We are to teach new converts the basic doctrines of God.
    - *"and they have received them"*—We are to help new converts live the truth.
    - *"and have known surely that I came out from thee, and they have believed that thou didst send me"*—We are to help new converts grow in knowledge and understanding, that they may know the certainty of the words of truth, and be able to provide the reason for the hope that is in them to anyone who asks. Read *Proverbs 22:21, Luke 1:1-4, 1Peter 3:15*.

Chapter 17 - Advocate

Our Support as Christians

Preserved in the Holy Father's name

[Verses 11-12] Having recommended the disciples to the Father, Jesus began to pray for them specifically. He was mindful of the danger ahead. He knew that in the world they would be subject to evil, temptations, hatred, and persecutions. (Back in *John 14:12*, Jesus expected the disciples to replicate His works in greater frequency and number—*"greater works than these shall he do; because I go unto my Father."*) Therefore, Jesus petitioned the Holy Father to continue to preserve them in His name, for two reasons:

1. That none would be lost, except for the son of perdition, which happened according to scripture. *John 10:28 And I give unto them eternal life; and they shall never perish, neither shall any man pluck them out of my hand. (29) My Father, which gave them me, is greater than all; and no man is able to pluck them out of my Father's hand.*

2. That they might be one, as Jesus and God are one. Why is this unity important?
   - Verse 21, *"That they all may be one; as thou, Father, art in me, and I in thee, that they also may be one in us: that the world may believe that thou hast sent me."*
   - Verse 23, *"I in them, and thou in me, that they may be made perfect in one; and that the world may know that thou hast sent me, and hast loved them, as thou hast loved me."*

Note:

Good-hearted ministers often disagree on things ranging from doctrine to methods of operation. It is easy to get caught up in emotions, especially when one thinks he is right. Unchecked emotions can give way to pride, which leads to anger, strife, and contention. Read *Proverbs 13:10, Proverbs 29:22*. As hard as it may be, efforts rooted in humility must be made to reconcile to the truth. Read *Philippians 2:3*. It is counterproductive to win an argument and lose a brother. You want God to smile on you and bless you for obeying His commandment to love one another. That said, realistically, not every effort ends in reconciliation, especially if a brother is contrary to the word of God. *Amos 3:3 Can two walk together, except they be agreed?*

[Verse 13] With His death just hours away and so much pressure on Him, Jesus could have postponed praying for the disciples till He returned to the Father. It would have been just as effective. But He prayed while He was with them (*"these things I speak in the world"*) so that they would be able to rejoice in tribulation (*"that they might have my joy fulfilled in themselves"*), knowing that their Lord had prayed for them.

Wow, our Lord prayed for us. How wonderful and comforting this is. No matter what persecution we go through, we can be tearful and cheerful, because Jesus Christ has committed us into the custody of the Father, having prayed for us.

Protection from the evil one

[Verses 14-15] Jesus realized the world hated the disciples, because He had chosen them out of the world (*John 15:19*) and had given them the Father's word that testified against the world. So the world would unleash its hatred on the messengers. Jesus' solution was not to remove (isolate) the disciples out of the world, but to protect (insulate) them from the evil or wicked one.

Christ has chosen us out of the unbelieving world unto a new and righteous way of living. We are in the world, but we are

Chapter 17 - Advocate

not of the world. We must not act like the world or embrace its philosophies. The Bible warns us about this in *Colossians 2:6-8*. Because we are not of the world, the world hates and persecutes us. However, it is important to realize that the sinners of the world are not our enemies. This includes all non-Christians and atheists. When the Apostle Paul told the Corinthians not to keep company with fornicators, he meant not to keep company with Christians who were committing fornication, but insisted that they should keep company with the fornicators of the world. Read *1Corinthians 5:9-11*. The reason being, it is our responsibility to show sinners the gospel truth. *2Timothy 2:24 And the servant of the Lord must not strive; but be gentle unto all men, apt to teach, patient, (25) In meekness instructing those that oppose themselves; if God peradventure will give them repentance to the acknowledging of the truth; (26) And that they may recover themselves out of the snare of the devil, who are taken captive by him at his will.*

The devil is our real adversary. Unfortunately, more Christians pray against flesh and blood (people they don't like) than pray against the principalities, powers, and rulers of the darkness of this world (the evil one). Among those who acknowledge the devil, many are apathetic toward him. They take him too lightly, as if he is a cute, harmless red cartoon character with two horns and a pitch fork. Few Christian parents teach their children how this ultimate predator came to be and his desires. So over time, the devil becomes imaginary and no threat in the child's mind. That's a perfect position for any predator.

Make no mistake, the devil is real, powerful, and smart. Of all of God's creation, the devil *"sealest up the sum, full of wisdom, and perfect in beauty."* Read *Ezekiel 28:12-19, Ezekiel 31:8-9*. We stand no chance against him. We are like potato chips to him. He is as *"a roaring lion, walketh about, seeking whom he may devour"* and *"hath desired to have you, that he may sift you as wheat,"* according to *1Peter 5:8* and *Luke 22:31*. His main goal in life is to be like the Most High God. His motivations are to steal, kill, and destroy souls. If he can't take us into the hell fire, he wants to take the fire of serving God out of us.

Still not convinced the devil is real? Do this... really purpose in your heart to do the right thing and to serve God. If your church attendance is infrequent, make sure you attend Sunday school, main service, and fellowship classes regularly. If you have not been baptized or discipled, do so. If you have not been sharing the gospel of salvation with the lost, do so. Give to and serve in your local church, and support missionaries, and see if the devil will leave you alone.

Oh, by the way, ever wonder why the word "Lucifer" has been completely removed from many Bibles? Do you think the devil has anything to do with it? I would be checking my Bible if I were you. What does *Isaiah 14:12* say in your Bible?

Unbelievers of the world hate Christians, because they are driven by the force of darkness. They are the devil's puppets. Therefore, we should not expect them to love us. To them, anyone who holds the Bible view is an intolerant, ignorant, non-progressive, and prejudiced hatemonger. Anyone who does not call evil good and good evil is vilified. People who stand against homosexuality are labeled as homophobes and risk losing their jobs. Employers are forced to provide immoral healthcare benefits for their employees. The list goes on, but all are symptoms of the real problem, which is the devil. Therefore, it makes sense for the Lord to pray this protection over His believers. With this confidence, we can minister the gospel of Jesus Christ to sinners, that they may receive forgiveness of sin and turn from darkness to light and from the power of Satan unto God. We should be on the offence and pray against the evil one. Pause and pray right now.

Chapter 17 - Advocate

Sanctified for His service

[Verses 16-19] Because the disciples were not of the world, but had to operate in the world, Jesus also requested the Father to sanctify (separate or set apart) them as holy through His truth. This was needful, because Jesus had sent the disciples into the world to spread the word in the same manner as the Father had sent Him. This was possible because Jesus had sanctified Himself (lived a sinless life), that the disciples might be sanctified through the truth (Jesus Christ). *Hebrews 10:10 By the which will we are sanctified through the offering of the body of Jesus Christ once for all.*

Consider *Jeremiah 1:5 Before I formed thee in the belly I knew thee; and before thou camest forth out of the womb I sanctified thee, and I ordained thee a prophet unto the nations.* Also consider *Romans 1:1 Paul, a servant of Jesus Christ, called to be an apostle, separated unto the gospel of God.* Now, every believer is a minister and priest unto God, therefore, we should live a sanctified life, entirely devoted to God, that we may be blameless (not flawless) in executing the office of the priesthood.

With this prayer, Jesus Christ has sanctified all believers as ministers and has sent all into the world to spread the word—to evangelize the lost and disciple new converts. If you are not doing this, your Christianity is off track.

Oneness with God

[Verse 20] Jesus, foreseeing abundant fruit, expanded His prayer to cover future believers who would believe on Him through the ministry of the disciples, as He uttered, *"Neither pray I for these alone, but for them also which shall believe on me through their word."*

Sinners are converted through the ministry of Christ's disciples—through their word, either in preaching or publication.

Jesus uses believers to deliver the gospel of salvation to sinners. *Romans 10:14 How then shall they call on him in whom they have not believed? and how shall they believe in him of whom they have not heard? and how shall they hear without a preacher? (15) And how shall they preach, except they be sent? as it is written, How beautiful are the feet of them that preach the gospel of peace, and bring glad tidings of good things!* You should be willing and able to preach the gospel in a moment's notice. A Christian who is incapable of sharing the gospel is like a soldier who is incapable of firing a gun.

[Verse 21] Specifically, Jesus prayed for the oneness of believers—*"<u>That they all may be one</u>; as thou, Father, art in me, and I in thee, <u>that they also may be one in us</u>: that the world may believe that thou hast sent me."*

New Testament believers comprising of Jewish and Gentile converts in one body and one God should endeavor to be united:

- In testimony—Jesus Christ is the Lamb of God who died for the sins of the world.

- In doctrine—one body, one Spirit, one hope, one Lord, one faith, one baptism, and one God and Father. Read *Ephesians 4:1-6*.

- In worship—a lifestyle of a living sacrifice, holy, and acceptable unto God. Read *Romans 12:1-2*.

- In affection—brotherly love toward one another and love toward God. If we have the love of God, we will stand out, and the world will acknowledge that we are the children of God. They may still hate us, but at least they will know that we are the children of God. They

Chapter 17 - Advocate

hate us because our testimony convicts them. Read *John 13:34, John 14:15,21, 1John 5:1-2*.

The purpose of this unity is so that the unbelieving world may perceive and believe that Jesus Christ is the Sent One, the Savior of the world.

So, do you think the world is convinced that Jesus is the Messiah by looking at Christians today? Far from it. If anything, they are running the other direction. At present, Christendom is messed up. Some of the words that describe Christendom today are hypocrisy, greed, divided, phony, unholy, and untrustworthy. The lost already have their fill of these. Why would they want more from Christians? Instead of love, life, and hope, lost people see organized religion—a mechanical unity of ecclesiastical machinery that is after their money. Is there any wonder that they want to get rid of us?

As bad as it sounds, there is hope. We may fail, but not God. Don't forget this is Jesus' prayer. It will be answered in due time.

[Verse 22-23] Jesus so desired for His believers to be one (like He and the Father are one) to the intent that the unbelieving world might believe that He was the Sent One. For this purpose, He bestowed the glory He received from the Father on the believers. He said, *"And the glory which thou gavest me I have given them; that they may be one, even as we are one: I in them, and thou in me, that they may be made perfect in one; and that the world may know that thou hast sent me, and hast loved them, as thou hast loved me."*

Essentially, believers are to be like God—in oneness, in glory, and in perfection (maturity or completeness). This obviously is not the current state of Christendom, but God will make it happen in the future. And the world will eventually know that Jesus Christ is the Sent One, and that God loves His children as He loved Jesus.

Read *John 14:20, John 16:27*. In the mean time, we are a work in progress under tutors and governors until the time appointed of the Father. *Ephesians 4:11 And he gave some, apostles; and some, prophets; and some, evangelists; and some, pastors and teachers; (12) For the perfecting of the saints, for the work of the ministry, for the edifying of the body of Christ: (13) Till we all come in the unity of the faith, and of the knowledge of the Son of God, unto a perfect man, unto the measure of the stature of the fulness of Christ.*

Glorified with Jesus

[Verses 24-26] Jesus' final request and will was for all the believers to be with Him in heaven, that they might behold His glory, which the Father gave Him. The justifications for this request were as follows:

1. The Father's love for Jesus.
   John 10:17 Therefore doth my Father love me, because I lay down my life, that I might take it again.

2. The believers' faith in Jesus as the Sent One.
   John 16:27 For the Father himself loveth you, because ye have loved me, and have believed that I came out from God.

3. Jesus' promise to declare the Father's name. According to verse 6, Jesus had manifested the Father's name to the believers, and here, Jesus promised to declare it again in heaven, that the love of God might be fulfilled in them and Jesus might dwell in them. *Psalms 22:22 I will declare thy name unto my brethren: in the midst of the congregation will I praise thee... (25) My praise shall be of thee in the great congregation: I will pay my vows before them that fear him.*

Chapter 17 - Advocate

What a wonderful grand finale and comfort! Imagine having eternal fellowship with Jesus in the 3rd heaven and gazing into His glory. *2Corinthians 3:18 says, "But we all, with open face beholding as in a glass the glory of the Lord, are changed into the same image from glory to glory, even as by the Spirit of the Lord."* We should pinch ourselves. How can sinners like us end up there? We owe it all to Jesus Christ.

Summary

I can't keep from repeatedly saying "Wow" when I read Jesus' prayer for me. The fact that my God prayed for me alone has set Him apart from all other gods. And what He prayed for me is the best benefit package anyone can hope for. *2Peter 1:4 Whereby are given unto us exceeding great and precious promises: that by these ye might be partakers of the divine nature, having escaped the corruption that is in the world through lust.* What is the persecution of the world compared to the promises of God? O Lord, how great thou art!

> O Lord my God! When I in awesome wonder
> Consider all the worlds Thy Hands have made;
> I see the stars, I hear the rolling thunder,
> Thy power throughout the universe displayed:
>
> Refrain:
> Then sings my soul, my Saviour God, to Thee,
> How great Thou art, How great Thou art!
> Then sings my soul, my Saviour God, to Thee;
> How great Thou art, how great Thou art!
>
> When through the woods and forest glades I wander
> And hear the birds sing sweetly in the trees;
> When I look down, from lofty mountain grandeur

And hear the brook, and feel the gentle breeze: [Refrain]

And when I think that God, His Son not sparing,
Sent Him to die, I scarce can take it in;
That on the cross, my burden gladly bearing,
He bled and died to take away my sin: [Refrain]

When Christ shall come with shout of acclamation
And take me home, what joy shall fill my heart!
Then I shall bow in humble adoration,
And then proclaim, my God, how great Thou art! [Refrain]

("How Great Thou Art" hymn by Stuart K. Hine)

18 – Truth

Historical Synopsis

After His prayer in the preceding chapter, Jesus and the disciples crossed the brook Cedron (Kidron) and resorted to the Garden of Gethsemane. There, He was betrayed by Judas Iscariot and was arrested by the men and officers from the chief priests and Pharisees. A brief altercation occurred when Peter cut off the right ear of Malchus, a servant of the high priest.

Jesus was first presented to Annas, who was a high priest (*Acts 4:6*) and the father-in-law of Caiaphas, the resident high priest that year. Annas, although believed to be deposed from the high priest position by the Romans, remained influential and exercised much of the power of the high priesthood along with Caiaphas. He was the godfather figure in that society, which could explain why they brought Jesus to him first.

Jesus was then brought before Caiaphas, who questioned Him about His disciples and doctrine. During questioning, one of the officers did not like Jesus' answer and slapped Him. While the entire event was unfolding, Peter denied Jesus three times before the cock crowed, fulfilling Jesus' saying in *John 13:38* concerning him.

Finally, Jesus was brought before Pilate in the hall of judgment. Pilate found Jesus faultless and offered to release Him, but the Jews chose Barabbas to be released instead, who was a robber and murderer.

The Book of John

This chapter can be outlined as such:

I. Truth betrayed – *John 18:1-11*
II. Truth arrested – *John 18:12-14*
III. Truth fulfilled – *John 18:15-18, 25-27*
IV. Truth prosecuted – *John 18:19-24, 28-37*
V. Truth declared faultless – *John 18:38*
VI. Truth rejected – *John 18:39-40*

Chapter 18 - Truth

Key Spiritual Lessons

The unbelievers of the world, in an effort to stamp out truth, effectively applies a principle from *Zechariah 13:7—"Smite the shepherd, and the sheep shall be scattered,"* by leveraging religions and politics (ecclesiastical and civil powers). They do so because their deeds are evil and they do not want to be reproved by the word of God. (The word of God is truth, according to *John 17:17*, and Jesus Christ is Truth.) As such, unbelievers remain in darkness and are spiritually blind. They fail to recognize truth at every level, which leads to their rejection of Truth, as we see in this chapter.

    I.   The captors failed to recognize Truth – *John 18:1-12*
    II.   The religious leaders failed to recognize Truth – *John 18:13-14, 19-24*
    III.   The government failed to recognize Truth – *John 18:28-38*
    IV.   The people failed to recognize Truth – *John 18:39-40*

The Captors Failed to Recognize Truth

[Verse 1] The name "Cedron" means "turbid." The brook Cedron or Kidron runs through the mountains between Jerusalem and Mount Olives and empties into the Dead Sea. It gets the name "turbid" for its cloudy or opaque water. The Jews dumped unclean and defiled things into it. Read *2Chronicles 15:16, 2Chronicles 29:16, 2Chronicles 30:14, 2Kings 23:4-6*. A canal from the temple also contributed blood and soil from sacrifices into the foul brook.

King David (a type of Christ) and his people also crossed this brook in sorrow when he fled from Absalom, his rebellious son.

Read *2Samuel 15:13-23*. Jesus also crossed this brook with His disciples in deep sorrow knowing what would befall Him.

Jesus went into the garden of Gethsemane, which means "an oil press." It was there that He said, *"My soul is exceeding sorrowful, even unto death"* and prayed, *"O my Father, if it be possible, let this cup pass from me: nevertheless not as I will, but as thou wilt."*

It was in a garden that man fell. Interestingly, man's healing also began in a garden.

[Verses 2-3] Judas, the traitor, who knew that Jesus often resorted to the garden of Gethsemane, came with a band of men and officers to arrest Him. The captors represent the unbelieving world, and below are the lessons:

- The unbelieving world knows exactly where to find us. There is no point in hiding. We should face them like Jesus did in verse 4.

- The unbelieving world will vastly outnumber us as rendered by the ratio of the captors to Jesus' disciples in verse 3.

- The unbelieving world comes with *"lanterns and torches and weapons"*, according to verse 3.
    - They have physical light (the world's knowledge, wisdom, philosophy, tradition), but are void of the spiritual light of God. The word of God is our spiritual light. *Psalms 119:105 Thy word is a lamp unto my feet, and a light unto my path.*
    - The world is spiritually blind and unable to recognize Truth, as the captors were unable to recognize Jesus with light from their lanterns

and torches when they came into the garden. Jesus had to tell them *"I am he."*
- The weapons of the world are carnal, but our weapons are spiritual and mightier. *2Corinthians 10:4 For the weapons of our warfare are not carnal, but mighty through God to the pulling down of strong holds.*

- The unbelieving world will first go after the head or the shepherd. This includes pastors, ministry leaders, and heads of families. Read *Matthew 10:16-18, Psalms 2:1-3.* Pray for God's protection over these people.

[Verses 4-9] Jesus greeted His captors by asking them *"Whom seek ye?"* They said they were looking for Jesus of Nazareth. As soon as Jesus acknowledged *"I am he,"* they fell backward to the ground. After recovering themselves and not knowing what had just hit them, Jesus asked them the same question again, to which they also replied *"Jesus of Nazareth."* Jesus willingly offered Himself, but told them to let the disciples go.

Below are the lessons:

- Engage unbelievers head-on with truth (the word of God). Like an unsaved person who reads and tries to make sense of the Bible, unbelievers are not able to comprehend truth even when they come face to face with it. We are to engage and tell the world that Jesus is He, the Savior of the world. This is evangelism.

- The captors dishonored Jesus by reproachfully calling Him *"Jesus of Nazareth"* of Galilee. In *John 7:52,* the Pharisees said, *"Out of Galilee ariseth no prophet,"* essentially calling Him a hoax. *Psalms 22:6 But I am a worm, and no man; a reproach of men, and despised of the people.* Since the world dishonors Jesus, it will also dishonor His believers. But this shouldn't stop us from confessing Jesus. He answered their reproach by confessing *"I am he."*

- The captors came specifically for Jesus. The world will specifically come after every effective believer. There is no hiding. Pray for each other and remember the Lord's prayer in chapter 17. Be resolute when you face oppression and persecution. You should have counted the cost when you decided to follow Jesus. He is not a free ticket to heaven. Most Christians today are ill-equipped to handle persecution. Prepare your family before the evil days come. Review "How should one prepare for persecution?" in Chapter 16.

- For thirty pieces of silver, Judas switched sides and stood with the captors. What is your price?

- The world with all of its glory and power cannot stand up to Truth. Like the captors, sinners of the world will fall backward, as if being slain, when they stand face to face with the great I AM. (Believers fall forward in worship, but unbelievers fall backward in judgment.) Jesus simply spoke the captors to the ground. He could have killed them on the spot. Instead He gave Himself up willingly. Read *John 10:18*. It was also a wakeup call— a little snarl from the Lion of the tribe of Judah. The world will experience the full roar when Jesus returns as the King of Kings and Lord of Lords.

- Jesus gave the captors a second chance by asking them again *"Whom seek ye?"* God is longsuffering and gives second chances, but there is a point when He will give up on a hardened heart and give the person over to his devices. Read *Romans 1:20-32*.

- Jesus was the good Shepherd who offered Himself so that His sheep might live. He commanded the captors to let the disciples go, so that the scripture might be fulfilled—*"Of them which thou gavest me have I lost none."* The captors made a wise choice in obeying the command and letting the disciples go, otherwise, Jesus would have hurt them. Remember the judgment of God that fell on Egypt when Pharaoh refused to let Israel go?

[Verses 10-11] Peter, in his attempt to defend Jesus, resorted to violence. He cut off the high priest's servant's ear, whose name was Malchus. But Jesus commanded Peter to put away his sword and not fight, because He must drink the cup (the wrath of God) that the Father gave Him.

We do not need to defend truth. Truth will defend itself. Truth predates us and will certainly outlive us. The word of God will stand. If you don't believe it, simply violate any of God's commandments (not that I recommend it) and see how it will work out for you. You will end up proving God right every time. Read *Isaiah 40:6-8, Isaiah 46:9-11, Proverbs 19:21*.

We just need to obey truth, even unto death, as Jesus received the cup from the Father and drank it. Don't get ahead of God like Peter. Simply trust and obey.

[Verse 12] It's too bad the captors were too blind to recognize Truth. Jesus had just spoken them to the ground and allowed them to bind Him, and they thought they finally got the malefactor (evildoer). They did not realize the powerful miracle that had just happened. When Jesus restored the blind man's sight in *John 9*, at least some of the unbelieving Jews questioned their own judgment, *"How can a man that is a sinner do such miracles?"* But the world is all about silencing Truth and willfully shuts its eyes to the miracles and ignores or spins all evidence.

The Religious Leaders Failed to Recognize Truth

[Verses 13-14] The captors led Jesus to Annas, who then sent Him bound to his son-in-law, Caiaphas, who was also the high priest that year. In *John 11*, Caiaphas recommended that Jesus should die in order to protect their civil and religious privileges.

The names Annas and Caiaphas mean "humble" and "as comely" respectively. How interesting of these lost, blind, and clueless religious leaders to have had godly names, but inwardly they were ravening wolves. The entire Sanhedrim was guilty of preconceived murder – *John 11:53*.

Both high priests failed to recognize Truth. If you also want to miss Truth, get religion. But if you want Truth, get Jesus Christ. He is not a religion. He is the living God with whom you can have a personal relationship.

[Verses 19-24] Caiaphas grilled Jesus about His disciples and doctrine in hopes of finding a reason to charge Him and put Him to death. Jesus did not expose the disciples, nor did He implicate Himself. Jesus insisted He had no secret doctrine. He openly taught in public places, synagogues, and temples. So, Jesus suggested that Caiaphas should ask those who heard His doctrine—*"Behold, they know what I said"*—presumably pointing to the officers who attempted to arrest Him in *John 7*, but returned and told the Pharisees, *"Never man spake like this man."* But one of the officers did not take kindly to Jesus' suggestion and slapped Him. Jesus did not avenge the assault, but in meekness asked the officer to bear witness if He had delivered any wicked doctrine in the course of His

Chapter 18 - Truth

ministry. For more detail on the proceeding, read *Matthew 26:57-68*.

Besides attacking the Shepherd, the unbelieving world also wants to go after His disciples and doctrines. It is interested in knowing who the Christians are, especially those who are actively serving the Lord. Religious profiling is nothing new, but is rapidly growing. It will come to a point where the entire world is against Christianity, especially during the antichrist's rule. The antichrist's economy will require everyone to bear the mark of the beast. Anyone who does not have the mark will stick out like a sore thumb and will suffer persecution.

The unbelieving world is looking for excuses to stop preachers from preaching the gospel. Its agents are monitoring pastors' sermons in churches or online. Ministers are scrutinized. Those who break the law, such as by cheating on taxes, give the world a reason to stop them. Don't be foolish, live a blameless life.

The unbelieving world is also interested in the doctrine of Jesus Christ, not because it wants to own it, but to resist and destroy it. The world is all about *"having a form of godliness, but denying the power thereof."* The world loves to put on a holy façade to draw people into its religious system and leads them astray with false teachings, new and improved doctrines (including new Bibles), fables, genealogies, philosophies, traditions, and heresies. The people in this religious system keep learning, but are *"never able to come to the knowledge of the truth."* The Apostle Paul counseled Timothy on how to handle this in *2Timothy 3:10-17, 2Timothy 4:1-5*.

[Verses 15-18, 25-27] Woven into this chapter is the account of Peter's denial of Christ. Jesus said in *John 13:36-38* that *"The cock shall not crow, till thou hast denied me thrice."* And it happened exactly as prophesied. Indeed, whatever truth says shall come to pass. Take heed that you are under its good grace.

Locked in this simple story is a warning to ministers who desire to import the world's system for the betterment of their ministries. This includes the world's methodologies and ideologies for obtaining salvation, achieving holiness, growing the church, teaching and admonishing children, discipling, counseling, and so on. To unlock the message, we should know that the palace of the high priest in verse 15 represents the religious system of the world.

Like a palace, the religious system of the world looks attractive and luxurious on the outside, and appears to have Jesus inside. The religious rulers kept Jesus in the palace, not to honor Him, but to kill Him. Jesus was not a free man; He was bound. The world's system, pretending to have the truth inside, but in reality it is killing the truth by watering it down. The messages sound good, but are ineffective in transforming lives. The word of God does not have free course. Biblical methods are perceived to be ancient and outdated compared to the world's ways, which are deemed more palatable and are endorsed by celebrities. Peter began to deny Christ as soon as he walked through the guard door to enter into the palace. Take heed, you too will begin to deny Christ the moment you dabble with the world's system.

Inside the palace, Peter stood with the servants and officers of the chief priests and Pharisees to warm himself by the fire of coals they made. If you dabble with the world's system, you will find yourself standing with their people and cozying up to them. Notice the progression. Verse 16: Peter stood at the door without. Verse 18: Peter stood with them, and warmed himself. Verse 25: Simon Peter stood and warmed himself.

You will find the world's system is able to attract all kinds of people and flourish into mega organizations. Read *Ezekiel 31:3-9*. Why not? The word of God is not the final authority. There is no accountability. People are welcomed to live their lives any way they want, as long as they are happy. *Judges 21:25 In those days there was no king in Israel: every man did that which was right in his own eyes.*

Peter denied Christ two more times inside the palace. The people you cozy up to will cause you to deny Christ, as they did to Peter. Your end will be bitter, just as when Peter recalled Jesus' words and went out and wept bitterly.

Notice the fire of coals inside the palace of the high priest? Coal fire in the Bible is a type of God's judgment. In other words, God's judgment is in the religious system of the world. These foolish people are stoking the fire and warming themselves by it.

Beware that you do not import any of the world's philosophies (more like fail-osophies) into your ministry. You would rather have a small church that honors God by teaching and preaching the word of God undiluted, than a mega seeker-friendly church that caters to the consumer culture by watering down the truth. You must come to terms that God's way is perfect and needs no improvement. *Isaiah 55:9 For as the heavens are higher than the earth, so are my ways higher than your ways, and my thoughts than your thoughts.* Never swap God's perfect way for the world's way. Do you know God's way for finding a spouse, raising children, and managing finances? Do you wonder why the divorce rate is high among Christians, or why children are so rebellious?

The Government Failed to Recognize Truth

[Verse 28] When the religious rulers were done interrogating Jesus, they handed Him to Roman governor Pontius Pilate to finish Him off. The religious rulers were careful not to defile themselves and avoided entering into the judgment hall so they might eat the Passover feast.

The Book of John

Religion uses vehicles such as the government to do its dirty job. Religion can reject and kill the truth and still look holy. Religion will waste no time getting rid of truth once it gets a hold of it, as the rulers went to Pilate's house early in the morning to get rid of Jesus.

I wonder how many churches are like this. They look good and holy on the outside, but inside they torture and water down the truth. The messages from the pulpit are ineffective. Too bad the people who attend these churches are ignorant of the truth. Otherwise they would run screaming. Did you know the Bible is written on about the eighth-grade level? It is not hard to understand, it is just hard to believe. These people have no excuse for not knowing the word of God.

[Verses 29-32] Pilate performed his duty well, even though he was disturbed by a group of rude Jews in the wee hours of the morning. Since they would not enter into the judgment hall, Pilate went out to them and demanded to know *"What accusation bring ye against this man?"* They rudely replied, *"If he were not a malefactor, we would not have delivered him up unto thee,"* insinuating that Jesus had done something really bad, but they provided no details. Without knowing the exact violation, Pilate wouldn't be bothered by the Jews and told them to judge Jesus according to their law instead. Then the Jews said, *"It is not lawful for us to put any man to death,"* further insinuating that the crime was worthy of death, which they could not inflict, because the Romans had removed the capital-punishment authority from them.

People who hate truth will make things up to accuse truth. Their claims are usually baseless or based on manufactured evidence. Don't believe their evidence. Stand firm on the word of God. They can accuse all they want, but they will be found liars. *Romans 3:4 God forbid: yea, let God be true, but every man a liar; as it is written, That thou mightest be justified in thy sayings, and mightest overcome when thou art judged.*

Chapter 18 - Truth

When someone says, "Here's what's wrong with the word of God," that person is a liar, because *"the law of the LORD is perfect"* and *"the testimony of the LORD is sure,"* according to *Psalms 19:7*. Truth is faultless against all accusations.

Truth shall stand. All of Jesus' sayings will be fulfilled. Read *Matthew 5:18, Matthew 24:35*. Jesus said He would be crucified by the Gentiles. If the Romans hadn't removed capital-punishment authority from the Jews, the religious rulers would have stoned Jesus rather than crucify Him. Read *Mark 10:33, John 3:14, John 12:32-33*.

These Jews, by rejecting Truth, ended up proving truth right. This is mind-blowing. Even when they falsely accused Jesus as a malefactor (evildoer), they still proved truth right, because Jesus was made sin for us. Everyone who is against truth will prove truth right. God is to be feared. *Luke 12:5 But I will forewarn you whom ye shall fear: Fear him, which after he hath killed hath power to cast into hell; yea, I say unto you, Fear him.*

[Verses 33-38] The religious rulers sentenced Jesus to death for blasphemy for making Himself equal to God. However, Roman law had no such condemnation, but it would hand down capital punishment to those who were a threat to Caesar. Since the chief priests had also accused Jesus in *Luke 23:2* by saying, *"We found this fellow perverting the nation, and forbidding to give tribute to Caesar, saying that he himself is Christ a King,"* Pilate asked Jesus, *"Art thou the King of the Jews?"* Pilate wanted to know if Jesus would be a king in a political or religious sense. If religious, he had no interest.

Jesus answered Pilate's question with a question, essentially asking, "Did you conclude by yourself that I am a king or did others tell you so?" If the former, the burden of proof was on Pilate. If the latter, the burden of proof was on the accusers.

The Book of John

Pilate wasn't happy with the answer and rebuked Jesus. He said he wasn't a Jew and therefore couldn't comprehend Jewish matters. But since the Jewish nation and the chief priests had delivered Him there, he had the responsibility to determine the relevancy of the charge. So Pilate demanded to know, *"What hast thou done?"*

Then Jesus revealed that His kingdom was not of this world. For if His kingdom were of this world, then would His servants fight and He would not be delivered to the Jews. In other words, there was no reason for the Roman government to be alarmed.

Then Pilate, who wanted to be sure of what he had just heard, asked Jesus to confirm, *"Art thou a king then?"* to which Jesus answered, *"Thou sayest that I am a king."* Jesus never explicitly claimed He was a king, but claimed He came to this world to testify to the truth. Furthermore, Jesus said, *"Every one that is of the truth heareth my voice."* Pilate obviously didn't get the message, because only those of the Truth would know who Jesus was. Read *John 10:27, John 8:47*.

By that time, Pilate concluded that Jesus was no threat to the Roman government and probably had enough of the religious mumbo-jumbo. He asked Jesus *"What is truth?"* and didn't care for the answer. He left the judgment hall to proclaim Jesus was faultless. Too bad for Pilate, who was face to face with Truth, but did not recognize it. Pilate thought he knew Jesus, but didn't care for the truth and as such missed the Savior. Jesus Christ is Truth and the Savior of the world. Unfortunately, many people have an idea of Jesus in their heads, but miss Him by 18 inches, the distance between the head and the heart.

1Timothy 2:2 says we should pray *"For kings, and for all that are in authority; that we may lead a quiet and peaceable life in all godliness and honesty."* We thank God for government servants who are Christians and for a peaceful environment in which to

Chapter 18 - Truth

exercise our faith, but we cannot count on any government to support Jesus Christ, because it does not recognize truth.

Governments cannot recognize truth, because they consist of mostly unbelievers who are spiritually blind and unable to discern truth. Jesus told Pilate that His kingdom was not of this world, meaning it is a spiritual kingdom. Read *Romans 14:17, Luke 17:21*. That went over Pilate's head, just as it went over Nicodemus' head when Jesus told him, *"Except a man be born again, he cannot see the kingdom of God."*

Governments also will not recognize truth, because that would mean making truth the final authority. If a government says *"Thy word is truth,"* then it must rule by the word of God.

It is interesting that even though Pilate did not recognize Truth, he concluded that Truth was faultless. Furthermore, he began his examination of Jesus as a man (verse 29), but ended calling Him a king (verse 37).

Only individuals who are of the Truth will hear Jesus' voice and will follow Him. If you are of the Truth, this should be your purpose in life—*"To this end was I born, and for this cause came I into the world, that I should bear witness unto the truth."* Remember John the Baptist's purpose in life? *John 1:6 There was a man sent from God, whose name was John. (7) The same came for a witness, to bear witness of the Light, that all men through him might believe. (8) He was not that Light, but was sent to bear witness of that Light.* Imagine that... living a purposeful life for God!

The People Failed to Recognize Truth

[Verses 39-40] According to *Matthew 27:18*, Pilate knew the religious rulers wanted to destroy Jesus because of envy. So, as a last-ditch effort to save Jesus, Pilate allowed the customary release of a prisoner of their choice, hoping that they would choose Jesus. The word "again" in verse 40 suggests that Pilate had offered this once before, but the chief priests and elders persuaded the multitude to ask for Barabbas instead, who was a robber and murderer. Read *Luke 23:20-25*. Pilate tried hard and pleaded with them—*"Why, what evil hath he (Jesus) done?,"* but couldn't prevail against the multitude. In the end, Pilate washed his hands before them and said, *"I am innocent of the blood of this just person: see ye to it."* And the people said, *"His blood be on us, and on our children."* Read about the account in *Matthew 27*.

There are two very important lessons here:

1. People who follow religion and religious rulers will end up crucifying Truth. Billions of people in various religions of the world will split hell wide open, because they do not have a personal relationship with Truth. It bears repeating, Jesus Christ is not a religion. He is Truth—the living God who died for the sins of the world. *1John 5:20 And we know that the Son of God is come, and hath given us an understanding, that we may know him that is true, and we are in him that is true, even in his Son Jesus Christ. This is the true God, and eternal life.*

2. Jesus Christ, the innocent Lamb of God, was killed so that sinners on death row could be pardoned. It was a good day for Barabbas. It is a good day for any sinner who accepts Jesus Christ as Savior.

Chapter 18 - Truth

Prophecies

When the captors met Jesus in verse 4, they could not recognize Him. As soon as Jesus revealed Himself as "I AM," they fell backward to the ground. This shows Israel didn't recognize Jesus as Messiah in His first coming. They fell to the ground, like the unfruitful branches that were cut down in *John 15*.

However, the captors recognized Jesus when He said to them "I AM" for the second time in verse 8. This shows Israel will recognize Jesus as Messiah at His second coming.

Pilate began his examination of Jesus as a man in verse 29, but ended calling Him a king in verse 37. Jesus Christ as God in the flesh came to this world as a humble man to bear witness of the truth, to destroy the works of the devil, and to give eternal life to all who would believe in Him. Jesus Christ will return again as the King of Kings and Lord of Lords.

Summary

It is good to reflect on Jesus' question, *"Whom seek ye?"* Hopefully you do not seek Jesus out of some religious duty, but seek Him as the Savior and Truth. May God grant you to know that Jesus Christ is Truth and that you may master truth as a *"workman that needeth not to be ashamed, rightly dividing the word of truth."*

19 – Lamb of God

Historical Synopsis

Pilate, having to juggle the difficult tasks of pacifying the Jews and releasing the innocent Jesus, came up with a plan to chastise Jesus before letting Him go (*Luke 23:16*). After scourging Jesus and inflicting Him with other severities and insults, Pilate presented the beaten-up Jesus wearing a crown of thorns and a purple robe to the Jews, and again pronounced that Jesus was faultless. But the religious rulers were dead set on seeing Jesus crucified. Pilate did not prevail, despite numerous attempts to deliver Jesus from death.

Jesus was crucified along with two thieves in Golgotha, near Jerusalem. The title on the cross, "JESUS OF NAZARETH THE KING OF THE JEWS," was written in Hebrew, Greek, and Latin. Below the cross, the soldiers parted Jesus' garments and cast lots for His coat.

While on the cross, Jesus bequeathed the care of His mother to the Apostle John. Having been on the cross for six hours and after receiving some vinegar, Jesus died. His body was claimed by Joseph of Arimathaea, who along with Nicodemus, provided the burial services.

This chapter can be outlined as such:

   I. Jesus is scourged and mocked – *John 19:1-15*
   II. Jesus is crucified at Golgotha – *John 19:16-27*
   III. Jesus dies on the cross – *John 19:28-37*
   IV. Joseph and Nicodemus bury Jesus – *John 19:38-42*

Chapter 19 – Lamb of God

Key Spiritual Lessons

Human interference with the plan of God, for good or bad reasons, is futile. God is sovereign. God will fulfill His word, every bit of it. We will see a number of fulfilled prophecies in this chapter. *Luke 16:17 And it is easier for heaven and earth to pass, than one tittle of the law to fail.*

Following are the key spiritual lessons:

I. Humans' futile efforts to protect Truth – *John 19:1-12*
II. Humans' futile efforts to destroy Truth – *John 19:13-22, 28-37*
III. Humans' shameless efforts to profit from Truth – *John 19:23-24*
IV. Believers stand by the cross and step up to the plate – *John 19:25-27, 38-42*

Humans' Futile Efforts to Protect Truth

[Verses 1-7] The Jews had been a constant source of trouble for the Romans with their uprisings and riots. As a governor, Pilate was under pressure to keep the peace and demonstrate his leadership to Rome.

After announcing Jesus was faultless, Pilate learned that He was a Galilaean. Since Galilee was in Herod's jurisdiction, Pilate was probably happy to get rid of Jesus and promptly transferred Him over to Herod, who happened to be in Jerusalem at that time. (This was Herod who beheaded John the Baptist.)

Herod, who had desired to see Jesus for a long time, was glad for the encounter, because he had heard of His fame. Herod

Chapter 19 – Lamb of God

asked Jesus many questions, but He answered not a word. So, Herod and his soldiers who accompanied him made nothing of Jesus and treated Him as a silly and contemptible person. After they finished mocking Him, they arrayed Him in a white robe and sent Him back to Pilate. Read about the account in *Matthew 27, Mark 15, Luke 23*.

In order to appease the Jews, Pilate decided to chastise Jesus for a show and planned to release Him afterward. Jesus was mercilessly scourged. The soldiers set a crown of thorns on His head, a reed in His right hand, and put on Him a purple robe. Then they mocked, slapped, hit Him on the head with the reed, and spat on Him.

Pilate presented the beaten-up Jesus to the Jews and hoped they would be satisfied. But the plan backfired. The Jews were not in the least moved. Instead, they cried out *"Crucify him, crucify him,"* even though Pilate repeatedly said, *"I find no fault in him."* The Jews also said Jesus ought to die, because He claimed to be the Son of God.

Words fail to describe the injustice, brutality, and atrocity that were done to the Lord Jesus Christ, who was innocent, righteous, and sinless. This is my least favorite chapter in the Gospel of John, perhaps because I am one of the reasons why Jesus suffered and died. Yet I am forever thankful that He died for my sins. Indeed, by His stripes I am healed. *Isaiah 53:3 He is despised and rejected of men; a man of sorrows, and acquainted with grief: and we hid as it were our faces from him; he was despised, and we esteemed him not. (4) Surely he hath borne our griefs, and carried our sorrows: yet we did esteem him stricken, smitten of God, and afflicted. (5) But he was wounded for our transgressions, he was bruised for our iniquities: the chastisement of our peace was upon him; and with his stripes we are healed.*

The Book of John

Pause to reflect for a moment. Every god demands worship, but the true God died for the sins of mankind. God became man in the person of Jesus Christ (verse 5: *"Behold the man!"*) This sets Him apart from all other so-called gods. *Romans 5:6 For when we were yet without strength, in due time Christ died for the ungodly. (7) For scarcely for a righteous man will one die: yet peradventure for a good man some would even dare to die. (8) But God commendeth his love toward us, in that, while we were yet sinners, Christ died for us.*

No matter how badly people treat Truth, He remains royal and righteous. When Herod was done with Jesus, he put on Him a white robe (picture of righteousness) before sending Him back to Pilate. Pilate's soldiers put a purple robe (picture of royalty) on Jesus when they mocked and tortured Him. They stripped Jesus of this purple robe before they crucified Him. The King of Kings gave everything up to die for the sins of the world.

[Verses 8-9] When Pilate heard that the reason the Jews wanted to kill Jesus was because He had asserted Himself to be the Son of God, he became more afraid. He knew in his conscience that Jesus was innocent, and his wife had also said to him, *"Have thou nothing to do with that just man: for I have suffered many things this day in a dream because of him."* So, Pilate went back into the judgment hall and asked Jesus, *"Whence art thou?"* He knew Jesus was a Jew from Galilee, but he was asking about Jesus' origin. In other words, "Are you a man or God?," but Jesus kept silent.

Everyone should consider *"Whence art thou?"* concerning Jesus. If you say He originates from heaven, then He is who the Bible says He is. *John 1:1 In the beginning was the Word, and the Word was with God, and the Word was God.* If you say He is just a good person or a prophet, then you missed your Savior. The Jews struggled with this question in *John 7:27-28, John 8:13-14,* and *John 9:29.*

[Verses 10-12] Pilate was upset that Jesus did not answer his question and reminded Jesus that he had the power to kill and to release. An ordinary person would oblige to answer and beg for his life. But Jesus wasn't at all concerned for His life and said, *"Thou couldest have no power at all against me, except it were given thee from above: therefore he that delivered me unto thee hath the greater sin."* These words might have confirmed Pilate's suspicion that Jesus was a divine being. Thereafter, he sought to release Jesus, but the religious rulers made it very hard for him. They knew that Pilate highly valued his affiliation with Caesar and certainly would not want the public to perceive him to be unfaithful to Caesar. So, the religious rulers played the Caesar card saying, *"If thou let this man go, thou art not Caesar's friend: whosoever maketh himself a king speaketh against Caesar."* This was a twist and a lie, because Jesus never claimed to be a king.

Pilate gave up on saving Jesus when the Jews played the Caesar card. This goes to show that human efforts to protect Truth are futile, because like most things, there are breaking points. Humans are inherently weak, selfish, and easily succumb to pressure. Thank God, Truth does not need anyone to defend Him.

Humans' Futile Efforts to Destroy Truth

[Verses 13-15] Pilate, being a governor and politician, chose to protect his reputation and prioritize Caesar over Jesus. He brought Jesus out of the judgment hall to a place called the Pavement, where he sat in the judgment seat. The day was *"the preparation of the passover,"* which was the day before the Sabbath (not the regular Sabbath, but a high day or Passover-Sabbath, according to verse 31). *Luke 23:54 And that day was the preparation, and the sabbath drew on.* The time, as documented by the Apostle John, was the sixth hour, which was about noon. However, according to Mark, Jesus was crucified at the third hour (9 a.m., *Mark 15:25*), died at the ninth hour (3 p.m., *Mark 15:34-37*), and buried at even (6 p.m., *Mark 15:42*). According to *Matthew 27:45* and *Luke 23:44*, Jesus was already on the cross at the sixth hour and darkness was over all the land till the ninth hour. So, it makes sense to treat the Apostle John's time as a rough instead of precise time.

Pilate, who had to be frustrated with the Jews for putting him in a predicament, sarcastically said, *"Behold your King!,"* for he knew the Jews falsely accused Jesus. But the Jews cried out, *"Away with him, away with him, crucify him."* He gave them a final chance to change their mind by asking, *"Shall I crucify your King?"* And the Jews gave their final rejection of Jesus and said, *"We have no king but Caesar."*

Pilate in the judgment seat is an example of man judging God. As Pilate ended up calling Jesus a king, every man who sees Jesus again will acknowledge the same. *Philippians 2:10 That at the name of Jesus every knee should bow, of things in heaven, and things in earth, and things under the earth; (11) And that every tongue should confess that Jesus Christ is Lord, to the glory of God the Father.*

The Jews' final rejection of Jesus was a fulfillment of *John 1:11, "He came unto his own, and his own received him not."* The prophecies that are fulfilled in this chapter are amazing. Jesus' suffering as a lamb headed to the slaughter and the method of death were prophesied and fulfilled. The day that Jesus died, the time of death, and the day of His resurrection perfectly coincided with the Feast of Passover, Feast of Unleavened Bread, and Feast of Firstfruits, which God instructed Moses to record about 1,300 years earlier. Try to figure the odds. All I can say is God is awesome and we serve an amazing God!

[Verses 16-18] In the end, the Jews won, and the soldiers led Jesus to be crucified. Jesus carried His wooden cross part way, and

Chapter 19 – Lamb of God

when He could no longer bear it, the soldiers compelled Simon the Cyrenian, who just came out of the country, to carry it for Jesus. He was crucified in Golgotha with two thieves.

Yet another prophecy was fulfilled. Jesus was numbered with the transgressors. *Isaiah 53:12 Therefore will I divide him a portion with the great, and he shall divide the spoil with the strong; because he hath poured out his soul unto death: and he was numbered with the transgressors; and he bare the sin of many, and made intercession for the transgressors.*

The fact that Jesus carried His own cross reminds us that we have our own cross to carry, especially if we are His disciples. *Luke 14:27 And whosoever doth not bear his cross, and come after me, cannot be my disciple.* This means we must die to self daily. *Luke 9:23 And he said to them all, If any man will come after me, let him deny himself, and take up his cross daily, and follow me.* We must lay aside our personal goals, desires, and ambitions so that God can reveal His for our life. We live to fulfill the mission that God has for us. Read *Luke 9:59-62*.

[Verses 19-22] Pilate wrote the title "JESUS OF NAZARETH THE KING OF THE JEWS" in Hebrew, Greek, and Latin, and nailed it to the cross. The religious rulers took exception to the message and wanted to remove "THE KING OF THE JEWS," but Pilate refused to do it.

It is amazing that a lost Gentile like Pilate could see and acknowledge Jesus as King when the Jewish leaders were blind to it, even until this day, because they reject Him as Messiah.

[Verses 28-30] After Jesus committed his mother to the care of the Apostle John, He knew He had fulfilled all prophecies concerning His sufferings, except for one, being offered vinegar for His thirst. And when He said, "*I thirst,*" they soaked a sponge with vinegar, put it on a reed of hyssop, and gave it to Him. As soon as this was done, Jesus said *"It is finished"* and gave up the ghost at the ninth hour (3 p.m., *Mark 15:34-37*). Thus were *Psalms 22:15* and *Psalms 69:21* fulfilled.

[Verses 31-37] Since it was the eve of the Sabbath, which began at 6 p.m., and the Mosaic law in *Deuteronomy 21:22-23* specified that a crucified victim must not remain on the cross overnight, the religious rulers asked Pilate to hasten the death by breaking the legs so that the victims could not push their bodies up to breathe. Thus, the soldiers broke the legs of both of the thieves, but when they came to Jesus, they noticed He had already died and therefore did not break His bones. But one of the soldiers, who wanted to be doubly sure, pierced Jesus' side with a spear, and out came blood and water.

Yet here, two more prophecies were fulfilled. The word of God is not only true, it is truth.

1. None of Jesus' bones would be broken. *Psalms 34:20 He keepeth all his bones: not one of them is broken.* Read *Exodus 12:46, Psalms 22:17*.

2. The Jews would look on Jesus whom they pierced. *Zechariah 12:10 And I will pour upon the house of David, and upon the inhabitants of Jerusalem, the spirit of grace and of supplications: and they shall look upon me whom they have pierced, and they shall mourn for him, as one mourneth for his only son, and shall be in bitterness for him, as one that is in bitterness for his firstborn.*

Observe that religious activities were in full observation, even though the religious rulers just crucified the Truth. They were so careful to maintain an outward appearance by not violating the Sabbath, but they crucified the Lord of the Sabbath. So, if you also

Chapter 19 – Lamb of God

want to miss Truth, simply pick a religion. But if you want Truth, get Jesus Christ by trusting Him as your Lord and Savior.

Also observe that no one ever died around Jesus when He was alive. The two thieves on the cross died after Jesus gave up the ghost. Lazarus was resurrected from the dead when Jesus visited him. Scores of people were healed from diseases by Jesus. He is the resurrection and the life! Believers of Jesus Christ have everlasting life!

Although the account of water and blood is unique to the Gospel of John, the apostle testified that he personally witnessed it and wanted us to know the record was true that we might believe in Jesus Christ. This is because water and blood are necessary for our salvation. By the spiritual water of the word (not the water of baptism) our souls are washed and purified. Read *Ephesians 5:26-27*. The Old Testament alluded to this with the practice of divers washings and of the shedding of the blood of innocent animals. Read *Hebrew 9:10, 19-26*. By the blood of Jesus Christ, the law of God is satisfied, our sins are forgiven, and we are justified and reconciled to God. Read *Romans 3:24-26*.

So, they nailed Jesus to the cross, and He died. Does this mean humans were able to destroy Truth? No, far from it. Everything happened according to God's will and plan. Nevertheless, it hasn't stopped lost people from their futile attempts to destroy truth (the word of God).

Humans' Shameless Efforts to Profit from Truth

[Verses 23-24] When the soldiers had crucified Jesus, they stripped Him naked and parted His blood-stained garments into four parts, one part for each soldier. The soldiers, however, decided to preserve Jesus' coat that was seamless and woven from top to bottom, and they cast lots to determine who should get it.

The soldiers' actions fulfilled yet another scripture. *Psalms 22:18 They part my garments among them, and cast lots upon my vesture.*

Jesus' coat was the robe of the ephod of the high priest. He wore the coat because He was the High Priest. Read *Exodus 28:31-32*. The coat was not destroyed, which shows Jesus' priesthood remains intact. The coat was seamless, woven from the top to bottom, and was most likely blue in color. Blue represents heaven, and the shape of the coat is the shape of the universe. *Psalms 104:6 Thou coveredst it* (the earth) *with the deep* (universe) *as with a garment: the waters stood above the mountains.* Read *Psalms 104:1-6*. The coat shows Jesus Christ originated from heaven and that He is greater than heaven, because the entire universe is but a coat for Him. *2Chronicles 2:6a But who is able to build him an house, seeing the heaven and heaven of heavens cannot contain him?*

The soldiers profiting from Jesus' garments represents the world's shameless efforts to profit from Jesus. The world is happy to make merchandise of Jesus. Just go to any Christian bookstore and see what percentage of the store is devoted to the only thing that matters, which is the Bible. In most stores, over 99% of the store is filled with Jesus stuff. Do you really need stuff to express or remind you of your Christianity?

Chapter 19 – Lamb of God

Believers Stand by the Cross and Step Up to the Plate

[Verses 25-27] Standing by the cross within earshot of the dying Jesus were three ladies all named Mary—Mary the mother of Jesus, Mary the wife of Cleophas, and Mary Magdalene, as well as the Apostle John. Jesus tenderly provided for his mother at His death. He gave her to John to be his mother. And to John He said, *"Behold thy mother!,"* to whom he now had a filial duty. From that time, the Apostle John took Mary to his home to care for her. (Joseph had apparently passed away.)

Jesus cared for people even when He was on the cross. That was because Jesus, being God, was merciful and gracious as always. *Hebrews 13:8 Jesus Christ the same yesterday, and to day, and for ever.*

As the times of the Gentiles draws to a close, we will see more atrocity toward Christianity. It is important that we stand by the cross like the three women and the Apostle John. We must listen to Jesus, for He will care for us and instruct us on what to do.

[Verses 38-42] Because he feared the Jews, Joseph of Arimathaea was a secret believer and disciple of Jesus. He begged Pilate for the body of Jesus and took it down from the cross. Nicodemus, who was also a secret believer, came to honor Jesus with burial spices of myrrh and aloes. Together, they wrapped Jesus' body in linen cloth with the burial spices according to the Jewish custom. Joseph also provided a new sepulcher for Jesus' burial. It was in a garden near the site of the cross.

A garden is where people plant and grow things. Jesus was the seed that the husbandman Father planted. *John 12:24 Verily, verily, I say unto you, Except a corn of wheat fall into the ground and die, it abideth alone: but if it die, it bringeth forth much fruit.*

The first Adam sinned in the Garden of Eden and ruined mankind. The last Adam (Jesus) was sacrificed and planted in a garden to provide salvation for mankind.

The secret believers came out of hiding to care for the body of Jesus. Now, the body of Jesus is the church. If you also are a secret believer, it is time for you to come out of hiding and step up to the plate for the service of God.

Summary

"*John 1:29b Behold the Lamb of God, which taketh away the sin of the world*" is a fitting verse to summarize this chapter. Every person should behold the Lamb of God crucified on the cross as the Israelites looked upon the brazen serpent on the pole for their healing. There is no other form of healing for sin, otherwise God wouldn't have had to sacrifice His only begotten Son. He did it because He loved the world. *John 15:13 Greater love hath no man than this, that a man lay down his life for his friends.* God is "*not willing that any should perish, but that all should come to repentance.*" Why should anyone die and go to hell when salvation is so accessible by faith?

There is no other salvation besides Jesus Christ. *Acts 4:12 Neither is there salvation in any other: for there is none other name under heaven given among men, whereby we must be saved.* May God give you grace and faith to behold the Lamb of God.

20 – The Christ

Historical Synopsis

Mary Magdalene, from whom Jesus cast out seven devils, went to the grave with sweet spices to anoint the body of Jesus at the rising of the sun on Sunday morning. She discovered the large stone covering the sepulcher had been rolled away and the body of Jesus was missing. She departed quickly to inform the disciples. When she told Peter and John, they did not believe her account and ran to the grave to see it for themselves.

Mary returned to the sepulcher and wept. Soon after she talked with the angels, Jesus appeared to her, but she thought He was the gardener and asked if He knew where she might be able to find the body of Jesus. But when Jesus called her name, she instantly knew that it was Him and called Him *"Rabboni,"* which means "Master."

In the evening of the same day, Jesus appeared to the disciples and showed them His hands and side, and they were glad to see Him. But Thomas, who was absent at the time, would only be persuaded if he could witness and feel Jesus' hands and side. Thomas' wish was fulfilled eight days later when Jesus reappeared to the disciples.

This chapter can be outlined as such:

    I.   Mary Magdalene's encounter with the risen Christ – *John 20:1-18*

The Book of John

II. The disciples' encounter with the risen Christ – *John 20:19-23*

III. Thomas' encounter with the risen Christ – *John 20:24-31*

Chapter 20 – The Christ

Key Spiritual Lessons

This chapter gives proofs of Christ's resurrection. While no one witnessed the actual resurrection, there were many eyewitnesses and proofs of the resurrection. Examples include the empty tomb (*Luke 24:1-3*), Mary Magdalene's encounter with the risen Christ (*John 20:16-17*), and the disciples' encounter with the risen Christ on three occasions: in locked rooms (*John 20:19,26*), on the shore of the sea of Tiberias (*John 21:1*), and on the Mount of Olives (*Acts 1:9-12*). Cleopas and his friend encountered the risen Christ on the road to Emmaus (*Luke 24:13-35*), and there was the eyewitness of more than 500 people including the Apostle Paul (*1Corinthians 15:4-8*). Besides these, the living Jesus performed many signs in the presence of His disciples that are not written in the Bible. The things that are documented are enough to help us believe that Jesus is the risen Christ.

This chapter shows three groups of people who will encounter the living Jesus represented by Mary Magdalene, the disciples, and Thomas. Mary Magdalene represents people who by faith seek Jesus early. The disciples represent people who are ignorant of scriptures, struggle with faith, and require evidences before believing. Thomas represents those who will only believe by sight.

Following are the key spiritual lessons:

I. Lessons from Mary Magdalene's encounter with the risen Christ – *John 20:1, 11-18*
II. Lessons from the disciples' encounter with the risen Christ – *John 20:2-10, 19-23*
III. Lessons from Thomas' encounter with the risen Christ – *John 20:24-31*

Lessons from Mary Magdalene's Encounter with the Risen Christ

[Verse 1] Mary Magdalene loved the Lord Jesus. She rose up early to minister to His body, but encountered the living Jesus instead. Proverbs 8:17 says, *"I love them that love me; and those that seek me early shall find me."* This teaches us to seek Jesus early in our lives. I have a good friend who told me he would consider Jesus at age 50. But there is no guarantee of tomorrow.

It was still dark when Mary Magdalene went to the grave. The perfect time to seek Jesus is when we are in darkness, because He is the light of the world. Read *John 8:12, John 12:46*. Realize that this world is in darkness and is ruled by the rulers of darkness. The god of this world (Satan) has blinded the minds of those who don't believe the gospel. Read *Ephesians 6:12, 2Corinthians 4:3-4*. Do not remain in darkness, but believe the gospel of Jesus Christ.

When Mary Magdalene was on her way to the grave, she wondered who would roll the large stone away from the door of the sepulcher, for she certainly did not have the strength. But when she got there, she noticed the stone was already rolled away. Read *Mark 16:1-4*. This teaches us to live by faith. The world's wisdom says Mary should have made sure the stone was removed before making the trip, otherwise it would be a waste of time. God's wisdom says, *"The just shall live by faith."* This doesn't mean we shouldn't dot the i's and cross the t's, but when it comes to serving God, there will be times we simply have to trust Him. The large stone blocking the sepulcher is like the Red Sea to Moses. Unless God performs His miracle, the mission cannot be accomplished. Christians love to say, God wants me to do this and that and go here and there. If so, the strongest validation is when the path contains an obstacle that only God can remove. This is because serving God requires faith. *Hebrews 11:6 But without faith it is impossible to*

Chapter 20 – The Christ

please him: for he that cometh to God must believe that he is, and that he is a rewarder of them that diligently seek him.

[Verse 11] Those who seek Jesus early will find that He is risen just as Mary saw an empty sepulcher. They will discover that the death, burial, and resurrection of Jesus was according to scriptures. *1Corinthians 15:3 For I delivered unto you first of all that which I also received, how that Christ died for our sins according to the scriptures; (4) And that he was buried, and that he rose again the third day according to the scriptures.*

[Verse 12] Mary saw two angels in the sepulcher. Those who are born again by faith will see supernatural things in the scriptures. They will also be able to see the Kingdom of God, according to *John 3:3*.

[Verse 13] But Mary Magdalene continued to be upset in spite of an angel's reminder of Jesus' words, how that He would be delivered into the hands of sinful men, and be crucified, and rise again on the third day. Read *Matthew 17:22-23, Luke 24:1-8*. For some reason, she either could not comprehend or would not believe in the resurrection and continued looking for the body of Jesus. She should have known the story of Lazarus, and probably knew him personally. Instead of believing in the word of God, Mary held on to her own conclusion, which was that someone had stolen the body of Jesus, and she was on a mission to get it back.

Some Christians are like Mary Magdalene. They are upset over many things, because they refuse to believe scriptures, choosing rather to live by their own notion and understanding. They say things like, "I know what the Bible says, but I just can't believe…" or "It is impossible…" The Bible is not hard to understand, it is hard to believe. The word of God is truth and will not fail. Always believe in the word of God, no matter how far fetched a promise may be. *Luke 1:37 For with God nothing shall be impossible.*

The Book of John

[Verse 14] As soon as Mary Magdalene turned herself back, she saw Jesus, even though she did not recognize Him. Turning back is a picture of repentance. People who have a hard time believing scriptures need to repent, and they will see the truth.

[Verse 15] Mary thought Jesus was the gardener and asked if He had taken the body of Jesus. This is so representative of Christendom today. Christians can read the Bible and still not see Jesus in it. Jesus Christ is in every page of the Bible in types and figures in both the Old and New Testament.

[Verse 16] But all became well when the risen Christ called her name. Mary instantly recognized Jesus and called Him *"Rabboni."* Her sorrow turned to joy. This is good news to young and weak believers. Even though they may not be able to recognize Jesus in the scriptures, they will hear when He calls their name. *John 10:3 To him the porter openeth; and the sheep hear his voice: and he calleth his own sheep by name, and leadeth them out.*

[Verses 17-18] Jesus asked Mary not to touch Him, because He hadn't ascended to the Father yet. He gave her a task to tell others about the resurrection. We too should proclaim the resurrection of Jesus Christ. He arose! After all, what good is a corpse? What can a corpse do for us? If Jesus didn't rise again, there is no reason to call on Him. Just as there is no reason to call on those gods whose bones remain in their graves.

> Low in the grave He lay, Jesus, my Savior,
> Waiting the coming day, Jesus, my Lord!
>
> Refrain:
> Up from the grave He arose,
> With a mighty triumph o'er His foes,
> He arose a Victor from the dark domain,
> And He lives forever, with His saints to reign.
> He arose! He arose!
> Hallelujah! Christ arose!

Chapter 20 – The Christ

Vainly they watch His bed, Jesus, my Savior;
Vainly they seal the dead, Jesus, my Lord! [Refrain]

Death cannot keep his Prey, Jesus, my Savior;
He tore the bars away, Jesus, my Lord! [Refrain]

("He Arose" hymn by Robert Lowry)

Lessons from the Disciples' Encounter with the Risen Christ

[Verse 2-10] According to *Luke 24:11*, the disciples did not believe Mary Magdalene's account of the empty tomb. To them, her words were as idle tales. So, Peter and John rushed to the grave to check it out for themselves. They too saw an empty tomb.

Peter and John represent people who are ignorant of scriptures (verse 9), struggle with faith, and need to see some evidence before believing. This is fine. If their hearts are genuine, God will show them enough evidence through His creation and truth to help their faith. *Romans 1:20 For the invisible things of him from the creation of the world are clearly seen, being understood by the things that are made, even his eternal power and Godhead; so that they are without excuse.*

Besides the empty tomb, Jesus gave Peter and John more proof of His resurrection, as they observed the linen grave clothes lying neatly and undisturbed, and *"the napkin, that was about his head, not lying with the linen clothes, but wrapped together in a place by itself."* The evidence refuted Mary's claim of a stolen body. Below are the reasons.

1. In those days, grave thieves were after the treasures and not the body. Think of the graves of the Egyptian pharaohs. The burial treasures were looted, but the

mummified bodies were left behind. In this case, the grave robbers would have taken the new fine linen that Joseph provided, instead of making off with a naked body.

2. If the thieves were after the body, they wouldn't have taken the time to neatly fold the linen clothes and head napkin.

After seeing the evidence, Peter and John were convinced of the resurrection and believed the scriptures. *John 2:22 When therefore he was risen from the dead, his disciples remembered that he had said this unto them; and they believed the scripture, and the word which Jesus had said.*

[Verses 19-20] So far, the disciples had only seen the artifacts of the resurrection. But that evening, Jesus appeared to the disciples to comfort them, because they feared the Jews, especially since it was rumored that they had stolen Jesus' body. Read *Matthew 28:11-15*. The religious rulers might come to apprehend and kill them. But they were comforted by Jesus' salutation of peace and were glad and fully convinced after seeing His hands and His side.

[Verses 21-23] Thereafter, Jesus re-commissioned the disciples into ministry—"*As my Father hath sent me, even so send I you.*" (Review the "Sanctified for His service" section in Chapter 17.) As Jesus was the Sent One of the Father to accomplish His will and mission, He now sent the disciples to fulfill the great commission. Read *Matthew 28:16-20*. For this, He gave them two things:

1. His peace. Jesus reiterated the peace that they would have in Him that they might do the work of ministry and endure persecution. *John 16:33 These things I have spoken unto you, that in me ye might have peace. In the*

world ye shall have tribulation: but be of good cheer; I have overcome the world. Read *John 14:27.*

2. His power. Jesus empowered the disciples for ministerial service by breathing on them the Holy Ghost. [Verse 23] With the indwelling Holy Ghost, they would be able to impact the eternal destiny of the people they ministered to according to their response to the gospel.

We can draw parallels to the above. We too are sent to fulfill the great commission, according to *John 17:17-20* and *Matthew 28:19-20.* The Lord Jesus is our peace. He is alive and we serve a living God. We need not be fearful. We also have the indwelling of the Holy Ghost, according to *Ephesians 1:13.* God also has given us the ministry of reconciliation, according to *2Corinthians 5:18-19.* The question is how faithful are we in fulfilling our mission? *1Corinthians 4:1 Let a man so account of us, as of the ministers of Christ, and stewards of the mysteries of God. (2) Moreover it is required in stewards, that a man be found faithful.*

Lessons from Thomas' Encounter with the Risen Christ

[Verse 24-29] Thomas, whose Greek name was Didymus, was absent when Jesus appeared to the disciples in verse 19. Despite his fellow disciples' testimony of the risen Christ, Thomas would not believe. He said, *"Except I shall see in his hands the print of the nails, and put my finger into the print of the nails, and thrust my hand into his side, I will not believe."* Thomas' wish was fulfilled eight days later when the disciples gathered together and Jesus appeared to them. Jesus said to Thomas, *"Reach hither thy finger, and behold my hands; and reach hither thy hand, and thrust it into my side: and be not faithless, but believing."* Thereafter, Thomas believed and said, *"My Lord and my God."*

The lesson is that it is better to believe the word by faith than by sight. Jesus reprimanded Thomas instead of giving him a mission. Jesus said, *"Thomas, because thou hast seen me, thou hast believed: blessed are they that have not seen, and yet have believed."*

Thomas represents two groups of people. At present, he represents those who will only believe in Jesus by sight. Like Thomas, these people will miss Jesus initially, but will see Him eventually. When they see Him, they will acknowledge Him as Lord. *Philippians 2:10 That at the name of Jesus every knee should bow, of things in heaven, and things in earth, and things under the earth; (11) And that every tongue should confess that Jesus Christ is Lord, to the glory of God the Father.* Don't be like Thomas. Believe in Jesus Christ now by faith. *John 20:31 But these are written, that ye might believe that Jesus is the Christ, the Son of God; and that believing ye might have life through his name.*

In the future, Thomas represents post-millennial saints, because faith will no longer be required, as everyone will physically see the Lord Jesus rule and reign on earth.

Prophecies

The prophecy in this chapter reveals the tribulation and salvation of the Jews. Because they rejected Jesus Christ the Messiah, the Jews will enter into a suffering period known as the Great Tribulation that lasts for seven years, with the worst in the last three and a half years. It is an extremely sorrowful and frightening period. This prophecy is depicted by Mary Magdalene weeping and searching for her Lord and the disciples meeting behind closed doors in fear.

Chapter 20 – The Christ

The Jews will see evidences, as Peter and John did, and will be able to reconcile Jesus Christ with the Old Testament scripture and know that He is the Messiah. This will happen when God lifts the veil that prevents them from seeing the truth. *2Corinthians 3:12 Seeing then that we have such hope, we use great plainness of speech: (13) And not as Moses, which put a vail over his face, that the children of Israel could not stedfastly look to the end of that which is abolished: (14) But their minds were blinded: for until this day remaineth the same vail untaken away in the reading of the old testament; which vail is done away in Christ. (15) But even unto this day, when Moses is read, the vail is upon their heart. (16) Nevertheless when it shall turn to the Lord, the vail shall be taken away.*

In their affliction, the Jews will mourn and seek the Lord Jesus early, as Mary sought the body of Jesus early while it was yet dark. *Hosea 5:15 I will go and return to my place, till they acknowledge their offence, and seek my face: in their affliction they will seek me early.* The Jews will run and hide from the persecution of the antichrist, which will be far worse than the atrocity they suffered from Hitler. Read *Matthew 24:15-22, Ecclesiastes 12:1-6.*

But as the scripture promised, and like clockwork, the Lord Jesus Christ will appear to rescue the Jews in their darkest moment. He will proclaim peace to them and they will be so glad to see Him. The entire nation of Israel will be saved in one day, and they will receive the Holy Ghost.

Summary

Sometimes I wonder what it would have been like to be born in Jesus' time and to see Him in person, hear His sermons, and to see Him alive after He was dead. Would I have believed Him then? To me, Christ's resurrection is the main differentiator that sets Him apart from other so-called gods—Buddha, Mohammad, Confucius, Hanuman, Siva, etc. They all died and perished. Jesus Christ rose from the dead to conquer sin and death. He is alive! He is the living God! Verse 31 says the written testimonies of Jesus Christ in the Bible are enough to convince people that He is the Christ, the Son of God. May God give all readers the faith to believe and accept Jesus Christ as God and Savior.

21 – Master Fisherman

Historical Synopsis

Having met Jesus twice after His resurrection from the dead, Peter decided to return to his old fishing profession. The six disciples who joined Peter in this endeavor were Thomas, Nathanael, James, John, and two unnamed disciples, which are thought to be Andrew and Philip since they were both of Bethsaida. They fished all night and caught nothing.

In the morning, Jesus stood on the shore and instructed the disciples to cast their net on the right side of the ship. Though they didn't recognize Him, they did what He said and caught 153 large fishes. The net was so heavy that they were not able to draw it into the ship. When Peter realized the man on the shore was Jesus, he was immediately conscious of his nakedness and quickly put on a coat and jumped into the sea.

On shore, Jesus had prepared a fire of coal with fish laid thereon, and bread. He instructed the disciples to bring the fish that they had caught and invited them to dine with Him. He distributed bread and fish to the disciples.

After they finished eating, Jesus asked Peter three times if he loved Him. With each affirmation of love, He told Peter to feed His sheep. Jesus also foretold that Peter would experience a violent death, but that his death would glorify God. (Ecclesiastical history confirms that Peter was crucified at Rome.)

The Book of John

This chapter can be outlined as such:

 I. Jesus turned an unfruitful fishing trip into the catch of the day – *John 21:1-14*
 II. Jesus instructed Peter to feed His lambs and sheep and to follow Him – *John 21:15-25*

bring the fish
feed my sheep

358

Chapter 21 – Master Fisherman

Key Spiritual Lessons

As the saying goes, "There is a price for everything." I wonder what would draw you away from serving the Lord Jesus? How about fame, fortune, a relationship with an unbeliever, or trappings such as drugs, sex, and alcohol? This chapter warns believers from turning away from serving the Lord. It also instructs believers to evangelize the lost and disciple new converts.

Following are the key spiritual lessons:

I.   The consequences of not serving the Lord – *John 21:1-8*
II. The time to fish for men is now – *John 21:9-10*
III. The secrets to a big catch – *John 21:11-14*
IV. The lambs and sheep need to be fed – *John 21:15-23*

The Consequences of Not Serving the Lord

[Verses 1-3] Despite seeing the risen Christ twice, Peter decided to return to his old fishing profession and abandon the work of the gospel. He was followed by six other disciples, and they went fishing in the sea of Tiberias. They were busy all night, but were unfruitful.

The name Tiberias means "from the Tiber (as river-god)." This "river god" represents anything that draws you away from serving the Lord. It could be your old religion, idols, or a sinful lifestyle. In verse 3, a ship was immediately available to take them fishing. The "river god" wants you back and is immediately available to receive you. Every Christian is only steps away from leaving the Lord. Never think for a moment that you are invincible.

The Book of John

Your decision to desert your post in ministry may cause others to also abandon theirs, especially if you are an influential person. You will be unfruitful as Peter and his pals were unfruitful. Self-serving Christians who benefit from the salvation of Jesus Christ, but don't labor in the work of the gospel, be forewarned—you will end up with nothing.

[Verses 4-5] When morning came, Jesus asked, *"Children, have ye any meat?"* and the disciples answered "No."

Every Christian is accountable to the Lord. One of these days, you will stand before Him and account for your life. A life with no service to Him is a life lived in vain. Never appear empty handed before the King of Kings and Lord of Lords who died for your sins. *John 15:16 Ye have not chosen me, but I have chosen you, and ordained you, that ye should go and bring forth fruit, and that your fruit should remain: that whatsoever ye shall ask of the Father in my name, he may give it you.*

According to verse 4, Jesus stood on the shore waiting for the disciples to return. You can sail away and run from the Lord, but you will eventually run out of gas and need to return to shore. Guess who will be there to greet you? It is foolish to think that a Christian can avoid doing the work of the gospel without any consequences.

[Verse 6] Peter and his pals had been fishing on the wrong side of the ship all night. They finally caught a lot of fish when they obeyed Jesus' instruction to cast the net on the right side of the ship.

The truth is, no matter what you do, you will always be on the wrong side if you do not serve the Lord. What can you do if God is against you? The Bible says, *"It is hard for thee to kick against the pricks."* Until you repent, you will not be fruitful. But if you repent

Chapter 21 – Master Fisherman

and follow His instructions, God can still use you and bless you with abundant fruit.

[Verses 7-8] When Peter realized the man on shore was Jesus, he immediately was conscious of his nakedness. He grabbed and put on his fishers coat and jumped into the sea. The rest of the crew came in the ship to meet Jesus while dragging the net full of fishes.

It is unclear why Peter cast himself into the sea. It could be that he was shocked, ashamed, and wanted to hide. It could also be that he was eager to meet Jesus, and thus swimming to shore from 100 yards (200 cubits) away was faster than the ship with a heavy net. Regardless of Peter's reason, all self-serving Christians will have a rude awakening when they find themselves in the presence of the Lord. I don't think any backsliding, self-serving Christian will be so eager to see the Lord.

The Bible ascribes nakedness to believers who are worldly rich, but spiritually bankrupt. Trust me, you don't want to be naked and ashamed before the Lord. *Revelation 3:17 Because thou sayest, I am rich, and increased with goods, and have need of nothing; and knowest not that thou art wretched, and miserable, and poor, and blind, and naked.*

The Time to Fish for Men is Now

Peter and his pals went fishing at night. Night in the Bible refers to the church age, a time of spiritual darkness in the world. The whole world is under the power of darkness. The god of this world (Satan) wants to keep everyone from seeing the light of the glorious gospel of Christ. *2Corinthians 4:3 But if our gospel be hid, it is hid to them that are lost: (4) In whom the god of this world hath blinded the minds of them which believe not, lest the light of the glorious gospel of Christ, who is the image of God, should shine unto them.*

You are living in the age of spiritual darkness (night time). Now is the appropriate time to go fishing for men. Share your conversion testimony with friends and family. Tell them what life was like before Jesus, how you met Jesus, and what life is like now with Jesus.

[Verses 9-10] When the disciples came to shore in the morning, they noticed Jesus had prepared a fire of coals with fish on it. There was also bread. Jesus instructed them to bring the fish they caught.

Morning in the Bible refers to the return of the Lord Jesus Christ to judge the world of sins. The Lord Jesus is the morning star, according to *Revelation 22:16*. Coal fire is a type of God's judgment. Fish represents lost men, and bread represents the word of God. Read *Psalms 18:6-13, John 6:35*. The encoded message here is that when Jesus Christ returns, unsaved men will be judged by the word of God. Read *John 12:46-48*.

For this reason, it is utterly important for Christians to evangelize. We must *"Bring of the fish which ye have now caught"* to Jesus, otherwise, they will be found guilty before God at the judgment and will spend eternity in the lake of fire.

It is necessary that you evangelize for the following reasons:

1. Necessity is laid upon you. *1Corinthians 9:16 For though I preach the gospel, I have nothing to glory of: for necessity is laid upon me; yea, woe is unto me, if I preach not the gospel!*

2. You are an ambassador for Christ. You have the word of reconciliation and own the ministry of reconciliation, according to *2Corinthians 5:17-21*.

3. You don't want to see your loved ones end up in the lake of fire. Morning will break and Jesus will return to judge the world. It is better for lost men to meet Him by faith at night, than to meet Him by sight in the morning, because bread (word of God) and a fire of coals (judgment) await them.

The Secrets to a Big Catch

[Verses 11-14] When Peter drew the net to land, there were altogether 153 large fishes. It is amazing that the net did not break. The disciples fellowshipped with Jesus as they ate bread and fish. That was the third time Jesus appeared to the disciples after His resurrection.

The secrets to a big catch are as follows:

1. Obey the word of God. If the Lord says cast the net on the right side of the ship, do not cast on the back, front, or left side. To be fruitful, you must abide in Christ and let His word abide in you. You cannot practice a sinful lifestyle and expect to be fruitful.

2. Get a net that does not break. The net represents the word of God. It will not break, no matter how many fish you catch.

3. Understand that it is the Lord who gives the bread and the fish. Read verse 13, *1Corinthians 3:5-7,* and review Chapter 6. Pray that the Lord will give you bread and fish the next time you go fishing for men.

I would like to emphasize the net. Many churches in the U.S. use programs and entertainment as the net. They draw many people and become mega churches. I wonder how many people will remain faithful when the programs and entertainment are removed. More importantly, how many of them are willing to serve the Lord.

I was in Odisha, India, and met some persecuted pastors and believers from various districts around Rayagada. The pastors preached Jesus Christ in subtropical jungle villages. Soon after receiving Christ as God and Savior, the converts suffered their first persecution from family members. They were told to deny Jesus or get out of the family. In some cases, men lost their wives when their father-in-laws took them back. The Hindu zealots also often threatened to kill them.

I visited the homes of some of the believers. The homes were nothing more than mud huts that I had to crawl inside. They had nothing of the world, but they told me they would die for Jesus. While my background prepared me for the poverty, I wasn't prepared for such strong faith.

I spent the next few days wondering how these believers, even the baby Christians, could have such a strong faith. I concluded that when they bought into Jesus Christ, they were drawn by the word of God and the promises therein. The pastors were poor and had nothing to offer except the word of God. These people weren't drawn to Jesus by programs and entertainment. I witnessed faith that withstood persecution. Such an incredible faith can only be powered by the word of God. So please, when you share Jesus with people, give them the word of God in its full, undiluted strength. Read *1Corinthians 2:1-5, 1Thessalonians 1:3-8.*

Chapter 21 – Master Fisherman

The Lambs and Sheep Need to be Fed

[Verses 15-17] Peter had previously promised to follow Jesus in *John 13:36-37*, even to lay down his life, but ended up denying Him publicly three times. Here, Jesus singled him out and gave him three opportunities to publicly express his love toward Him. With each affirmation of love from Peter, Jesus instructed him to feed the lambs and sheep. (The lambs are the tender part of the flock—believers who are young in the Lord. The sheep are the mature believers.)

While fishing is evangelism, feeding the lambs and sheep is discipleship. Evangelism and discipleship are two sides of the same coin. Without evangelism, there will be no one to disciple. You are commanded to evangelize and make disciples (feed the lambs and sheep). Read *Matthew 28:19-20*. As you grow and mature in the Lord, it will be your turn to disciple others. You must be discipled before you can disciple others. Pray that God will put someone in your life who will invest in you—someone who will guide and help you find your way in the Bible and answer your questions. Find a church that understands and practices discipleship.

A disciple is an obedient follower (learner or apprentice) of Jesus Christ whose fruit is the character qualities of God. *Luke 6:40 The disciple is not above his master: but every one that is perfect shall be as his master.* In other words, the reason a person would want to be a disciple of Jesus Christ is to be like Him.

Discipleship is *"Follow me, and I will make you fishers of men."* Read *Matthew 4:19*. As such, discipleship is a process of learning from the master fisherman—the Lord Jesus Christ. As you read the four gospels, you will get a sense that the disciples were clueless or dull of understanding most of the time. Jesus did not choose them because they had a master's or Ph.D. degree in divinity. They were mostly unlearned and ignorant men. But as they walked with and learned from Jesus, they gained knowledge and understanding. Likewise, you may not currently know the Bible intimately, but God will increase your knowledge and understanding as you continue to read and demonstrate obedience to His word.

Discipleship is not a program or curriculum where you get a certificate of completion at the end. It is discipleship, not a diploma! It is also not a set of high-quest lessons. Learning does not make a person a disciple, but living the learning. Discipleship is a radical call to obedience to the word of God. Consider *Luke 6:46, "And why call ye me, Lord, Lord, and do not the things which I say?"* The Bible is not a restaurant menu where you pick and choose what you like. Mary gave excellent advice in *John 2:5, "Whatsoever he saith unto you, do it."*

Discipleship is OJT (on-the-job training). Many disciplers fall short by simply transferring information and not leading and showing by example. Disciples need to practice what they learn. It is like the hands-on lab exercise at the end of each technical chapter that is designed to solidify the concept and understanding. Disciplers should take the disciples and model the lessons. For example, go hand out gospel tracts and witness to strangers together.

Discipleship is a process of committing the word of God from one faithful Christian to another over generations. *2Timothy 2:2 And the things that thou hast heard of me among many witnesses, the same commit thou to faithful men, who shall be able to teach others also.* It is pointless and a phenomenal waste of time to disciple an unfaithful person. Never waste time chasing after a person who doesn't want to get caught. Jesus never begs people to follow Him.

Discipleship is definitely not for everyone, because there is a high price to pay. You must first count the cost. In the Kung-Fu martial art, all disciples understand the price of learning and of practice. They will give up their life to protect the organization.

Chapter 21 – Master Fisherman

Peter knew ahead of time that he would experience a violent death by following Jesus. Jesus gave the following three conditions for being His disciple:

1. You love Jesus more than anyone else in your life. This makes sense, as what kind of disciple does not make his master paramount is his life? Review "The necessity of making Christ preeminent in your life" section in Chapter 3.
    a. *Luke 14:26 If any man come to me, and hate not his father, and mother, and wife, and children, and brethren, and sisters, yea, and his own life also, he cannot be my disciple.*

2. You bear your cross daily. This means you must die to self by presenting your body a living sacrifice. Lay aside your personal goals, desires, and ambitions so that God can reveal His for your life. Live to fulfill the mission that God has for you.
    a. *Luke 14:27 And whosoever doth not bear his cross, and come after me, cannot be my disciple.*
    b. *Luke 9:23 And he said to them all, If any man will come after me, let him deny himself, and take up his cross daily, and follow me.*

3. You are willing to forsake (surrender your claim, say goodbye to) all worldly possessions.
    a. Read *Luke 14:28-33*, particularly verse 33, "*So likewise, whosoever he be of you that forsaketh not all that he hath, he cannot be my disciple.*"
    b. Read *Matthew 19:16-22*.
    c. Billy Graham said, "Salvation is free, but discipleship costs everything we have."

[Verses 18-23] Jesus gave Peter the opportunity to make good on his declaration of love for Him. Besides the care of the lambs and sheep, Peter followed the Lord to the end, even glorifying God with his death, which was prophesied in verse 18.

While following Jesus, Peter turned around and saw John also was following. Peter asked Jesus, *"What shall this man do?,"* meaning in what work and service would John be employed. Jesus basically told Peter it was no concern of his, but that Peter should focus on following Him. Jesus' exact answer was, *"If I will that he tarry till I come, what is that to thee?"* The disciples who were present overheard and misconstrued the saying to mean that John would not die.

This section teaches what it means to follow Jesus (in addition to the notes in Chapter 1):

1. Verse 18 – Following Jesus is to submit to the will of God. Peter had no say in what God had in store for him.

2. Verse 19 – Following Jesus may cost you your life. It is a sobering decision.

3. Verse 20 – Following Jesus means no turning back. You cannot serve two masters, according to *Matthew 6:24*. You must burn the bridges to the past.

4. Verses 20-21 – Following Jesus is a decision of personal accountability. You follow Jesus and don't worry about what others do or don't do. You personally are accountable to the Lord for what He has bid you to do.

Summary

Our duty toward God is to bring the fish and feed the sheep. Our duty toward the world is to proclaim the gospel of Jesus Christ. The harvest truly is plenteous, but the laborers are few. May God show you a field that you can labor and invest in. May God bless you and make you as a fruitful vine by the sides of His house.

Works Cited

- Matthew Henry's Complete Commentary on the Bible

- John Gill's Exposition on the Whole Bible

- Jamieson, Fausset, and Brown's Commentary on the Whole Bible

About the Author

I grew up in a small fishing village in northern Malaysia, bordering Thailand. My family practiced Taoism in a Muslim country. We worshiped idols and ancestors. My dad maintained three altars at home—for the god of wealth, the god of the earth, and ancestors. He offered a daily drink offering of tea, oil for the lamps, and incense in the morning and evening. He asked the gods and ancestors for protection and blessings. On festival days he set out meat offerings of chicken or duck and sweet cakes, which ended up as our dinner.

We went to temples on special occasions, such as for fortune-telling, to celebrate the birthdays of our favorite gods, to get the best dates for travel, weddings, building, moving, or starting a new business, and to ask for healing and financial blessings, normally in the form of lottery numbers. Indeed, everyone that I knew asked for three common things—wealth, health, and more wealth. No one ever kneeled down to an idol and said, "Forgive me, I am a sinner."

I was sick a lot in my early years. Grandma frequently took me to the temple, which was only about 100 yards away. At one point the priest decided that I should be adopted by the god of heaven. And so I was given to him. That meant I had to appear before the god of heaven once a year with offerings and thanksgiving. I can't remember if my sickness went away, but obviously I survived. When I was 15, my grandma decided I needed to be redeemed from the god of heaven, otherwise I would not prosper. It didn't mean anything to me, but I did what I was told. I went to the temple with incense and offerings and thanked the god of heaven for his protection and told him that I didn't need him anymore.

Our concept of gods and ghosts was simple. We believed them and didn't want to offend them. They could be for us or against us, so we worshiped and bribed them for our personal benefit.

Hell was real. Asians who practice Taoism know that they will die and go to hell. This knowledge was passed down to me by my grandparents in my early years. When Christians in the U.S. told me that I was going to split hell wide open, this was no new revelation.

I was taught that the hell god will judge the dead according to their works. Those with excellent good works will cross the chasm on the golden bridge without punishment and be reincarnated as privileged humans. Those with good works that outweigh their bad works use the silver bridge without punishment, but will be reincarnated as humans with fewer privileges. Those who were bad will be severely punished and tortured in hell.

About the Author

However, I was taught that punishments could be reduced if living relatives burned hell money, houses, cars, and maids made of bamboo and paper as offerings to the hell god. I watched my dad burn those things to the hell god soon after my grandpa died. He burned stacks of hell notes, which came in extremely large denominations, as much as $2 billion apiece. The total amount had to be in the gazillions. I thought to myself that things must be very expensive down there. At the end of the burning, a small twister wind came and picked up the ashes. I was freaked out, but was comforted when my dad told me that the hell god had received the offerings.

I was further taught that the Wheel of Reincarnation and the Pavilion of Forgetfulness are in the Tenth Court of hell. After serving their sentences, sinners arrive at the Tenth Court to receive their final judgment from the hell god. Thereafter they are brought to the Pavilion of Forgetfulness, where an old lady, Meng Po, hands them a cup of magic tea, which makes them forget their past lives. They then go through the Wheel of Reincarnation where some are reborn as humans and some as animals, depending on their past

The Book of John

deeds. Some are reborn into a life of ease and comfort, while others into sorrow and suffering.

Life in a small fishing village was good, slow, and peaceful. People knew each other and dropped by for a visit without an appointment. My family didn't have much. I spent a lot of time at my neighbor's house watching black and white TV. It was a piece of furniture with a small tube. I grew up watching Wild, Wild West, Gun Smoke, Bonanza, The Andy Griffith Show, Looney Tunes, and Disney programs. I love Bugs Bunny to this day.

Behind the closed doors of most Chinese families, parents put intense pressure on their children to succeed. My parents always compared me to other kids. When I did not achieve at school, I would hear them say, "You lousy...," "You stupid...," "You useless..." It was their way of challenging, motivating, and preparing me for the real world. Most Chinese parents in their generation adopted this motivation method. Today I thank them, because they toughened me for the competition on a global platform. The intense pressure was driven by two main reasons. 1) The official retirement age is 55. Males particularly have to succeed by age 30, so the ramp up is short and steep. There is no time to party. 2) The Chinese society is very materialistic. People are judged by their possessions. A Chinese male who does not own a house, a Mercedes Benz, and a Rolex watch by age 30 is considered an underachiever. (Bear in mind, those things cost several times more over there than in the U.S.) The guys who don't get rich by age 30 have a tough time getting a date. So life to me was about money, fast money, and lots of money, by hook or by crook, and I joined the materialistic society.

I was transferred to Kuala Lumpur, the capital of Malaysia, in my freshman year for higher education. The move was like dropping someone who couldn't swim into an ocean with no floatation. I went from the serene and beautiful beaches of the South China Sea to a rat-race, glitzy concrete jungle. I had to learn so many new things, almost all at once. I was so handicapped

About the Author

compared to the city kids. My attire, mannerisms, and speech betrayed me. Things like disco and break dancing while holding a stereo the size of small luggage was so foreign to me. Thankfully I was able to make rapid changes and excelled in school. Unfortunately I was also exposed to the five vices of happiness—eating, drinking, womanizing, gambling, and smoking. That was the definition of a successful and happy man.

While I was in college, my parents decided to send all my siblings to Kuala Lumpur for education and bought a house for us to live in. My sister attended the St. Mary girls' school and was the first to become a Christian in my family. Soon after, my parents retired and moved in. The next thing I knew, mom was reading the Bible. That infuriated me. Christianity divided my family—the ladies were Christians, the boys were Taoists. From then on I hated the Christian religion and my Christian friends. I treated them badly.

I was one of the earliest computer science graduates in Malaysia. I had a computer job before I graduated and worked in the industry for a few years. Computers, especially personal computers, were so new at the time. It took two men to carry an 80 MB hard drive. I wish I kept the Apple II and the Mac. I still have a stack of punch cards and a stack of hard drives the size of a large pizza to remind me of the good old days.

I was increasingly dissatisfied with the open discrimination by the Malaysian government against the Chinese and Indians, and decided to move abroad. I was choosing between Australia and the U.S. Since I grew up watching American TV programs, I chose and came to the U.S. in 1990 with the hope of seeing cowboys in person and making lots of dollars so I could return to Malaysia to live like a king.

Life in the U.S. was a reboot and tough in the beginning. Yet again I found myself having to assimilate into a foreign culture. I ended up in Kansas City and fell in love with the place and the people. The Midwesterners were so friendly and helpful.

One day a coworker invited me to church. I reluctantly agreed, because she was my supervisor. I can't remember what was said during the service, but I went forward to the altar during the invitation. Pastor Gary Staab greeted me and offered to teach me the Bible. We met each Saturday morning at his house for about a year. He taught me the basic doctrines and principles from the Bible. I realized the significance of my sins for the very first time. (I previously thought sin was no big deal because the hell god could be bribed, and there was reincarnation.) I learned the truth that sin condemned me to death, and all my good works were unable to cleanse me or purchase the required redemption. I was separated from God. I looked for a solution in my old religion, but none of the idols, monks, and priests could give me eternal life. I discovered eternal life was a gift from God through Jesus Christ. In 1994, by faith I accepted Jesus Christ as my Lord and Savior for the pardoning of my sins.

God is sovereign. A Taoist kid from a little-known small fishing village set off in search of worldly success and happiness, but by the grace of God, found eternal life, true riches, peace, and purpose. I am forever in debt to and thankful for the Lord Jesus Christ. I am also thankful for the faithful people whom God put in my life to teach and guide me in His truth.

I am now serving the Lord in the juvenile detention ministry, Friends of International Students ministry, and am partnering with native pastors in India and Nepal. Feel free to email me with your comments and suggestions at TheBookofJohn777@yahoo.com.

An inspirational suspense novel from Purple Dreamer Publishers available on Amazon

In 1987, Julie Bradley kidnaps her daughter, stunning everyone who knows her. She has no other alternative to keep her abusive ex-husband from getting at their daughter. Julie's policeman ex-father-in-law wants his granddaughter back, in spite of the horrific things his son has done to her. Like bloodhounds, law enforcement is always one heart-pounding step behind them. For how long can they escape? Will Julie's primitive motherly instincts be enough to match the will of the enemy? Three things keep Julie grounded: her journal, a Psalm, and her daughter. One thing is certain, they will never live ordinary lives.

Get free inspirational materials at MasterTruth.com

Jody Shee

Ditch Depression Devotional

31 Days to Biblical Hope, Peace and Emotional Balance

A 31-day devotional guide to biblical hope, peace and emotional balance available on Amazon

Depression does not take God by surprise. What seems like a crisis to us is an opportunity to Him. Relief starts with an understanding of His viewpoint. This 31-day devotional looks at the topic of depression four ways: Common causes; depression's spiritual benefits (there are some!); God's loving rescue; and Bible character overcomers. This book is especially useful to new believers, singles and moms. Besides a short daily reading, it includes: Daily "going deeper" sections for those who want to explore the topic further; a life-altering assignment to complete by the end of the book; links to helpful songs; and online free frameable verse pictures. While it is meant for personal use to complete in one month, it is also appropriate for use in a classroom or small-group setting with a free online leader's guide available on mastertruth.com.

Made in United States
Troutdale, OR
03/24/2025